Rational Choice and Moral Agency

*

Rational Choice and Moral Agency

*

David Schmidtz

PRINCETON UNIVERSITY PRESS

PRINCETON, NEW JERSEY

Copyright © 1995 by Princeton University Press
Published by Princeton University Press, 41 William Street,
Princeton, New Jersey 08540
In the United Kingdom: Princeton University Press, Chichester, West Sussex

Library of Congress Cataloging-in-Publication Data

Schmidtz, David, 1955–
Rational choice and moral agency / David Schmidtz.
p.   cm.
Includes bibliographical references and index.
ISBN 0-691-03401-X
1. Ethics.   2. Rationalism.   I. Title.
BJ1012.S346   1994
170′.42—dc20   94-19059

This book has been composed in Linotype Sabon

Princeton University Press books are printed on acid-free paper
and meet the guidelines for permanence and durability of the
Committee on Production Guidelines for Book Longevity of the
Council on Library Resources

Printed in the United States of America

1   3   5   7   9   10   8   6   4   2

IN MEMORY OF GREG KAVKA

*

* Contents *

Preface and Acknowledgments ✳

GRAPPLING WITH QUESTIONS about how people should live—how they should treat each other and how they should treat themselves—is what made me a philosopher. Philosophers, needless to say, have pondered such questions for thousands of years, and Plato's *Republic* remains a point of departure. Those who are familiar with Plato's dialogue may think of Thrasymachus as exemplifying the person who has the soul of a tyrant and is therefore at war with himself: torn by appetites, seduced by vainglory, incapable of internal harmony. Glaucon, too, is at war with himself, although in a different way. Glaucon embraces morality, but he also embraces prudence, and he sincerely worries that the two may be incompatible. When he asks whether the moral life is profitable, he asks in earnest.

In this book, I reflect on the war within Glaucon. I argue that prudence and morality are natural allies. I will not argue that prudence and morality never conflict, for even natural allies sometimes fight, but I do hope to show that conflict is the exception rather than the rule. Moral acts are not always prudent acts, and vice versa, but for Glaucon, a truly moral way of life is a truly prudent way of life.

This book presumes that readers have had a course in the history of ethics, but in only a few spots (Chapter 6 in particular) does it presume more than that. The existing literature often is immensely helpful, and I am grateful for the many works (including Plato's *Republic*) that provide a springboard for mine. Nevertheless, what led me to philosophy was not a need to know what scholars have said about how people should live, but rather the question itself. A substantial part of this book is about what other people have said, and I acknowledge intellectual debts whenever I am aware of them. However, examining the literature is a secondary aim only, for the question of how one should live is more important than what any of us has to say about it. My ambition is to meet the question head-on.

Not without help, though. Over the years, I have presented parts of the book at the following universities: Arizona, Bowling Green State, British Columbia, Calgary, California-Davis, California-

Irvine, Colorado, Cornell, Kansas, Oklahoma, Virginia, and Yale. Special thanks to the people at Kansas State, North Carolina-Chapel Hill, and Waterloo for their splendid hospitality during my extended visits there.

I thank Neera Badhwar, Lesley Ann Beneke, Michael Della Rocca, Shelly Kagan, Alan Nelson, William Nelson, Lainie Friedman Ross, Geoff Sayre-McCord, Elizabeth Willott, two anonymous referees, and my editor, Ann Wald, for commenting on the entire manuscript. For comments on one or more chapters, I thank Bob Adams, Dorit Bar-On, Jules Coleman, Tyler Cowen, Peter Danielson, Harry Frankfurt, Walter Glannon, Tom Hill, Sr., Roderick Long, Bill Lycan, Eric Mack, Ruth Marcus, Scott MacDonald, John Majewski, Mark Migotti, Christopher Morris, Philip Pettit, Charles Raff, John Ross, Carol Rovane, Stephen Scott, Russell Shafer-Landau, Doran Smolkin, Sergio Troncoso, and Stuart Warner.

Among the students whom I should single out for special thanks are: Burton Bauchner, Amber Carpenter, Mark Chenoweth, Parag Chordia, Janie Chuang, Molly Clay, Tamer Francis, Reyaz Kassamali, Robert Pollock, Nancy Won, and Jon Zerolnick. Thanks also to Yale University for a 1990–1991 Morse Fellowship during the tenure of which I began to write this book.

An earlier version of Chapter 2 appeared in *Journal of Philosophy* 89 (1992): 445–66. Chapters 3 and 4 each draw on material that originally appeared in *Ethics* 104 (1994): 226–51; copyright by the University of Chicago. All rights reserved. An earlier version of Chapter 5 was published in *Social Philosophy and Policy* 10 (1993): 52–68. I thank these journals for permission to use that material here.

Finally, I will always be grateful to Elizabeth Willott for accepting my invitation to the high school prom, for dragging me along to a visiting lecture by Joel Feinberg one cold winter's night when I was still a biology major, and (several years later) for not thinking I was out of my mind when I said I wanted to quit my job at the post office and go back to school to study philosophy.

PART I
RATIONAL CHOICE

*

Introduction

THIS BOOK EXPLORES CONNECTIONS between rationality and morality. Its purpose is to find out how being rational and being moral fit together with being human. I conclude that insofar as we decide on a case-by-case basis whether to be moral, most people most of the time have reason to be moral. Moreover, for beings with a human psychology, it is eminently rational to be moral as a way of life. If we cared only about ourselves, we would have too little to care about. Life would be pointless, or nearly so. Therefore, it makes sense for us to care about other people, even if our reasons to care about other people are not logically compelling. It also makes sense to respect people, both to secure their respect in return and so that we can think of ourselves as deserving their respect.

It makes sense to respect and comply with constraints imposed on us by moral institutions as well. Indeed, it is of the essence of moral institutions that they do what they can to close the gap between individual and collective rationality. However, although complying with moral institutions is part of being moral, there is more to it than that. Being moral also has a personal component, one that involves working to earn self-respect. The different parts of morality connect to rationality in different ways, sometimes circuitous ways, but they do connect.

Before we can reach these conclusions, though, we need to characterize rationality and morality. Part I develops a model of rational choice. My initial hypothesis was that the main reason why standard rational choice theories leave so little room for morality is that they are radically oversimplified as models of humanly rational choice. Part I considers what being rational is like in the real world, where people must deal with their own psychology, with their own biological nature, and with radical uncertainty both about current circumstances and about how and when those circumstances will change.

My model explains when nonmaximizing strategies are rational and when maximizing strategies are not. It explains why it is rational for human beings not only to be cognizant of external constraints but to operate within self-imposed constraints as well. It

3

explains how rational choice can range over the choice of ends as well as means. The model explains how goals we have yet to embrace can be rationally compared and what to do when they cannot be rationally compared. It also explains how a purely self-regarding human agent would have reason to internalize non-instrumental concern and respect for other people, given the option of doing so. And humanly rational agents do have that option.

One might anticipate that such conclusions will inevitably rest on an idiosyncratic notion of rationality, perhaps even a question-begging notion. On the contrary, as Chapter 1 explains, I begin with the standard means-end model used by all rational choice theorists. Besides being the thinnest and most uncontentious of rational choice models, the means-end model connects in an obvious way to reasons for action. That is, we have reason for seeking to choose effective means to our ends (that is, for being rational) insofar as it actually helps us to achieve our ends. The only serious objection to the means-end model is that, some would say, it is an incomplete and oversimplified model of human rationality. In fact, it is incomplete. Chapters 3 and 4 develop an expanded notion of rational choice—reflective rationality—that shows how humanly rational choice can range over the choice of ends as well as means. A model of reflectively rational choice, however, must be careful about how it departs from the means-end model, for, when developing a new model, there is a risk of inadvertently changing the topic, that is, reconciling morality with something I call rationality but which really is something else. Most of all, a model of rationality must connect to reasons for action for human beings.

Accordingly, Chapter 3 explains how reflective rationality transcends means-end reasoning not by abandoning means-end reasoning in favor of something else but simply by applying means-end reasoning in a more self-aware way. In particular, being reflectively rational involves being aware of certain strengths and limitations inherent in the structure of human psychology. (For example, reflective rationality involves being aware that we cannot be expected to spend our whole lives in rational-choice mode, and neither can the people on whom we depend.) Our psychological structure has a bearing on what our ends can be and on what strategies can reasonably be expected to serve our ends. Indeed, our psychological structure is such that it is not a tautology that seeking effective means to our ends helps us achieve our ends. On the contrary, the extent to which means-end reasoning serves our ends is a complicated empirical question.

To serve its purpose within the context of this book, the model must capture enough of the complexity of real-world, humanly rational choice to help us understand how being moral could fit into the life of a humanly rational agent. It also must constitute an ideal to which real-world human beings have reason to aspire. The five chapters comprising Part I discuss what humanly rational choice is like. Parts II and III show how humanly rational choice connects to moral agency.

CHAPTER 1

Why Be Rational?

Does man think, then, because he has found
that thinking pays—because he thinks it
advantageous to think?
Ludwig Wittgenstein (1958, p. 134)

A Source of Normative Force

SUPPOSE A STUDENT COMES to my office asking which courses she should take next semester. I respond by asking her what she wants to do. She says she wants to major in philosophy. I ask why. She answers in a way that reassures me that she has no illusions about the philosophy major. She has a sense of what it is like to study philosophy and understands that she has only a slim chance of being able to make a living as a professional philosopher. Knowing all this, she definitely wants to be a philosophy major.

So, I tell her she ought to meet the logic requirement. Now I take it that what I told her is true. I could be wrong about the logic requirement, but if I am wrong, it is because I have made a factual error. (Perhaps my department does not have a logic requirement.) I might be wrong about what she ought to do, but it remains the case that, because she has ends, there are things she ought to do. Given that she really has the goal of majoring in philosophy and that meeting the logic requirement really is part of what she must do to complete the major, she really *ought* to meet the logic requirement.

Something in the situation allowed us to derive a normative conclusion, a conclusion about what she ought to do. We did not formally derive an "ought" from an "is". Nor would there be much point in trying. As the student and I sit in my office pondering her future, the so-called is-ought problem is the least of our concerns.[1]

[1] This refers to the question of whether we can validly deduce statements about what ought to be the case from statements about what is the case. See David Hume (1978, pp. 469–70) or G. E. Moore (1903, pp. 10–12).

The is-ought problem is a philosophical analog of a real problem, and the two of us are pondering the real thing, not its philosophical analog. The real problem involves deciding what she should do given the information at hand. Although we may not have derived an ought from an is, we did derive an ought.

What allowed us to conclude that she ought to meet the logic requirement? First, we had information about her ends. Second, we had information to the effect that meeting the logic requirement would be a means to her ends. We derived a normative conclusion from facts about a person's ends and facts about what would achieve those ends, which means that facts about ends have a certain potency, a certain *normative force*: They give us reasons for action.[2] As Bernard Williams says, "*Should* draws attention to the reasons I have for acting in one way rather than another" (1985, p. 18). In particular, to have goals is to have reasons for acting in one way rather than another. If acting in one way rather than another would serve my ends, then I have reason to act in one way rather than another.[3]

This is one source of reasons for action: If doing X would best serve a person's ends, then the person has reason to do X. If this is not the only source of reasons for action, then we may need to qualify the last statement, adding the phrase "all other things equal" in recognition of the possibility that other normative considerations could conflict with means-end considerations. Whether or not other sources of normative force exist, we have identified at least one way in which normative considerations come into existence. They come into existence along with ends.

Are ends the only things that give us reasons for action? Or, can we have reasons for action independently of whether the action would serve our ends? If we can, then acknowledging and internalizing such reasons might serve our ends. Part of this book is about how other kinds of normative force—including the peculiar kind of ought associated with moral constraints—could emerge

---

[2] As the phrase is used here, "normative force" is related to, but not identical to, motivational force. An end's normative force lies not so much in its tendency to move the agent as in the fact that being conscious of wanting some things rather than others gives the agent reasons to act in some ways rather than others. The distinction is adapted from J. David Velleman (1989, chap. 7).

[3] I use 'end' and 'goal' (ditto for ought/should, decision/choice, desire/want, and person/agent) interchangeably.

from such humble beginnings. Suppose we begin with a rudimentary self-regard born of biological instinct and an ability to evaluate alternative means to our ends. Beginning from there, how do we come to have other kinds of reason for action?

How do people come to care about themselves in the way we care about ourselves? This may seem like something to take for granted, but the easiest things to take for granted are sometimes the hardest things to explain. It is easy to explain in biological terms why we want to survive, or to have sex, but some of us want people to spell our names correctly. Some of us want dishes with matching patterns. Why?

How do people come to care about others in the way we care about others? Again, it is easy to explain in biological terms why we care about the survival of our children, but some of us care who wins the World Series. Our concerns sometimes extend not only beyond our children but even beyond our species. We feel sickened by the extinction of nonhuman species even when they have no commercial value and are found only in countries we will never see. Why?

Our goals give us reasons for action. I say this without presuming that the goals themselves are reasonable. In fact, later chapters insist that our goals are subject to rational critique; we have reasons to have some goals rather than others. There may even be ends, like the end of completing a philosophy degree, that we do not acquire until we become convinced that pursuing such an end is reasonable. Nevertheless, once we have an end, simply having it gives us reasons for action. For example, whether or not we can justify having a goal of survival, it remains that if our goal is to survive, there are certain things we have reason to do. Accordingly, we can make sense of the fact that even biologically given ends, like the end of survival, can give us reasons for acting in some ways rather than others. To have an end is to have something with normative force, something that gives us reasons for action, whether we in turn have reason to have the end.

Of course, not all reasons for action are equally powerful. Further, questioning our ends may sometimes serve our ends, and if the exercise reveals that we have no good reason to be pursuing a certain end, that can undercut the end as a source of reasons for action. The following chapters have more to say about the rational critique of ends. This chapter discusses rationality as a particular kind of normative consideration.

ENDORSEMENT

What do we mean when we call something rational? My answer is distinct from, but also inspired by, an answer recently defended by Allan Gibbard. Sketching Gibbard's view helps explain my own. Gibbard (1990, p. 6), says that to call something rational is to endorse it (see also Richard Fumerton [1990, p. 111]). More precisely, according to Gibbard, to call something rational is to express acceptance of norms that permit it (p. 7).

There is something attractive in Gibbard's approach. It directs attention away from the thankless task of defining the term 'rational' as it appears in ordinary language. Instead, he invites us to focus on the connection between being rational and having reasons for action. Some of the details of Gibbard's approach are worth challenging, though, partly as a way of explaining why I take a slightly different approach. For example, when Kate calls X rational, is Kate really expressing *acceptance* of norms that permit X, or is she merely expressing a belief that X is permitted by certain norms? More generally, must I accept a norm in order to express my belief that it permits X? I think not. If my dinner companion seems flustered about conventional table manners, it would not be strange for me to say, "That's the right fork, for what it's worth." In this way, I genuinely endorse her choice of forks by expressing my belief that her choice is permitted by norms of etiquette that *she* accepts (and about which she would like to be more knowledgeable). But I express my belief without implying that I accept those norms myself. I merely know about them.

Thus, in matters of etiquette, using a norm as a basis for endorsement does not presuppose that one accepts the norm. The same holds true when we endorse a choice as rational. If my dinner companion tells me she has accepted a proposal of marriage, it would not be too strange for me to convey, if not in these exact words, "I'm happy for you. For you, it's rational, partly because you accept the legal and religious norms that help to make up the institution of marriage. Although I reject those norms myself and thus will never marry, I can see that for you getting married makes perfect sense." Although I do not reject out of hand Gibbard's analysis in terms of norm acceptance, I worry that people could call something rational with more detachment than his analysis seems to allow. Accordingly, I will use the more general of

9

Gibbard's two formulations: To call something rational is to endorse it.

Although I prefer the more general formulation, in one respect it is too general. Gibbard is right that calling X rational falls into the genus of ways of endorsing X. But it is less clear that calling X rational is coextensive with that genus. When we call something rational, are we merely endorsing it in a generic way, or are we offering a specific kind of endorsement? The latter seems more natural. At a restaurant, when the waiter brings the salad and my companion hesitantly picks up the smaller fork, I might say, "That's the right fork." Am I calling it rational to pick the smaller fork? Not to my knowledge. The norm by which I endorse her selection of the smaller fork is a norm of etiquette rather than of rationality. I can express a norm of etiquette, one that mandates using the small fork to eat salad, without expressing or implying the thought that using the small fork is rational. I can endorse X (and even express acceptance of norms that permit X) without at the same time calling X rational.

I also suspect that our calling something rational does not quite entail that we endorse it. As Gibbard points out, we can call something rational in a sour tone of voice (p. 50). On the other hand, we can offer an endorsement without being cheerful. A grudging endorsement is still an endorsement. Must the endorsement we express when we call a choice rational be without reservation? In part, this depends on whether we take the term to express an "all things considered" judgment or something more narrow. If in calling a choice rational we mean that it is the thing to choose, all things considered, then we can have no reservations about it beyond the reservation that we might be mistaken about its being rational. In contrast, if we express a less comprehensive kind of endorsement when we call a choice rational, then we may have reservations about it (and may convey that fact by speaking in a sour tone of voice) despite being convinced that it is rational.

I do not want to leave the impression, however, that something momentous hangs on how we decide to use the term 'rational'. Gibbard says that settling what it is rational to do settles what to do, period (p. 49). I think we could go either way. For our purposes, it makes no difference, because whether we follow Gibbard in reserving the term 'rational' to refer to an "all things considered" sort of judgment, it remains the case that moral considerations sometimes conflict with other considerations when we are settling what to do. Such conflicts are internal to rationality in Gibbard's "all things considered" sense, but they still occur, no matter how we use the terms. Whether we identify rationality with the entire genus of normative endorsement, we are left needing to consider how moral and nonmoral considerations weigh against each other when we are deciding what to do. I will return to the question of how moral endorsement differs from other kinds of endorsement. The next two sections discuss when something warrants the endorsement we imply when we call it rational.

WARRANTED ENDORSEMENT

Gibbard says that when we call something rational, we are doing more than offering a mere description of it. He is right. Calling something rational is also (or at least tends to be) an expression of endorsement. Gibbard chastises people who "take the characteristics that go to make something rational and have them constitute the meaning of the term" (p. 10). In my words, Gibbard's point is that the descriptive features that occasion endorsement are less central to the meaning of rationality than is the element of endorsement itself. People quarrel over whether particular choices are rational, and generally the dispute is not terminological. If my student argues with her parents about whether it is rational for her to major in philosophy, they will not be arguing about what the term means. They all understand that to call a choice rational is to endorse it. They argue precisely because they agree that to call a choice rational is to endorse it, and they disagree about whether majoring in philosophy is worthy of the endorsement implicit in calling it rational.

This is plausible, as far as it goes. Yet, to call a choice rational is to try to say *something* about it. Calling a choice rational is not mere description, but it is not mere endorsement either. Earlier, I suggested that Gibbard views the term 'rational' as not merely descriptive. Actually, Gibbard thinks the term is not descriptive at all. Gibbard insists that to call a choice rational is not to attribute a property to it, not even the property of being permitted by accepted norms (p. 8). Now, if he is saying there is no particular property in terms of which we can analyze the meaning of the term 'rational',

11

he might be right. It is hard to say. But the real question concerns whether there are particular qualities in a choice to which we *refer* when we pick it out as rational. And if there is nothing in the choice that leads us to call it rational, then there is no reason for our endorsement. In that case, something has gone awry.

The point for us to stress, then, is that calling X rational does more than simply convey endorsement. It also conveys that we think we have good reasons for endorsement. Even if Gibbard is correct in saying that no particular property ascription is implied by the term's meaning, we nevertheless are not using the term properly unless we take X to have some property or other that gives us a basis for endorsement. Think about it from a listener's point of view: When we call something rational, people understand us to be saying not just that we endorse it but also that we think we have *reasons* for endorsement. To call X rational is not to endorse X in the way one might whimsically endorse pistachio as a flavor of ice cream. Rather, to call X rational is to imply a belief that X *warrants* endorsement. Listeners may not interpret us as having specified a reason for endorsement, but they will interpret us as thinking we have a some sort of reason for endorsement. I accept Gibbard's claim that to call something rational is to endorse it. Yet, there remains a question about exactly what, descriptively speaking, we pick out for endorsement when we call a choice rational.

Sometimes, at least, we call a choice rational because we think it will serve the chooser's ends. Understood in this way, to call a choice rational is, first, to endorse it, second, to have a reason for endorsement, and third, to have as one's reason for endorsement that the choice will serve the chooser's ends.[4] When I call a choice rational, I may be saying that it will in fact serve the chooser's ends or that the chooser has good reason to think it will (whether or not it actually does so). In any case, rational choice, as understood

---

[4] What do we mean when we call a *person* rational? We are endorsing the person neither as a means to the person's ends nor as a means to someone else's ends. Typically we are saying that the person is using his or her cognitive capacities in a way that effectively serves his or her ends. Similarly, to call a choice rational is to endorse it as a means to the chooser's ends, but such endorsement implies an assumption that the choice involved deliberation. Otherwise, the endorsement is not apt. For more on conditions that support endorsement, and countervailing conditions, see the next section.

here, involves seeking to choose effective means to one's ends. This is the heart of my characterization of rational choice. It does not have a lot of content, but we will see that it has enough to support the conclusion that, for most people, being moral is rational.

BELIEFS AS INPUTS AND BELIEFS AS OUTPUTS

Whether the chooser's *beliefs* are rational is another issue. What an agent has reason to choose depends on what the agent believes, but I say this without presupposing any particular theory of rational belief. Practical rationality, or rational choice, is about making choices in light of what one believes. Being rational in the practical sense involves seeking to choose effective means to one's ends, given one's beliefs. I acknowledge that issues of epistemic rationality arise at an earlier stage when one forms beliefs. If we were talking about belief rather than choice, our grounds for endorsement might well be something other than means-end efficacy.[5]

Although a theory of rational choice need not be committed to any particular theory about rational belief, I do want to comment on a curious property of beliefs that is crucial to any theory of rational choice aspiring to have practical significance for human beings. What I have in mind is that the processes by which we acquire and revise beliefs can be compromised by our choices. For example, when we make choices we could not justify to others (or would feel uncomfortable trying to justify), such a state tends to induce irrational belief-forming processes: projection, repression, spurious rationalization, and so on. Clearly, such processes can hurt us. They can obscure the nature of our ends. They can lead us to overlook incongruity in the means we choose to our ends. They can block our pursuit of self-understanding.[6]

Because the consequences of irrational belief-forming processes can be momentous, it is of the essence of humanly rational choice that it involves recognizing and coping with the fact that we cannot

---

[5] Robert Nozick advises, "Believe [hypothesis] *h* only if the expected utility of believing *h* is not less than the expected utility of having no belief about *h*" (1993, p. 92). Means-end efficacy is thus a necessary condition for rational belief in Nozick's theory, but not the only one. For example, hypothesis *h* must have at least minimal credibility and must be more credible than the alternatives.

[6] See Velleman (1989, especially chap. 1) on the desire for self-understanding.

13

take our own rationality for granted. If we care about rational choice, we have to care about the rationality of our belief-forming processes to the extent that their reliability is predictabily affected by our choices. In a discussion of moral motivation, T. M. Scanlon observes that the desire to be able to justify one's actions to others on grounds they could not reasonably reject may not be universal, but it is quite strong in most people (1982, p. 117). I mention the point here because, when we feel others *could* reasonably object to a choice, that feeling can count against the choice's rationality, insofar as such feelings tend to trigger psychological defense mechanisms that compromise the reliability of our belief-forming processes.[7]

In different words, practical rationality proceeds from whatever beliefs a person has, and so the epistemic rationality of beliefs as inputs into choices is a peripheral issue here. However, we do need to distinguish between beliefs (as inputs into decisions) and changes in beliefs (as outputs of decisions). The epistemic rationality of our beliefs as outputs of our choices is a central concern.

When a choice induces spurious rationalization as part of its output, it thereby compromises the reliability of the person's beliefs as inputs into future choices; it lowers the quality of inputs into future choices, which typically would be contrary to practical rationality. Therefore, even in the most narrowly practical terms, we cannot ignore issues of epistemic rationality. There is no need here for a *theory* of epistemic rationality, but we do need to be aware that, human psychology being what it is, our choices affect the reliability of our belief-forming processes. This is just one of the many ways in which our choices affect us, though, and that more general topic—our choices and how they affect us—is this book's main concern.

If we set out to formulate a sufficient condition for rational choice, we might need to say more about the role of beliefs as inputs into our choices. We might need to say something like: A

---

[7] Unfortunately, even if it is true that we strongly desire to justify ourselves to others on grounds they could not reasonably reject, it is also true that we desire simply to be accepted by others. Therein lies a source of psychological pressure that can undercut moral motivation, because there can be a big difference between what people do accept and what they should accept (or could not reasonably reject). Later chapters, especially Chapter 9, return to this point.

choice is rational if it serves an agent's ends, assuming the agent is cognizant of how it will serve his or her ends and makes the choice on that basis. Fleshing out such a qualification might call for a theory of epistemic rationality. But no matter what caveats we would need to introduce if we were attempting to formulate a sufficient condition, there remains a close link between rational choice and means-end efficacy.

We can describe that link by saying means-end efficacy is a *supporting condition* for rational choice. A supporting condition is a qualified sufficient condition, qualified in the sense of being sufficient in the absence of countervailing conditions. In different words, a supporting condition is sufficient to shift the burden of proof. Analogously, in a court of law, certain kinds of evidence are regarded as sufficient, in the absence of countervailing evidence, to establish legal liability. For example, under a certain set of liability rules, if the plaintiff can show that you ran over his bicycle, that suffices to establish your legal liability unless you can show in turn that the plaintiff was negligent in leaving his bicycle on the ground behind your car. In the same way, evidence that a choice will serve the chooser's ends warrants our endorsing the choice as rational, barring countervailing evidence (for example, barring evidence that the chooser was not cognizant of the manner in which the choice would serve his or her or its ends).

In this qualified way, the fact that a choice will serve the chooser's ends suffices as grounds for endorsing the choice as rational. Of course, actual means-end efficacy is neither necessary nor strictly sufficient as grounds for calling a choice rational, but we do not need necessary and sufficient conditions.[8] When we see people choosing effective means to their ends, we have grounds for calling their choices rational, so long as we recognize the possibility of countervailing evidence. For example, we might resist calling a choice rational, even though it served the chooser's ends, if the chooser had no idea that it would serve his or her ends in the way it did. An objectively warranted choice may yet have been unwarranted in a subjective sense.

[8] Projects that begin by trying to analyze key concepts in terms of necessary and sufficient conditions tend to bog down in minutiae before they can get started. For most philosophical projects, supporting conditions are more to the point. I will rely on them again in my analysis of moral agency (see Part II).

Objectively Warranted Endorsement

Previous sections sketched the view that to call a choice rational is to endorse it as a means to the chooser's ends. This section distinguishes between warranting endorsement in an objective sense and warranting endorsement in a subjective sense. I then consider how the distinction leaves the strategy of maximizing expected utility open to rational criticism.

Perhaps endorsement can be warranted only from the perspectives of particular people. I judge my choices rational according to whether they warrant endorsement from my perspective. I judge your choices rational according to whether I think they warrant endorsement from your perspective. Even so, to endorse a choice as rational is to endorse it not arbitrarily but on particular grounds. If we endorse a choice as serving the chooser's ends, then whether the choice actually warrants such endorsement is a matter of fact, not a matter of opinion. This is not to deny that this matter of fact might turn on facts that are agent-relative. Whether choosing to pursue a career in philosophy will serve my student's ends may be a factual question, but the answer will of course depend on facts about her. The rationality of her choice does not turn on her opinion per se, and thus is to that extent objective, but it does turn on her ends. Thus, given my means-end conception of rationality—a conception that can hardly be considered unusual—it follows that whether a choice warrants endorsement as rational is a question the answer to which is both agent-relative and objective.

Why does this matter? Gibbard says we do not need objective standards in order to get guidance. Consider a variation of an example of Gibbard's (p. 18). A hiker is lost in the woods, wanting very much to get back to town. There is an objectively best path in this case, for there is a path that as a matter of fact would best serve the hiker's ends: a straight line back to town. Nevertheless, the rational path in this case is not identical to the objectively best path. The rational path is the path that follows the river. Why? Because the hiker is operating under incomplete information. (He is, after all, lost.) Because he has no idea which direction constitutes a straight line back to town, he concludes that following the river has the highest expected utility. Although the river path is a roundabout way of getting back to town, it is the path most likely to eventually bring him safely back. The river path is thus subjectively justified. It is subjectively justified in the sense that, given what the hiker knows about the situation, the river path seems most likely to serve his ends. If it actually serves his ends, then it is an objective success as well.

What does Gibbard conclude? Gibbard reasons that either we do not know enough to follow an objectively best path, one that best serves our ends, or if we do know enough, then the path we follow is also subjectively best. Either way, what we follow is the subjectively best path. Objective standards are either useless or superfluous (p. 43).[9] Gibbard seems to think nothing more needs to be said, that the idea of a subjectively right path is intelligible independent of objective standards of rightness.

This is not so. On the contrary, the idea that there is a subjectively best path presupposes that the hiker has standards of objective rightness. Suppose the story continues. The hiker's downstream trail leads him ever deeper into the woods. The sun goes down, his legs will carry him no farther, and it begins to look as though he will freeze to death. At this point, does the hiker review his strategy, find that it was impeccable by subjective standards, and die happy? Not at all. In fact, he has cause for regret, for his subjectively justified strategy is an objective failure. His strategy had the highest subjective probability of success. The point of the subjectively justified strategy, though, was to maximize the likelihood of objective success, where objective success consisted of getting safely back to town. A subjectively right strategy is a means to the end of getting the hiker back to town, and whether it serves that end is an objective matter.

Gibbard thinks there is "no need, then, for an account of what it means to call an act wrong in the objective sense" (p. 43). However, as I understand the term 'objective' (Gibbard must have something else in mind), this is not true. On the contrary, we need a sense of objective right and wrong to have a *purpose* in formulating subjective strategies and to distinguish between the successes and the failures of subjectively justified strategies. It is important to

[9] Allan Gibbard (1990) makes these remarks in a discussion of moral rightness, but he views rationality as encompassing all considerations of what it makes sense to do. I could be wrong, but the context strongly suggests that he intends his remarks to be about rationality in general.

be subjectively right (that is, to choose a strategy that, to the best of one's knowledge, is most likely to achieve the end) if and only if it is important to be objectively right (that is, to actually achieve the end). Maximizing expected utility is a means to the end of maximizing actual utility. More generally, being subjectively justified is a means to the end of being objectively right.[10]

Two points of clarification: First, I am not arguing with Gibbard about whether the hiker is rational. I agree that the hiker is rational and that he is rational precisely because his strategy is subjectively justified (that is, it has the highest subjective probability of getting him back to town). I claim, though, that objective standards of rightness, far from being superfluous, are crucial to an understanding of subjective justification. There is a distinction not between subjective and objective rationality as such but rather between the subjective justification we can have in choosing means and the objective success we can have in achieving ends.[11] There can be no conception of a strategy's subjective justification except in the context of a conception of the strategy's objective success.

Second, saying this does not commit us to holding that some ends are better than others independent of people's preferences. Some ends may well be better in that sense, but I have not relied on any such idea here. Suppose we grant that what it is rational for a person to choose ultimately depends on the person's actual present purposes. Consider what this supposition does not imply. It does not imply that people, as rational agents, must take their present purposes as a simple given. On the contrary, it is a fact about hu-

[10] The same conclusion holds when the hiker knows that the river path will take him back to town but also knows that the river path is not the shortest path. In that case, the hiker maximizes expected utility not by seeking the path with maximum actual utility but rather by seeking a merely satisfactory path. Must rationally seeking a satisfactory alternative always be a way of maximizing? See Chapter 2.

[11] There may also be a distinction between subjective and objective rationality. Insofar as a choice is rational if it warrants endorsement as a means to the chooser's ends, we can say a choice is subjectively rational if it is subjectively warranted and objectively rational if it is objectively warranted. I do not use this distinction in what follows, but it would hold up under any number of ways of drawing the prior distinction between subjective and objective. For example, we could distinguish between the best alternative as far as the agent knows and the best alternative in fact, although I think we express that distinction less ambiguously when we speak in terms of subjective justification versus objective success.

man beings that our ends can change, which suggests that a person's existing corpus of ends sometimes might be well served by processes that predictably cause the corpus of ends to change. For example, our desire to be healthy might be well served by developing nutritional and exercise goals. Further, a preexisting end of being healthy is best served if we come to like jogging and eating broccoli for their own sake, not only for the sake of their conduciveness to our health. Taking our present ends as simple givens could lead us to overlook opportunities to further them.

Even more puzzling, there may be cases in which one has no real means of weighing alternatives until after one makes some basic choices. Even when there is nothing prospectively to be said for one alternative compared to another, it can still be true that whichever one we choose, we will in retrospect be glad we chose it. This is because our choices can change us in such a way that we come to have a framework within which previous choices emerge as suitable for the people we are becoming. In simpler words, we tend to accommodate ourselves to our choices; we grow into them.[12]

Static rationality involves assessing means to present ends we take as given. We can talk about rational choice in a static sense, so long as we realize that static rationality is not the only thing there is to talk about. There is a conversation that comes to an end when we have identified means to the chooser's actual present ends. But there is another conversation that begins when we reflect on how people's present capacities and present ends evolve as a consequence of their choices. This, too, is a conversation about rational choice, but it is rational choice of a different kind, a reflective kind of rationality that we understand better if we keep in mind that it is different.

"Why Be Rational" as an Empirical Question

Because there is a difference between being subjectively justified and being objectively right, we cannot jump from saying rational choice involves seeking to choose effective means to one's ends to saying rational choice involves seeking to maximize expected utility. Consider: Why would anyone seek to maximize expected util-

---

[12] Chapters 2 and 4 explore this issue.

ity? Presumably, one thinks that maximizing expected utility will have actual utility, which is to say, one thinks that maximizing expected utility will serve one's ends. Maximizing expected utility is a strategy. A strategy is something we adopt as a means to an end. Whether a strategy serves its purpose is an objective and contingent matter. Therefore, there is no strategy, not even maximizing expected utility, that we can simply equate with being rational.[13] Even if we can say the hiker's end is to maximize actual utility, it remains an open question whether a strategy of maximizing expected utility is an effective means to that end. Maximizing *expected* utility cannot possibly be the hiker's end; by hypothesis, he *did* maximize expected utility, yet he manifestly did not get what he wanted.

Part of the point of asking "why be rational" is to draw attention to the fact that it is tautologous that we have reason to do what serves our ends, and yet it is not tautologous that we have reason to be utility maximizers or to affect a deliberate and calculating demeanor. To endorse a choice as rational is to endorse it as a means to an end. This is the basic concept. To get to the conclusion that it is rational to employ a utility-maximizing strategy or to affect an unemotional demeanor, we need empirical premises, premises that are sometimes true in the real world but that often are not. If rational choice is thought of as involving a certain way of pursuing goals, then it will be an empirical question whether people are better off pursuing goals in that way.

For example, there are limits to the rationality of being deliberate and calculating. Some situations call for spontaneity or for a certain lack of concern. A well-ordered life makes room for a certain amount of disorder, both because some disorder is inevitable and also because good things sometimes come from it.[14] Effectively serving one's ends need not always involve being fully in con-

---

[13] John C. Harsanyi does equate rationality with maximizing expected utility, at least in the context of decision making under conditions of risk or uncertainty (1982, p. 44), as does Richard Fumerton (1990, pp. 101, 109). See also "Reason and Maximization" in David Gauthier (1990).

[14] Also, as Michael E. Bratman observes, we are "planning creatures. On the other hand, the world changes in ways we are not in a position to anticipate; so highly detailed plans about the future will often be of little use and not worth bothering with" (1990, p. 19). We form partial plans and sometimes are appropriately casual about matters of detail.

trol of the situation or even being fully in control of oneself. Some of life's most precious moments are moments when we are merely "along for the ride." For any strategy or character trait having a close empirical association with rationality, there will be limits to how rational it is to cling to that strategy or that persona, for there will be circumstances in which things that normally serve our purposes would be counterproductive.

Being rational typically involves carefully weighing costs and benefits, but carefully weighing costs and benefits is itself an activity with costs and benefits, and so if we step back to weigh the costs and benefits of being rational, we may foresee situations in which being rational in that sense is not worth the price. There might be times when we will lose opportunities if we stop to think them over carefully. There may also be times when stopping to think them over would change the nature of the alternatives. For example, buying your spouse a bracelet only after carefully deliberating about anticipated costs and benefits might not be the same kind of act as buying your spouse a bracelet in a burst of carefree affection. The latter kind of act might serve your purposes better.

So much for things contingently associated with being rational, things like hard-headed strategies and calculating demeanors. These things usually serve us well, but they are sometimes out of place. Setting aside contingent associations, then, rational choice essentially involves seeking to choose effective means to one's ends. Given this understanding of rationality, can there be limits to how rational it is to seek effective means to one's ends? Can there be limits to how rational it is rational to be? I think so. There are times when means-end reasoning is counterproductive. If Tom is just getting involved in a new romantic relationship, for example, he might be well-advised to relax and let things happen. Thinking too hard about how to achieve his goals could make him look unromantic, and thus be precisely what stops him from achieving his goals.[15]

---

[15] This might be an example of a case where calling Tom's choice rational would not be a way of (even grudgingly) endorsing it. Calling Tom's choice rational might be our way of trying to explain to Tom where he went wrong. We may be telling Tom that truly rational people realize that, in a romantic context, a rational-chooser frame of mind is not what the situation calls for. I thank Jim Hamilton for this point.

Why be rational, then? This is not an idle question. It has an answer, namely, that being rational—seeking effective means to our ends—generally serves our ends. This is not a tautology. It is an empirical claim. While we always have reason to endorse effective means to our ends, we do not always have reason to endorse means-end reasoning itself, for there are times when means-end reasoning cannot survive self-scrutiny, when means-end reasoning would be counterproductive. In such cases, means-end reasoning can lead us to reject means-end reasoning as a way of guiding action. Means-end reasoning is not guaranteed to pass its own test.

When means-end reasoning would not serve one's ends, then choosing to engage in means-end reasoning would not be rational by the lights of a means-end account of rational choice. Note that we can scrutinize means-end reasoning in terms of its means-end efficacy without questioning the underlying means-end account of rational choice. We can hold that rational choice involves seeking to choose effective means to one's ends and at the same time acknowledge, without inconsistency, that being in a rational-chooser frame of mind is not always to our advantage.

Further, to summarize earlier remarks, there are limits to the rationality of strategies and behavioral patterns commonly but contingently associated with rationality. A given strategy or persona is rational insofar as it serves the agent's ends, and sometimes the things that normally serve an agent's ends would be out of place. Rationality does not always dictate being strategic, or being calculating, or being self-controlled. It usually does not dictate being inhibited, and it almost never dictates being humorless.

Making Room for Morality

As I mentioned earlier, if we follow Gibbard and equate rational choice with what makes the most sense, all things considered, then our question about the difference between being rational and being moral resurfaces as a question about the difference between morality and prudence as domains within "all things considered" rational choice. For some purposes, it might also be useful to define a domain of epistemic rationality. We could, for example, distinguish epistemic from prudential rationality by saying the former concerns the pursuit of truth[16] whereas the latter concerns the pursuit of one's long-range welfare.

While rational choice involves seeking to choose effective means to our ends, moral agency, as a first approximation, involves having certain ends and pursuing them within certain constraints. Conflict between rational choice and moral agency so conceived is not inevitable, but neither is convergence. We are left wanting to know which contingent factors can get us from a means-end form of rationality to the substantive ends and self-imposed constraints of morality.

Prudential rationality counsels us to seek effective ways of serving our ends, and in particular our long-range self-interest. Morality counsels us to do what is right. Each counsel seems incontestable on its own ground. From time to time, though, we need to choose. We can do what is in our best interest or what is right, but not both. It would be nice if we could settle which of the two—prudence or morality—has the stronger case, but the fact is that each has the stronger case on its own ground. Our only recourse is to explore the extent to which each, on its own ground, makes room for the other. Therein lies the strategy of this book.

Some people see rational choice as essentially tied not only to a formal notion of means-end efficacy but also to a substantive notion of self-regard. However, I see rational choice's tie to self-regard as merely contingent. It so happens that people tend to have predominantly self-regarding ends. Since our ends tend to be substantially self-regarding, rational choice tends to be aimed at self-regarding ends, but that is not the same as thinking those or any other substantive ends are an essential part of the concept of rational choice. There might be ways in which morality is coextensive with rationality without being coextensive in the same way with self-regard. Nor is morality exclusively tied to other-regard. Just as

---

[16] It is probably better to say the epistemic domain involves pursuing truth with respect to specific questions that come up in the course of one's particular pursuits, rather than pursuing some more Platonic notion of Truth. On this view, the goals defining the epistemic domain have little content in abstraction from the goals that define our pursuits in other domains and that raise particular issues with respect to which we want true beliefs. In this respect, then, goals defining the epistemic domain are parasitic on goals defining other domains.

there are rational reasons for other-regard, so, too, are there moral reasons for self-regard (see Chapter 8).

Identifying substantive grounds for moral endorsement is hard work reserved for later chapters, but without getting into questions about the content of moral reasons, let me say something here about their form. Deontology consists, in part, of a view that moral imperatives are categorical, which is to say their imperative force is not contingent on what the agent happens to desire. Against this, Philippa Foot says we "should be prepared to think that moral considerations give reasons for action only in ordinary ways" (1978, p. 154). When Foot speaks of giving reasons for action in ordinary ways, she means reasons appealing to interests and desires. I am not so sure moral considerations give reasons for action only in ordinary ways. Maybe there are other ways. Still, only the ordinary ways are uncontroversial. My plan, then, follows Foot insofar as it explores the extent to which moral considerations do in fact give reasons for action in ordinary ways.

This approach does not presuppose that moral imperatives are like this: "If I want to be moral, I should keep promises." Even if this imperative is true, it is still misleading at best as an account of why, morally speaking, I ought to keep promises. The reason why I morally ought to keep promises has little to do with whether I happen to want to be moral. (By way of comparison, consider: "If I want to be moral, then I *want* to keep promises." We can agree that whether I want to keep promises can depend on whether I want to be moral, but this tells why I might want to keep promises rather than why I ought to.)

Hypothetical imperatives are imperatives such that, were we to put them in "if, then" grammatical form, their if-clauses would be couched in terms of appeals to the agent's interests and desires. Hypothetical imperatives can appeal to a desire to be moral, but such an appeal makes them nonetheless hypothetical. Unlike Foot, I am perfectly content with the idea that moral imperatives are categorical. They present themselves to us as imperatives we ought to obey whether or not we want to. Morally speaking, we should keep promises, period, whether or not we want to be moral. The lesson to take from Foot's argument is not that moral imperatives are hypothetical but rather that moral motivation is contingent. Even if moral imperatives are categorical, our motivation to obey them is hypothetical—contingent to some degree on what we desire.[17] I explore this contingency later, asking how people can be led by ordinary interests and desires to internalize reasons for action that transcend ordinary interests and desires (see Chapters 5 and 6).

A related point is this: the categorical nature of moral imperatives is not what makes them moral. Etiquette and prudence also embody imperatives with a kind of normativity grounded in something other than an appeal to inclination. If we say X is a lie, or X is rude, or X is unhealthy, we are endorsing an abstention from X on grounds going beyond appeal to occurrent desire. If we say that what Kate is doing is immoral (or is rude or is unhealthy) and Kate responds by saying "I'm grateful for your concern, but as it happens I don't care about such things," we will feel she has missed the point, for the normative force of what we said was not contingent on what Kate desires. On the contrary, the force is categorical.[18] Kate ought to care about such things, and not caring about them is shocking. Still, although any of these failures would be shocking in their own way, not all of them are moral failures. Although norms of etiquette are categorical, they have none of the special normative force of moral imperatives.

Morality's special normative force—what makes it different from mere etiquette—is its teleology. Moral imperatives have a characteristic importance and urgency in virtue of being grounded in principles that are very general, nonarbitrary, and at the heart of what makes it possible for human beings to flourish in communities. Norms of etiquette are categorical, but to be categorical is not necessarily to be important. Norms of etiquette are in many ways quite like norms of morality, but they do not have the kind of central and ineliminably pervasive importance in human affairs

---

[17] Philippa Foot herself has come to regret her use of Kantian terminology (1978, p. xiii). It turns out that she distinguishes between hypothetical imperatives and hypothetical ought-statements, which leads her to say that rules of etiquette (and morality), although they may be hypothetical imperatives, nevertheless embody nonhypothetical uses of 'should' (p. 161). I suspect, then, that Foot and I have no substantive dispute about the point expressed in the above text. We would agree about the sense in which moral imperatives are categorical.

[18] Or perhaps it would be better to say we are voicing an *assertoric* imperative. Assertoric imperatives (see Kant, 1981, pp. 31–33) appeal to ends that human beings in general (perhaps even rational beings in general) are presumed to have. If a person denies having those ends, the denial would raise questions about the person's rationality.

that moral norms have.[19] The distinction, though, is largely one of degree. Really bad manners (like barging to the front of a line to buy tickets) shade into immorality. Really trivial immorality (like breaking a promise to bring dessert for a potluck party) shades into bad manners.

CONCLUSION

This chapter began by arguing that normative force—a reason for action—comes into being along with a person's ends. When one has ends, one has reasons to act in some ways rather than in others. Specifically, one has reasons to seek means to those ends. Along the way, we saw how this account makes room for a notion of objectivity. Indeed, without standards of objective rightness, there would be no point in trying to be subjectively justified. A subjectively justified course of action is chosen as a means to an end, and whether it achieves its end is an objective matter.

My goal in characterizing rationality in means-end terms is not to be comprehensive but rather to start with a minimal account, uncontroversial as far as it goes, and then see how far we can go with it. In the end, I will not deny that being rational involves more than seeking means to one's ends, but neither will I start by assuming that rationality involves more than that.

One of the main reasons to be skeptical about means-end accounts of rational choice is that they seem to leave us with nothing to say about ends themselves. However, we will see that the means-end conception is not as obviously incomplete an account of rational choice as it might first appear to be. In Chapter 3, we will see that, for beings like us in situations like ours, rational choice extends to the evaluation of ends as well as means. This extension of rational choice is not a departure from the basic means-end concept, for it brings ends under the scope of rational choice by bringing in empirical facts about human nature rather than by expanding the concept per se.[20] Surprisingly, the idea that means-end efficacy is a reason for endorsement will prove to be all we need, in terms of *normative* premises, to transcend instrumental rationality

---

[19] Chapters 6 and 7 pursue this further.

[20] Specifically, the extension takes account of the initial survival instinct and a certain capacity for reflection, as explained in Chapter 3.

and develop a conception of rationality ranging over ends as well as means.

As one might infer from what has been said so far, my rational choice theory is more closely tied to empirical considerations than is customary. My view is that decision theory has to be descriptive in part, because in order to have normative significance, it has to engage both our purposes and our capacities as they really are. To have normative force for us, a model has to tell us about means to ends (selfish and otherwise) we actually have, and it has to tell us about means that are actually available to us. What we ought to value depends on what we can value and on what would be good for us, which in turn depend on what we are like. The descriptive and normative facets of my theory will be intertwined throughout this book, because that is how it has to be for anyone aspiring to produce a normative theory relevant to beings like ourselves.

The first part of this book offers a theory about why we have the goals we do, and why we employ the strategies we employ—why we are not simple maximizers. More accurately, Part I offers a theory about why our goals and strategies are appropriate for beings like us. It is less concerned with the biological evolution of our goals and strategies and more concerned with why we have reason to be glad we have other-regarding ends and why we have reason to be glad we are not relentless maximizers. We are better off as we are. Our self-regarding ends are better served as parts of a package containing other-regarding ends than they would be by a package that cut out the other-regarding elements.

With respect to strategies, one might presume doing as well as possible involves *aiming* to do as well as possible. We saw that this is not a tautology but a controversial empirical claim, one that is sometimes true but often false. In general, as Chapter 2 explains, our goal of having life as a whole go as well as possible is best served by a combination of day-to-day strategies that often do not involve seeking optima.

Choosing Strategies

Two Kinds of Strategies

Suppose i need to decide whether to go off to fight for a cause in which I deeply believe or to stay home with a family that needs me and that I deeply love. What should I do? My friends say I should determine the possible outcomes of the two proposed courses of action, assign probabilities and numerical utilities to each possibility, multiply through, and then choose whichever alternative has the highest number.

My friends are wrong. Their proposal would be plausible in games of chance where information on probabilities and monetarily denominated utilities is readily available. In the present case, however, I can only guess at the possible outcomes of either course of action. Nor do I know their probabilities. Nor do I know how to gauge their utilities. The strategy of maximizing expected utility is out of the question, for employing it requires information that I do not have.

Nevertheless, my friends have not given up trying to help, and so they point out that I could simulate the process of maximizing expected utility by assuming a set of possible outcomes, estimating their probabilities, and then making educated guesses about how much utility they would have. I could indeed do this, but I decide not to, for it occurs to me that I have no reason to trust the formula for maximizing expected utility when I have nothing but question marks to plug into it. Better strategies are available, and explaining what they are is the purpose of this chapter.

This section distinguishes between optimizing and satisficing strategies and between moderate and immoderate preferences. The following three sections discuss, in turn, when satisficing strategies are rational, when they are not, and when cultivating moderate preferences is rational. Later sections offer a way of characterizing rational choice in situations where the agent's alternatives are incommensurable.

In the simplest context, one has a set of alternatives clearly ranked in terms of their utility as means to one's ends. If one is an *optimizer*, one chooses an alternative that ranks at least as high as any other. In contrast, if one is a *satisficer*, one settles for any alternative one considers satisfactory. In this static context, though, it is hard to see the point of choosing a suboptimal alternative, even if it is satisfactory.

In a more dynamic and more typical context, we are not presented with a set of nicely ranked alternatives. Instead, we have to look for them, judging their utility as we go. In this context, optimizing involves terminating one's search for alternatives upon concluding that one has found the best available alternative. However, although optimizing involves selecting what one judges is best, it need not involve judging what is best, all things considered, because sophisticated optimizers recognize that considering all things is not always worth the cost. There may be constraints (temporal, financial, and so on) on how much searching they can afford to do. A person who stops the search upon concluding that prolonging the search is not worth the cost is also employing an optimizing strategy, albeit one of a more subtle variety.[1]

Satisficing, in contrast, involves terminating the search for alternatives upon concluding that one has identified a satisfactory alternative. What distinguishes satisficing from optimizing in the dynamic context is that the two strategies employ different *stopping rules*.[2] Thus, if options emerge serially, a subtle optimizer might choose a known option in preference to the alternative, namely, searching for something better with no guarantee of ever finding it.

[1] Michael Stocker (1990, pp. 311–16) argues that optimizing, even in this subtle sense, is both morally and rationally problematic.

[2] I borrow the term 'satisficing' from Michael Slote (1989, p. 5), but my characterization of satisficing differs from his. My understanding is closer to that of Herbert A. Simon. Simon's (1955) idea is that, given our limited capacity to acquire and process information, we economize on our limited capacity by setting a concrete goal and then reasoning back to conclusions about what course of action would achieve that goal. This is what Simon means by satisficing. The notion of satisficing as a stopping rule is implied, and later becomes explicit (see Simon, 1979, p. 3). See also James March (1988, p. 270). Simon treats satisficing as a surrogate for optimizing under particular information constraints and, so far as I know, treats our limited information as an external constraint. I think such constraints are often more accurately viewed as being partly self-imposed. Within the context of constraints that are in part self-imposed, the distinction between satisficing and optimizing becomes more interesting.

The difference between satisficing and this more subtle kind of optimizing has to do with what the two strategies take into account in reaching a stopping point. At any point in the search, we may let the expected utility of stopping the search equal U, the utility of the best option we have discovered so far. The expected utility of continued search equals the probability of finding a better option, $P(fbo)$, multiplied by the utility of finding a better option, $U(fbo)$, minus the cost of further search, $C(fs)$. At some point, the satisficer stops because he believes U is good enough. In contrast, the subtle optimizer stops because she believes that $P(fbo)U(fbo) - C(fs) < 0$. Even if the two stopping rules happen to converge on the same stopping point, they do so for different reasons and require different information.[3]

Unlike the optimizer, who stops searching when she either has considered all her options or has run up against things like time constraints, the satisficer stops the search upon identifying an alternative as good enough.[4] For example, suppose you enter a cafeteria seeking a nutritionally balanced and reasonably tasty meal. You then proceed down the cafeteria line surveying the alternatives. If you are satisficing, you take the first meal that you deem nutritionally and aesthetically adequate. If you are optimizing, you continue down the line surveying alternatives until you reach the end of the line or run out of time. You then take the meal you consider optimal, either in comparison to the other known options or in comparison to the alternative of further search. A satisfactory meal may or may not be optimal. Likewise, as cafeteria patrons know only too well, the best available meal may or may not be

---

[3] For further discussion of how the two stopping rules differ and how they might usefully be combined, see the Appendix to this chapter.

[4] There may not be any precise way to characterize 'good enough'. Options promising disease, imprisonment, or premature death are typically held in low esteem, however, so the notion has certain objective elements. But what people consider good enough also seems relative to expectations. As expectations rise, the standards by which an option is judged good enough also tend to rise. This fact can be tragic. It can rob people of the ability to appreciate how well their lives are going, all things considered. Of course, it is rational to set *goals* with an eye to what is attainable, raising one's sights as higher goals become attainable. But raising the standard by which we deems our situation satisfactory is harder to fathom. Perhaps people are psychologically incapable of aiming at higher goals without simultaneously reformulating their notions of what is satisfactory. I do not know.

satisfactory. Of course, if you switch from one stopping rule to the other, you might end up choosing the same meal, but you will be choosing it for a different reason. Therefore, neither rule is reducible to the other. (One could employ both stopping rules simultaneously, of course, resolving to stop as soon as one finds a satisfactory alternative, or runs out of time, or has considered all available alternatives—whichever comes first.) Nor can satisficing be equated with the more subtle kind of optimizing that takes the cost of searching for more-than-satisfactory alternatives into account. Satisficers select the satisfactory alternative because it is satisfactory, not because they calculate that stopping the search at that point would maximize utility.

With this characterization of satisficing in mind, we can now clarify the difference between satisficing and *moderation*. Satisficing contrasts with optimizing. Being moderate, however, contrasts not with optimizing but with being immoderate. Being an optimizer does not entail being immoderate, and being a satisficer does not entail that one would be satisfied with a moderate bundle of goods. A person could be both a moderate and an optimizer, for the maximally satisfying bundle of goods for a given person may well be of moderate size. Likewise, a person could be both a satisficer and an immoderate, for a given satisficer may have wildly immoderate ideas about what counts as satisfactory. Consider a person whose goal in life is to be a millionaire (not a billionaire, mind you, just a millionaire) by the age of thirty.

When Satisficing Is Rational

There is an apparent incongruence between the theory and practice of rational choice. Theory models rational choice as optimizing choice, yet, in practice, satisficing is ubiquitous. We could explain away the incongruence by saying that when people think they are looking for something satisfactory, what they are really looking for is something optimal. But satisficing can be reconstructed as a subtle kind of optimizing strategy only on pain of attributing to people calculations they often do not perform (and do not have the information to perform) and intentions they often do not have. This section explains satisficing in terms of thought processes we can recognize in ourselves. Satisficing emerges as a real alternative to

31

optimizing, and thus as a strategy that can be evaluated, criticized, and sometimes redeemed as rational.

We begin with the observation that people have a multiplicity of goals. For example, a person can desire to be healthy, to have a successful career, to be a good parent, and so forth. Some goals are broad and others narrow, relatively speaking. Further, a given goal might be encompassed by another in the sense that the narrower goal's point—the reason for it being a goal—is that it is part of what one does in pursuit of a larger goal. For example, Kate might want to upgrade her wardrobe because she cares about her appearance because she wants a promotion because she cares about her career. Suppose she believes that achieving her various goals is instrumental to or constitutive of achieving a broader goal of making her life as a whole go well. To mark the difference in breadth between Kate's concern for her life as a whole and her concern for particular aspects of her life (such as her health or her career), let us say Kate seeks a *local* optimum when she seeks to make a certain aspect of her life go as well as possible. Kate seeks a *global* optimum when she seeks to make her life as a whole go as well as possible.[5]

Optima can be defined as such only within the context of the constraints under which goals are pursued. (Thus, when economists speak of maximizing utility, it goes without saying that they are talking about maximizing utility subject to a budget constraint.) We pursue goals subject to the limits of our knowledge, time, energy, ability, income, and so on. More intriguing, however, is that we typically operate under additional constraints that we have deliberately imposed on ourselves, as if the constraints imposed on us by external circumstances were too loose. For example, if Tom spends an evening at a casino, he is externally constrained (by his savings and his borrowing power) to spend no more than, say, fifty thousand dollars. What actually defines his set of options over the course of the evening, though, is the hundred-dollar budget constraint that he *chose* to impose on himself.[6]

[5] I borrowed the terms 'local' and 'global' from Jon Elster (1984, p. 9), although a rereading of his text reveals that the way he uses the terms bears little resemblance to the way they are used here. (He says the definitive difference between locally and globally maximizing machines is that the latter, unlike the former, are capable of *waiting* and *indirect* strategies.)

[6] For someone wanting to construct a tractable mathematical model, it might be easier to ignore the felt experience of pursuing local goals under self-imposed

To give another example, in fleshing out the task of buying a house, we need to make some prior decisions. We decide how long to look, how much money to spend, what neighborhoods to consider. We knock only on doors of houses displaying "for sale" signs rather than on every door in the neighborhood. To some extent, these constraints are imposed on us by mundane external factors, but they also have a striking normative aspect, for they are in part rules of conduct we impose on ourselves; we take it upon ourselves to make our constraints more precise and more limiting so as to make our choice set more definite. Local optimizing would often be neurotic and even stupid if local goals were not pursued within compartments partly defined by self-imposed constraints. The constraints we impose on our narrower pursuits can keep narrower pursuits from ruining the larger plans of which they are part.[7]

If we look at life as a whole, we see that life as a whole will go better if we spend most of it pursuing goals that are narrower than the goal of making life as a whole go better. That is why it is rational to formulate and pursue local goals. But it is rational also to prevent narrower pursuits from consuming more resources than is warranted by the importance (from the global perspective) of achieving those narrower goals. Accordingly, when we pursue narrower goals, we pursue them under self-imposed constraints.

Although the constraints we impose on ourselves are imposed from a more encompassing perspective, it is only within the narrower perspective that we become subject to self-imposed constraints. (Of course, we are subject to external constraints, limited incomes and such, from any perspective.) Self-imposed constraints can be applied only *to* narrower pursuits and can be applied only *from* the perspective of a more encompassing pursuit. In more fa-

---

constraints and concentrate instead on the global perspective, from which self-imposed constraints appear, more or less, as preferences about how to operate within external constraints. I want to explain satisficing in terms of thought processes we can recognize within ourselves, though. For my purposes, the fact that we have both broader and narrower perspectives cannot be ignored.

[7] As Jules Coleman has pointed out to me, what David Gauthier (1986, p. 170) calls constrained maximization is a particularly interesting kind of local optimizing under self-imposed constraints. Constrained maximizers seek maximum payoffs in Prisoner's Dilemmas subject to this constraint: They will cooperate (and thus pass up the opportunity to unilaterally defect) if the expected payoff of cooperating is higher than the known payoff of *mutual* defection, which it will be if and only if they expect their partners to cooperate.

33

miliar terms, the point is that, because we have broader objectives, there are limits to what we will do for the sake of our wardrobe, or for the sake of a promotion, or for the sake of a career.

Having distinguished between local and global optimization, we can now explain when satisficing is rational. Michael Slote believes the optimizing tendency can be self-defeating. He says, "A person bent on eking out the most good he can in any given situation will take pains and suffer anxieties that a more casual individual will avoid." And he asks us to consider "how much more planful and self-conscious the continual optimizer must be in comparison with the satisficer who does not always aim for the best and who some-times rejects the best or better for the good enough" (1989, p. 40). In short, that one has an opportunity to pursue the good is not by itself a compelling reason to pursue the good. Surely, Slote has an important point. Just as surely, however, his point applies to local optimizing rather than to optimizing as such. From the global per-spective, seeking local optima can be a waste of time. Global opti-mizers seek local optima only when doing so serves their purposes. For that reason, satisficing is a big part of a global optimizer's daily routine. A compulsive seeking of local optima is associated with being immoderate, perhaps, but not with being a global optimizer. Effort can have diminishing returns, so a global optimizer will be careful not to try too hard. Local optimizing often gives way to satisficing for the sake of global optimality.

From the global optimizer's point of view, the process of buying a house provides a good example of how satisficing can be rational. When we choose a house, we might proceed by seeking the best available house within certain constraints—within a one-month time limit, for example. We impose such a limit because we have goals other than living in a nice house. Looking for a house com-petes with our other goals for our time and energy. Or, we might look for a satisfactory house and cease looking when we find one. Most of the people I have asked say they would optimize within constraints, but would not deem satisficing irrational. Like local optimizing, satisficing can serve our larger plans by setting limits on how much effort we put into seeking a house at the expense of other goals that become more important at some point, given the diminishing returns of remaining on the housing market. An opti-mizing strategy places limits on how much we are willing to invest in seeking alternatives. A satisficing strategy places limits on how much we insist on finding before we quit that search and turn our attention to other matters.[8]

The two strategies need not be inflexible. People sometimes have reason to switch or revise strategies as new information comes in. If we seek a satisfactory house in an unfamiliar neighborhood and are shocked to find one within five minutes, we may stop the search, acknowledging the stopping rule we previously imposed on that activity. On the other hand, we may conclude that, having formulated our aspiration level under unrealistically pessimistic assumptions, we should resume our search with a satisficing strategy revised to reflect a higher aspiration level. Or, we may switch to a local optimizing strategy, spending another day or two looking at houses, then taking the best we have found so far. Or we may do both, looking until we either reach our new aspiration level or reach our time limit. In this way, the two strategies often are interactive.

Likewise, suppose we started out planning to seek the best house we could find within a one-month time limit but have so far been terribly disappointed with our options. In this case, when after two weeks we finally find a house that meets our plummeting aspiration level, we may find ourselves embracing a sadder but wiser aspiration level as a stopping rule, abandoning our original plan to seek a local optimum relative to a one-month time constraint.

Typically, the more concrete our local goals are, the more reason there is to satisfice. If we do not know exactly what we are looking for, then we usually are better off setting a time limit and then taking what we like best within that limit. But if we know exactly what we are looking for, then it is rational to stop searching as soon as we find it.[9] So, having detailed information about our *goals* weighs in favor of using that information in formulating aspiration levels as stopping rules. Conversely, the more we know about our *set of alternatives*, the easier it is to identify which alternative has the highest utility, which weighs in favor of seeking local optima.

---

[8] The Appendix to this chapter uses graphical analysis to illustrate the difference between the two kinds of self-imposed limit.

[9] Jay Rosenberg tells me that, before he began looking for a house, he made a list of desirable features, telling himself he would take the first house having 85 percent or more of those features. As it happens, the first house he looked at scored 85 percent. He stopped looking, bought the house, and has lived there ever since.

The stakes involved are also pertinent—indeed crucial. The less we care about the gap between satisfactory and optimal toothpaste, for example, the more reason we have to satisfice, that is, to look for a satisfactory brand and stop searching when we find it. Note the alternative: Instead of satisficing, we could optimize by searching among different brands of toothpaste until we find the precise point at which further search is not worth its cost. But an optimal stopping point is itself something for which we would have to search, and locating it might require information (about the probability of finding a better brand of toothpaste, for example) that is not worth gathering, given the stakes involved in the original search for toothpaste. Against this, one might object to my assumption that we need precision in the search for an optimal stopping point. Why not seek to learn *roughly* when looking for better toothpaste is not worth the cost? In the search for a stopping point that we might graft onto the original search for toothpaste, it can be more rational to seek to be tolerably close to an optimum than to seek to be at an optimum.

But that is my point: There are cases where we do not care enough about the gap between the satisfactory and the optimal to make it rational to search for the optimal. Searching for optimal toothpaste can be a waste of time, but so can searching for the optimal moment to quit looking for toothpaste. One way or another, satisficing enters the picture. There will be times when even the most sophisticated optimizing strategies will be inappropriate, for they require information that we may not have and that may not be worth acquiring. And a less sophisticated "all things considered" strategy will nearly always be inappropriate. Rational choice involves considering only those things that seem worthy of consideration, which is to say it involves satisficing, that is, having a stopping rule that limits how comprehensive a body of information we insist on gathering before stopping the search and turning our attention to other matters.

There is also something to be said for having a moderate disposition—a disposition that allows one to be content with merely satisfactory states of affairs. Consider that starting a search too soon can be every bit as wasteful as stopping a search too late. Searching for a house is costly. It is costly partly because people have other goals; the time and energy you spend searching for a house could have been spent on other things. Even if you find a better house than you already have, the process of moving will also be costly. Moreover, it takes time living in and enjoying a house in order to recoup these costs. If you move every month, you will always be paying the costs and never enjoying the benefits of better housing. Moving into a house is part and parcel of a decision to stay a while, for it is only in staying that you collect on the investment of time and energy you made in moving. The general lesson is that costly transitions to preferred states of affairs require intervening periods of stability so that transition costs can be recovered and thus rationally justified. The stability of the intervening periods requires a disposition to be content for a while with what one has—to find something one likes and then stop searching.

Further, even if transition costs are relatively minor, there still can come a point when we should abandon the search for, say, a better job or a better spouse, not because such goals are unattainable or even because the transition costs are too high but rather because such goals eventually can become inappropriate. At some point, we have to start collecting the rewards that come only when we make a genuine commitment—when we stop looking for something or someone better. We need to be able to satisfice within various local compartments (those defining our searches for spouses, jobs, and so on) in order to make our lives as a whole go well.

When Satisficing Is Not Rational

Slote says "choosing what is best for oneself may well be neither a necessary nor a sufficient condition of acting rationally, even in situations where only the agent's good is at stake" (p. 1). For example, a person who is moving and must sell his house might seek, "not to maximize his profit on the house, not to get the best price for it he is likely to receive within some appropriate time period, but simply to obtain what he takes to be a good or satisfactory price" (p. 9). When the seller receives a suitable offer, he may rationally accept it immediately, even though there would be no cost or risk in waiting a few days to see if a higher offer materializes. "His early agreement may not be due to undue anxiety about the firmness of the buyer's offer, or to a feeling that monetary transactions are unpleasant and to be got over as quickly as possible. He may simply be satisficing in the strong sense of the term. He may be moderate or modest in what he wants or needs" (p. 18).

Slote does not offer an analysis of rationality. Nor do I want this chapter's argument to rest on any particular analysis of rationality. I do, however, offer this as a necessary condition of rationality: One's choice is rational only if one does not recognize clearly better reasons for choosing any of one's forgone alternatives. This necessary condition is compatible with the means-end supporting condition introduced in Chapter 1. Further, it begs none of the questions that concern us here. It does not entail that rational choice is optimizing choice. Rather, it allows that one could rationally choose an alternative because it is satisfactory, terminating the search of one's choice set at that point.[10] Moreover, it also allows that if one has two satisfactory alternatives, one could choose the more moderate of the two on the grounds that it satisfies a preference one happens to have for moderation.

On the other hand, although a suboptimal option may be good enough to be worthy of choice in a given case, that does not mean it is worthy of being chosen in preference to something that is clearly better. If one has two choices and one alternative is satisfactory but the other is not, then the satisfactory choice is rational because it is *better*. But suppose one has two choices and both are satisfactory. (For example, suppose your house is for sale, and you simultaneously get two satisfactory offers, one for $200,000 and another for $210,000, and you prefer the larger offer.) In this case,

---

[10] That is, an optimizer might choose a satisfactory option in preference to searching for better options that might never materialize. Slote, however, says we intuitively recognize the rationality of taking the first satisfactory offer even in abstraction from the real-world risks and anxieties of having to sell one's house (1989, p. 18). However, if we are going to talk about common sense allowing a seller to immediately accept the firm offer even though the seller has the option of waiting a few days in hope of a higher offer, then we have to stick to conditions under which common sense holds sway. We do indeed have intuitions about what to do in risky situations, but we cannot, as Slote wants to do, simply *stipulate* that our intuitions regarding risky situations have nothing to do with the fact that in the real world such situations are risky. In the real-world housing market, to turn down an entirely satisfactory offer in quest of something better is to court disaster, to tempt fate. This is one reason why it is common sense, and rationally explicable common sense, for a global optimizer to be hesitant about turning down a satisfactory offer. Even from a local perspective, the expected gain from further search may not be worth risking the potential loss.

one does not give a rationale for choosing the inferior alternative merely by pointing out that the inferior alternative is satisfactory. The inferior option is satisfactory, but since this is not a difference, it cannot make a difference either. By hypothesis, the superior option is also satisfactory.

Why, then, should we choose the superior option? Presumably because it is better. Whatever it is in virtue of which we deem that option superior is also a reason for us to choose it.[11] Oddly, Slote denies this. It can be rational to choose the inferior option, Slote insists. Nor do we need a reason to choose the inferior option, Slote argues, because rationality does not always require people to have a reason for choosing one alternative rather than another (p. 21). For example, Kate might rationally grab a blouse out of her closet in the morning without being able to explain why she chose that one over the similar blouses hanging beside it. To call her irrational simply because she cannot explain her choice would be a mistake.

This seems right, as far as it goes; not all choices have to be or can be explained. To deem a choice rational, however, is to imply there is an explanation of a certain kind. A person can be rational without being aware of reasons for everything she does, but the things she does for no reason are not rational, and we do not show them to be rational merely by pointing out that they were done by a rational *person*. The person who simply grabs a blouse may be choosing, perhaps rationally, to forgo the opportunity to rationally choose which of her several blouses she wears. If Kate is running late for the train, then under the circumstances anything that counts as a blouse will also count as satisfactory, so she leaves to impulse the selection from her set of blouses. (In this case, the process of searching among alternative blouses virtually vanishes— there is hardly any choice at all. If she instead gives herself a few seconds to make sure she avoids the blouses with valentine or hammer-and-sickle patterns on them, then she will be choosing within a very small but still real local compartment.)

There may be a blouse in her closet that, given time, would emerge as best. Kate judges, however, that it is not worth her time to wait for this to happen. She is not literally compelled to simply pick something, but it serves her broader ends to forget about seek-

[11] Philip Pettit (1984, p. 172) makes the same point.

ing the optimal blouse and instead just grab something out of the closet. If Kate is running late for the train, she has reason to simply grab a blouse in preference to the clearly inferior alternative of wasting precious time seeking the optimal blouse. Initially adopting an end and creating a compartment within which to pursue it is itself a goal-directed activity and, from the standpoint of the global optimizer, not one to be engaged in frivolously. Therefore, we can endorse her *method* of selecting a blouse even though we anticipate having no particular reason to endorse her actual selection.

On the other hand, *deliberately* choosing the worse over the better would be irrational, and we do not give ourselves reason to soften this verdict merely by reminding ourselves that rational people sometimes leave their choices to impulse. Rational choice theory can tell us a story about why Kate finds herself going to work in a green blouse with orange polka dots, but the story will require an implicit or explicit distinction between more and less encompassing perspectives. Without the distinction, an optimization story would be blatantly false, for she does not in fact choose the optimal blouse, and a satisficing story would have neither explanatory nor justificatory power, for the point of choosing a merely satisfactory blouse when better ones were available would remain a mystery. To see the point of what she does at the local level, we have to step back and look at her actions from a broader perspective. From a broader perspective, Kate may have good reason to simply grab a blouse out of the closet, knowing it will be satisfactory even if it is not her favorite. However, it cannot be rational to choose something because it is satisfactory while at the same time having a clearly better option already in hand.

WHEN MODERATION IS RATIONAL

We saw that, when deciding between two satisfactory alternatives, it does not help to point out that one of them is satisfactory. We could, however, choose on the grounds that one of them is more moderate. Consider an example of Slote's. He says it "makes sense" for someone to desire "to be a really fine lawyer like her mother, but not desire to be as good a lawyer as she can possibly be. This limitation of ambition or aspiration may not stem from a belief that too much devotion to the law would damage other, more important parts of one's life. In certain moderate individuals, there are limits to aspiration and desire that cannot be explained in optimizing terms." (p. 2).

I agree that common sense can recognize moderate aspirations as rational, but to note this fact in an off-the-cuff way is hardly to provide an explanation of moderate aspirations. Our common-sense recognition is precisely what has to be explained. If all we have is an intuition that an act makes sense, but cannot say what the act makes sense *in terms of*, then we would be jumping to conclusions if we said we were approving of the act as rational. In contrast, if we explain a show of moderation in terms of its conduciveness to overall satisfaction, then we have explained it as rational. We have not merely claimed it makes sense; rather, we have actually made sense of it. We have shown that we had reason to choose as we did, while not having better reasons to choose differently.

How, then, might we explain having moderate career goals? First, there is the issue of trade-offs mentioned by Slote. One might cultivate an ability to be content with moderate career goals, not because one prefers moderate success to great success but because one cares about things other than success. Thus, one point of cultivating modest desires with respect to wealth is that it might improve a person's ability to adhere to a satisficing strategy with respect to income, thus freeing herself to devote time to her children, her health, and so on.

There are also ways in which moderation can have instrumental value that do not depend on the need to make trade-offs. There can be reasons for striving to be as good a lawyer as one's mother even if one wants to be as good a lawyer as possible. For example, a person might aim at being as good as her mother as a stepping-stone to becoming the best lawyer she can be. The modesty that enables a person to concentrate on successfully making smaller steps may eventually put her within reach of loftier goals. There is also value in concreteness. A person may have no idea how to go about becoming the best possible lawyer, but she may have a much clearer idea about how to become as good as her mother because the more modest goal is more concrete. Further, even given two equally concrete goals, an optimizer might very well choose the lesser on the grounds that only the lesser goal is realistic. Thus, one might become a better lawyer by emulating one's highly competent

41

mother than by wasting one's time in a fruitless attempt to emulate her superstar partner.

Finally, we can at least conceive of moderation being a preference in itself—not just a quality of a desire but itself the thing desired.[12] One might explain the cultivation of such a preference on the grounds that moderation is less distracting than extravagance, with the consequence that the moderate life is the more satisfyingly thoughtful and introspective life. In various ways, then, moderation can have instrumental or even constitutive value from the global perspective. Insofar as moderate preferences can be deliberately cultivated, their cultivation is subject to rational critique, and can thus be defended as rational.

When Seeking Optima Is Not Rational

To seek optima strikes us as generally a reasonable strategy, but it is not necessarily so. Earlier, I noted that local optimizing can be a waste of time from a global perspective, but this is not the only circumstance that can make it inappropriate to seek optima. For one thing, a set of alternatives need not contain a well-defined optimal choice at all, let alone one that can be easily identified. To borrow a fanciful example from John Pollock (1984, p. 417), suppose you are immortal and that you are also fortunate to have in your possession a bottle of EverBetter Wine. This wine improves with age. In fact, it improves so steadily and so rapidly that no matter how long you wait before drinking it, you would be better off, all things considered, waiting one more day. The question is, when should you drink the wine?

A rational *person* presumably would simply drink the wine at some point (perhaps after artificially constraining himself to drink the wine by year's end, then picking New Year's Eve as the obvious choice within that time frame), but the person would not be able to defend any particular day as an optimal choice. Indeed, it is part of the story that no matter what day the immortal chooses, waiting one more day would have been better. There are no constraints with respect to which he can regard any particular day as the optimal choice, unless he imposes those constraints on himself.

[12] I thank Mark Ravizza for this point.

42

There is something rational about choosing New Year's Eve, but the rationality lies in something other than how that day compares to the alternatives. Although the immortal could not defend choosing New Year's Eve in preference to waiting one more day, the choice is defensible in the sense that he did not have a better alternative to picking *something or other*. Indeed, picking something or other was optimal, because it was better than the only alternative, namely, sitting on the fence forever. The distinction between local and global optimizing thus allows us to explain without paradox the sense in which choosing New Year's Eve was rational. Picking something or other—and thus closing the compartment within which he seeks to set a date for drinking the wine—was rational from the global perspective despite the fact that from within that compartment, it was not possible to have a rationale for the choice of any particular day.[13]

The EverBetter Wine story is fantasy, of course, but it shows that we can at least imagine cases in which a set of alternatives has features making it inappropriate to seek the set's optimal member. Seeking optima may serve our ends, but if this is so, it is not a necessary truth but rather a contingent truth about the world and the kind of choice sets we find within it. In the EverBetter Wine case, the set of alternatives has no optimal member. Consider a more realistic story with a somewhat similar structure. Suppose a house comes up for sale in January. Out of curiosity, you take a look and find that you prefer it to the house you now own. When you look into the cost of selling your house and buying the new one, you find that the only cost you care about in the end is the cost and inconvenience of actually moving your belongings and settling into the new house. Suppose this cost, all things considered, amounts to one thousand dollars. Moreover, it is clear to you that such moving costs will be amply repaid over time. You can see that the stream of revenue or utility from the new house will be worth one hundred dollars per month more than what you will receive if

---

[13] Edna Ullmann-Margalit and Sidney Morgenbesser (1977, pp. 758–59) say one *picks* between A and B when one is indifferent between them and prefers the selection of either A or B to the selection of neither. What I call "picking something or other" presumes the latter but not the former condition, for one could be in a picking situation even if one was not indifferent between one's alternatives. In the EverBetter Wine case, one cannot find even a pair of alternatives over which one is indifferent. Even so, one still is forced to simply pick.

you stay where you are. Thus, the cost of the move will be repaid in ten months. This is hardly a wild fantasy, and, so far, buying the house is intuitively reasonable.

Now, to make the story more improbable, suppose you change houses in January and, four months later, it happens again. You find another house for sale. The move will cost another thousand dollars, but the new house will be worth a hundred dollars per month more than the one you now own. However, if you choose to move in May, that choice will make your January move retroactively suboptimal, with a net loss of around six hundred dollars. Should you move?

Perhaps opportunities to move to ever-better houses will surface again and again. You do not know.[14] But you do know this: For any move to be optimal, something must subsequently make you stay put long enough to recover the cost of that particular move. If you keep waiting for and expecting the day when the world stops presenting you with such opportunities, and if that day never comes, then sooner or later you will have to begin turning your back on them. As in the EverBetter Wine story, there is no particular point at which it is especially rational to stop moving. Indeed, whenever you finally reject an opportunity to move, it will be true that if you moved one more time before stopping, you eventually would be better off. Nevertheless, you have come to see that there is a point in committing yourself to being satisfied for a time with the house you have. Recall that optima are defined with respect to constraints. If you resolve in May that, once you choose, you will not look at another house for at least ten months, then choosing to move is optimal with respect to that self-imposed constraint. Your January move will then have been a waste of money, but your move in May will be worthwhile, provided that your self-imposed constraint remains firm.

Satisficing strategies strike us as reasonable in part because of contingent facts about ourselves and our world. For creatures as limited as ourselves, satisficing often makes a lot of sense. Perhaps less obvious is that the intuitive reasonableness of optimizing is no less contingent. Seizing on opportunities to make optimal moves serves a purpose partly because the real world is such that

[14] If you knew that ever-better opportunities will keep coming in a steady stream, the optimal long-run strategy would be to make a big move up every ten months, skipping intervening steps.

we can take for granted that there will time between moves to enjoy our improved situation. In the real world, opportunities to improve our situation do not come along so rapidly that we find ourselves stepping higher and higher without having time to enjoy the steps along the way. The real world limits our access to opportunities to improve our situation, and if such limits did not exist, we would have to invent them. We would have to give ourselves time to enjoy our situation even if that meant rejecting opportunities to improve it.

I argued that seeking optima is only contingently rational. The argument goes beyond the idea that different local goals can come into conflict. To be sure, there can be conflicts between the pursuit of local optima and the attainment of global optima, and such occasions give us reason not to pursue local optima. This section, though, articulates a different kind of reason not to pursue local optima, because the conflict discussed here could occur even if one had no goals beyond, for example, living in the best possible house. The nature of the conflict is that, ironically, seeking to live in the best possible house could leave us with no time to actually live in the best possible house.

Trade-offs among Incommensurable Values

As explained in previous sections, moderate preferences and satisficing strategies can be of instrumental value from the global perspective. I speculated that moderate preferences might even be considered essential constituents of the good life and thus have more than merely instrumental value. Satisficing strategies, however, can be of instrumental value only. This is because to satisfice is to give up the possibility of attaining a preferable outcome, and giving this up has to be explained in terms of the strategic reasons one has for giving it up. Local optimizing must likewise be explained, for it, too, consists of giving something up, namely, the opportunity to invest one's efforts in some other compartment.

Global optimizing, however, is not open to question and subject to trade-offs in the ways that local optimizing and satisficing are. Local goals can compete with each other, but there are no goals that compete with optimizing at the global level, at least not in the arena of rationality. A global optimum is not one among several competing goals; rather, in encompassing our lives as a whole, it also encompasses our competing goals. It represents the best way to resolve the competition from the standpoint of life as a whole. Local optimizing can be a waste of time from the global perspective, but global optimizing cannot.

What, then, is the nature of the global perspective? Do we ever actually assume the global viewpoint or is this merely a theoretical postulate? The answer is that we can and do assume the global viewpoint every time we do what we call "stepping back to look at the big picture." We do sometimes ask ourselves if the things we do to advance our careers, for example, are really worth doing. We do not spend all our waking hours looking at the big picture, of course. Nor should we, for when we look at the big picture, one thing we see is that it is possible to spend too much time looking at the big picture. Reflection is a crucial part of the good life, but it is only a part. Part of attaining a global optimum involves being able to lose ourselves for a time in our local pursuits.

In the previous section, we saw that, at least in fantasy cases, there can be rational choice regarding a set of alternatives even when the set has no optimal members. The lesson applies to more realistic situations as well. In particular, as Isaac Levi notes, a person torn between ideals of pacifism and patriotism need not feel that his eventual choice is best, all things considered. Rather, he may feel that his eventual choice is best according to one of his ideals and worst according to another. What we have in such a case is what Levi (1986, pp. 13ff.) calls "decisionmaking under unresolved conflict of values." If you have several goals, none of which are subordinate to any other, and you find yourself in a situation where these goals are in conflict, the globally optimal trade-off may not exist. And such situations (involving concerns for one's loved ones and for one's ideals, for example) may be rather common.

Yet, even in situations where there is no such thing as a global optimum, we can still take a global perspective. We can still look at our lives as a whole even if nothing presents itself as optimal from that perspective. Indeed, conflict of values is precisely that from which broader perspectives emerge. We confront the big picture precisely when we stop to consider that there is more to life than pursuing a career, or buying a house, or raising children. It is from broader perspectives that we attempt to resolve conflicts of values, with or without an algorithm for resolving them in an optimal fashion.[15]

One might think unresolved conflict is a sign of poorly chosen values. Why should would-be global optimizers risk adopting goals that could leave them having to make decisions under unresolved conflict? One reason is that some of our goals realize their full value in our lives only when they develop a certain autonomy, when we pursue them not as means of making our lives go well but as ends in themselves. We begin to tap the capacity of our ideals, our spouses, and our children to enrich our lives only when we acknowledge them as having value far beyond their capacity to enrich our lives. (Cherishing them becomes more than an instrumental means of making life go well; it becomes constitutive of life going well.) And goals we come to cherish as ends in themselves inherently tend to become incommensurable.[16] We may, for instance, find ourselves in a position where we cannot fight for a cause in which we deeply believe without compromising the care that our loved ones need from us and that we wholeheartedly want them to have. Nevertheless, this is the price of the richness and complexity of a life well lived. To have both ideals and loved ones is to run the risk of having to make decisions under unresolved conflicts of value.

Because some of our values are incommensurable, we sometimes have no method by which to identify optimal trade-offs among conflicting local goals. In such cases, the goal of making life as a whole go as well as possible remains meaningful, although there may not be any course of action that unequivocally counts as pursuing it. Even if would-be global optimizers cannot identify optimal options, they can still reject alternatives that fail to further any of their goals. In particular, if no better way of resolving the conflict emerges, simply picking something or other will emerge as

[15] As Allan Gibbard (1990, p. 321) says, we have ways of coping other than by resolving everything.

[16] T. K. Seung and Daniel Bonevac (1992) distinguish between *incommensurate* rankings (in which no alternative comes out best) and *indeterminate* rankings (in which several alternatives come out tied for best). Most of what follows is about incommensurate rankings. In contrast, most of the cases discussed in Ullmann-Margalit and Morgenbesser (1977), like the case in which a shopper chooses among identical cans of tomato soup, are about indeterminate rankings.

optimal compared to the alternative of remaining on the fence, for we eventually reject fence-sitting on the grounds that it fails to further any of our goals.

This may seem a grim picture of rational choice at the global level, but there are two points to keep in mind. First, when faced with a situation in which we must simply pick something, we are likely to have regrets about paths not taken, but we naturally adapt to the paths we take, and regret can fade as we grow into our choice. Thus, an alternative somewhat arbitrarily picked from a set within which no optimum exists can eventually come to be viewed as optimal from the perspectives of people we are yet to become, even if it could not have been considered optimal at the moment of choice. Second, this discussion of underdetermined rational choice concerns a worst-case scenario. Global optimizers carry out the highest-ranked life plan when they have one. Often, however, there is no highest-ranked plan for life as a whole and thus no well-defined global optimum; there is only a need to cope with competing and sometimes incommensurable local goals. In the worst case, no course of action unambiguously qualifies as making life as a whole go as well as possible, except insofar as it is unambiguously better to move in some direction rather than none. But this gives us enough to avoid paralysis even in the worst case. By hypothesis, simply picking something emerges as the best the agent can do, and thus to pick something is to optimize with respect to the choice of whether to spend more time sitting on the fence.

It would be natural to say rational choice is choice "all things considered." The trouble is that we often find ourselves not knowing what to consider, and it would be bad advice to tell us to consider all things. We can consider all things within a limited range, perhaps, but the limits of that range will themselves tend, in large part, to be matters of choice. We start out knowing that in some sense we want each aspect of our lives to go as well as possible, yet we realize that our resources are limited and that our various pursuits must make room for each other. When looking at our lives as a whole, what is most clear is that rationally managing a whole life involves managing trade-offs among life's various activities. If the benefits that will accrue from our various pursuits are known and commensurable, then managing the trade-offs is easy, at least theoretically; we simply maximize the sum of benefits. However, in many of the everyday cases discussed in this chapter, the benefits are neither known nor commensurable with other benefits. Even so, we can effectively manage trade-offs among particular pursuits by setting limits on how much of our lives we spend on particular pursuits. We can also set limits on how much benefit we insist on getting from particular pursuits. To impose the latter kind of stopping rule on a particular pursuit is to embrace what I have called a satisficing strategy.

Both kinds of constraint play a role in rational choice. Why? Because if we recognized only temporal limits, say, then we would automatically spend our full allotment of time in a given compartment even when we already had an acceptable option in hand. But if we also have strategically limited aspiration within that compartment, then finding an acceptable option will trigger a second kind of stopping rule. The second stopping rule closes the compartment and diverts the unused portion of the compartment's time allotment to other compartments where our need to find an acceptable option has not yet been met. Cultivating moderate preferences may also be advantageous in a supplementary way insofar as moderate preferences may help us adhere to the kind of limit we impose on a pursuit when we embrace a satisficing strategy.

Against the idea that our most important goals tend to become incommensurable with each other, one might suppose our global end is simply to flourish or to be happy—and that our local goals therefore *must* be commensurable in such terms. This would be a tidy climax to an otherwise rather untidy story about rational choice under unresolved conflict of values, but the tidiness would be superficial. One hardly gives people an algorithm for resolving conflicts when one advises them to be happy. What makes such advice vacuous is that flourishing and being happy cannot be concrete goals at the global level in the way that finding a house can be at the local level. Of course we *want* to flourish, but we *aim* to flourish only in an especially metaphorical sense. The fact is that we flourish not by aiming at flourishing but by successfully pursuing other things, things worth pursuing for their own sake.

Likewise, happiness can be a standard by which a life as a whole is judged, perhaps, but it cannot be a goal at which a life as a whole is aimed. We do not become happy by pursuing things there would otherwise be no point in pursuing. Rather, there must be a point in striving for a certain goal before striving for it can come to have any potential to make us happy. To aim at happiness is to aim at a

49

property that can emerge only in the course of aiming at something else.[17] So, the point about happiness and flourishing leaves us where we started, having to choose among things we value for their own sake, hoping we will be happy with our choice.

We might add that happiness derives from a variety of local sources, and the different elements of a person's happiness are not interchangeable. Our various local pleasures are not fungible; different dollar bills are all the same, functionally speaking, but different pleasures are not all the same, and they are not experienced as interchangeable units of the same kind of stuff. We can find happiness in our careers or in our marriages, but the vacuum left by a shattered career cannot be filled by domestic bliss.[18]

An Infinite Regress of Perspectives?

The global perspective is the perspective encompassing our lives as a whole. Decision making at this level disciplines the amount of time we devote to particular local compartments. It seems that we are capable of taking a perspective this broad even in worst-case scenarios where there is no well-defined global optimum. But even if we suppose we can take a perspective encompassing our whole lives, why should we suppose this is the broadest perspective we can take?

Perhaps there can be broader perspectives than what I call the global perspective. Indeed, the following chapters argue that we do have access to a larger perspective, that there are aspects of morality that we cannot appreciate except from a larger perspective, and that it can be rational to try to achieve this perspective. On the other hand, it would be unrealistic to suppose there is an infinite regress of levels. There is no need to prove that an infinite regress is impossible, but because the idea of an infinite regress is unrealistic, it is important to show that my theory does not *presuppose* an infinite regress.

---

[17] As Bernard Williams (in Smart and Williams, 1973, p. 113) puts it, one has to want other things for there to be anywhere that happiness can come from. See also the eleventh of Joseph Butler's *Fifteen Sermons* (1874, p. 139).

[18] I thank Nick Sturgeon for a discussion from which this point emerged. See also Michael Stocker (1990, chap. 6) and, of course, John Stuart Mill's *Utilitarianism* (chap. 2).

The threat of infinite regress arises in the following way. I said we cannot spend all our time looking at life as a whole; we must be able to lose ourselves (or perhaps I should say, find ourselves) in our local pursuits. How much time, then, should we spend pondering conflicting values? How much time should we spend looking at life as a whole? From what perspective do we choose to limit the amount of time we spend looking at our lives from the global perspective? Perhaps we need a "superglobal" perspective in order to answer these questions. After all, how could we decide how much time to spend at a given level unless we did so from a still more encompassing perspective?[19] It seems my theory can explain the time we allot to a given perspective only by supposing that we retreat to a broader one, ad infinitum.

But the theory presumes no such retreat. There are simpler, more realistic ways to explain the amount of time we spend looking at life as a whole.[20] First, there are things, like sleeping, that we do as the need arises; since we do not *decide* how much time to spend sleeping, we do not decide from a broader perspective, either. Indeed, we might be better off sleeping as we feel the need rather than trying to set aside a calculated amount of time for sleep. Perhaps the same holds true of the activity of looking at life as a whole. Insofar as our purpose in looking at life as a whole is to resolve conflicts arising between various aspects of our lives, so that life as a whole may go well, there will come a time when taking a global perspective has served its purpose. At that time, the compartment in our lives reserved for the activity of resolving local conflicts naturally closes until subsequent conflict forces it open again. There is no residual conflict awaiting resolution at a higher level.

Thus, the question of how much time to spend in contemplation need not itself require contemplation. Rather, we take whatever time it takes to genuinely resolve a conflict, or else we reach a point where we must simply pick something. More generally, we stop contemplating when we judge that pursuing our local goals has

[19] Holly Smith (1991) worries about the same sort of problem.

[20] The simplest way to explain the amount of time spent at the global level would be to say we take whatever time we need to consider *everything*. The trouble is that we do not have time to consider everything that might be relevant to life as a whole, any more than we have time to consider everything that might be relevant to the purchasing of a house. The explanation will have to be more complicated than this; hence the line of thought pursued in the following text.

come into conflict with—and has become more important than—the activity of thinking about how to juggle them. (For example, we would not dwell on the big picture if we were starving. Conflicts are rarely so important that contemplating them could preempt securing our immediate survival.) In this scenario, we are driven *to* the global level by local conflict and eventually are driven *from* that level by a need to get on with our lives.[21] The question of how much time to spend looking at life as a whole resolves itself.

We also can imagine a second kind of scenario in which the question does not resolve itself but is instead answered by deliberate calculation, in the same way that we could imagine deliberately calculating how much time to spend sleeping. Could we make a conscious decision of this kind without taking a superglobal perspective? Yes, we could. Consider that contemplation is an activity that must find its place in our lives along with other activities. For example, I might spend the month of July in a rented cabin, not doing anything to pursue my career, but just thinking about why I ever wanted to be a philosopher and about whether my original reasons still hold. This compartment in my life is reserved for contemplating my career. It is separate from the compartment or compartments within which I actually pursue my career. I also have a compartment, similar in many respects, within which I contemplate life as a whole. But although the *subject* I contemplate is the whole of my life, the contemplation itself is not. The contemplation is only one of many activities about which I care.

Now, if I need to decide how much time to reserve for contemplating life as a whole, I take a global perspective, trying to gauge how important such contemplation is to my life as a whole. Notice, then, what is unique about the compartment I reserve for the activity of contemplating my life as a whole. The compartment is unique because its boundaries are set by the activity that takes place within it. In the course of contemplating life from the global perspective, I decide how much time to reserve for any given activ-

---

[21] We also can be driven to a global perspective by the resolution of conflicts. Thus, when we finish a major project that had forced other pursuits to take a back seat, we often take time to evaluate self-imposed constraints and decide how to divide our extra time among previously neglected projects. And what drives us from the global perspective is the eventual resolution of a local conflict between savoring the big picture (a satisfying activity indeed when just finishing a major project) and the need, say, to start making dinner.

ity, including contemplation in general and contemplating life as a whole in particular. In this scenario, as in the previous one, no boundary-setting issue is left to await resolution at a higher level.

We have outlined two possibilities. In one case, we use whatever time it takes to resolve conflicts, subject to preemption by activities that in the short run are more important than conflict resolution. In this case, no decision is required. The discipline is automatic. In the second case, we discipline the compartment from within, as our contemplation of trade-offs leads us to conclude that we should reserve time for contemplation along with our other local activities. Therefore, we do not need a superglobal perspective to decide how much time to reserve for the activity of taking the global perspective. Such decisions are precisely the kind we make from the global perspective itself, if we need to make them at all. Unless we introduce something that competes with the goal of making life as a whole go as well as possible (such as, perhaps, the recognition of moral obligations), there is no reason to step back from a global perspective to something even broader.

CONCLUSION

This chapter sets out part of a normative ideal of rational choice suitable for the kind of beings we happen to be, beings who would only hurt ourselves if we tried to maximize our overall utility in every waking activity. It defines satisficing and local optimizing as strategies for pursuing goals within constraints that are in part self-imposed. Satisficing emerges not as an alternative to optimizing as a model of rationality but rather as an alternative to local optimizing as a strategy for pursuing global optima.

Under normal conditions, we employ a combination of heuristics, such as: (1) compartmentalizing our pursuits so as to narrow the scope of any particular optimization problem to the point where our limited knowledge becomes sufficient to identify an optimal solution; (2) accepting self-imposed constraints for the same reason as well as to keep particular pursuits from preempting more important ones; and (3) satisficing, which has the effect of closing compartments as soon as they serve the purpose for which they were created. Under normal conditions, where we lack the information we need to assign probabilities and utilities, this combination of strategies is more effective at making our lives as a whole go well than the alternative of plugging guesswork into a formula for maximizing expected utility. Thus, it is no wonder we so rarely make any attempt to calculate expected utilities, for the truth is that we usually have better things to do.

When goals are in conflict, there may not be any well-defined sense in which one way of resolving the conflict is, from the viewpoint of one's life as a whole, better than the alternatives. Of course, we do well to cultivate moderate preferences so as to reduce the frequency and severity of conflicts of value. But at the same time, there are limits to what one should do to avoid situations of underdetermined choice, for the risk of finding oneself in such situations is a risk we assume in the process of becoming rationally committed to particular ends as ends in themselves. A life with no regrets (about decisions made under unresolved conflict) is preferable, all other things equal, but if the lack of regret is purchased at a cost of not having goals that can come into unresolvable conflict, the price is too high. A person who adopts a number of goals as ends in themselves risks finding himself in situations where global optima do not exist, but there are reasons why a global optimizer would take that risk.

Admittedly, these conclusions about rational strategy are not particularly neat and tidy, certainly not in comparison to the simple maximization model. But tidying up the conclusions at the expense of realism would be a mistake, for the conclusions are meant to be about us, not about mathematically tractable caricatures of us. Rational choice theory developed along the lines indicated here and in chapters to follow has more power than simple maximization models to explain the ways in which we actually live, but it does not thereby become merely a self-congratulating description of how we live. Rather, it remains (or becomes) a tool for evaluating and criticizing the ways in which we actually live. It sets out a normative ideal of rational choice that it would be natural and healthy for us to try to live up to.

* *Appendix* *

THE DIFFERENCE BETWEEN SATISFICING
AND LOCAL OPTIMIZING

The first section of Chapter 2 distinguishes between satisficing and local optimizing as stopping rules. Some readers may find it helpful to consider a graphical representation of that distinction. We might represent a choice among alternatives in two-dimensional Cartesian space with utility on the y-axis and our set of alternatives arrayed along the x-axis. If we know the shape of the utility curve, we simply pick the highest point. No controversy arises (see fig. 2.1).

Chapter 2 concerns what to do when we are looking at a blank; that is, we may suppose there is some curve or other, but often we do not know what it looks like (see fig. 2.2).

Further, suppose we look at our lives from a global perspective, wanting life as a whole to go well. What do we see? We do not see one big graph, blank or otherwise. Rather, we see a collection of little graphs, some of which are more or less blank. The question then arises: Within a particular compartment, how do we make decisions when we do not know the utility function's shape? The answer is that we search the set of alternatives. We see how much utility a_1 has. We see how much a_2 has, and so forth. And since other decisions (searches) are also calling for our limited resources, we pick something at some point.

At what point do we rationally stop searching and pick something? The answer is that we impose two kinds of constraints on our search of the particular local utility space. We impose vertical constraints on how many alternatives we will consider (or if we

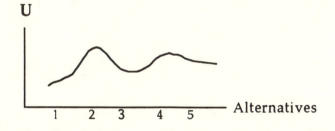

Figure 2.1. Searching Among Alternatives With Known Utilities

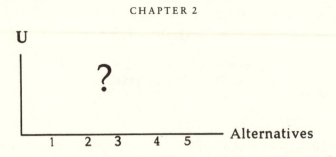

Figure 2.2. Searching Among Alternatives With Unknown Utilities

defined the x-axis differently, constraints on how much time or money or whatever resources we invest in the search). In other words, we operate with limited *inputs*. Or we impose horizontal constraints on how much utility we insist on getting before we stop searching. In other words, we operate with limited aspirations, limits on aimed-at *output*. Or we do both. Then, when we run up against either kind of limit, we stop searching in that local utility space, pick something, and turn our attention to some other local utility space. (see fig. 2.3).

In Figure 2.3, the horizontal line represents the point at which $U = U^*$, where U^* is the level of U with which the agent will be satisfied. As mentioned earlier, we can let the expected utility of continued search equal the probability of finding a better option, $P(fbo)$, multiplied by the utility of finding a better option, $U(fbo)$, minus the cost of further search, $C(fs)$. In that case, the vertical line in Figure 2.3 represents the point along the x-axis at which, the agent judges, it becomes true that $P(fbo)U(fbo) - C(fs) \leq 0$, where $P(fbo)U(fbo)$ is the expected utility of further search and $C(fs)$ is the cost of further search.

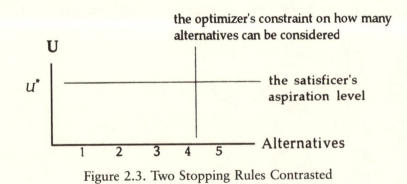

Figure 2.3. Two Stopping Rules Contrasted

In Figure 2.3, vertical constraints are constraints on inputs, and they define the search as local optimizing, taking the best alternative we discover prior to hitting that constraint. Horizontal constraints are constraints on aimed-at output, and they define the search as satisficing, taking the first alternative we find with that high a utility. The two strategies can be employed simultaneously, of course. Chapter 2 argues that this is how we actually live and that a global optimizer would have no reason for wanting to do things differently.

The vertical constraints partition our various activities in terms of how much of our total resources are allotted to those activities. Note that we do not need to be able to prioritize our activities in order to ration our resources among them. If necessary, we can arbitrarily set vertical constraints on how much (time, money, and so on) we are willing to spend within a particular compartment. As illustrated by the story about imposing time constraints on our search for optimal toothpaste, we tend to be satisficers when gathering information about where to set vertical constraints. The less we know about what our different endeavors mean to us, relatively speaking, the more arbitrariness there will be when we set the vertical constraints that delimit the different compartments. By the same token, the more comparability we have in terms of the relative importance of our different activities, the less arbitrary will be the boundaries we draw between them.

CHAPTER 3

Choosing Ends

'Reason' has a perfectly clear and precise meaning. It signifies the choice of the right means to an end that you wish to achieve. It has nothing whatever to do with the choice of ends.
Bertrand Russell (1954, p. 8)

THREE KINDS OF ENDS

RATIONAL CHOICE, on a means-end conception, involves seeking effective means to one's ends. From this basic idea, the social sciences have developed an instrumental model of rationality. The instrumental model goes beyond a means-end conception by inferring from it not only that rational choice involves seeking effective means to one's ends but also that rational choice involves nothing beyond this. Ends must be taken as given, as outside the purview of rational choice. All chains of justification eventually come to an end in something unjustified.

Or so the story goes. This chapter, though, shows that it is possible to have a chain of means and ends whose final link is rationally justified. One might assume that justifying final ends requires a conception of justification foreign to rational choice theory. It does not. Admittedly, defenders and critics alike agree that "the theory of rational choice disclaims all concern with the ends of action."[1] But such quietism about ends is not necessary. A means-end conception of rationality can be consistent with our intuition that we can be rational in a more reflective sense, calling into question ends we happen to have and revising them when they seem unfit.

One could define ends as items we *ought* to pursue, but I define

[1] David Gauthier (1986, p. 26) . Michael Resnik puts it dramatically: "Individual decision theory recognizes no distinction—either moral or rational—between the goals of killing oneself, being a sadist, making a million dollars, or being a missionary" (1987, p. 5).

58

ends descriptively, as items we do pursue, which leaves open whether it is possible to have ends we not only pursue but which were rational to adopt as items to pursue. This chapter looks beyond a purely instrumental model to something more reflective, a model in which agents choose and criticize ends as well as means.

There is, of course, a problem. The instrumentalist model is standard equipment in the social sciences, in part because it is useful, but also in part because it is hard to imagine an alternative. Evaluating a proposed means to a given end seems straightforward. We simply ask whether it would serve the given end. But when we talk about being reflectively rational, we are talking about evaluating ends as such. Now, we evidently can and do judge some ends as not worth pursuing, but how?

My answer draws on distinctions between four kinds of ends, three of which are well-known among philosophers. Suppose I wake one morning wanting to go for a two-mile run.

1. Perhaps I have this goal as an end in itself; I want to run two miles just for the sake of being out there running. In this case, the goal of running two miles is a *final* end.

2. Or perhaps I want to run for the sake of some other goal. I run because I want to be healthy. In this case, running two miles is an *instrumental* end, instrumental to the further end of being healthy.

3. Or suppose I want to run two miles because I want some aerobic exercise. In this case, running two miles is not exactly a mere means to the further end of getting some exercise. Rather, running two miles constitutes getting some exercise. So, in this third case we can speak of going for a run as a *constitutive* end.[2]

A variety of subsidiary criteria often help us to assess the relative merits of alternative constitutive ends. For instance, if my further goal is to get some aerobic exercise, and it occurs to me that I could ride my stationary bicycle rather than run two miles, I could ask myself which is easier on my knees, which will use less time, whether the bicycle's noise will bother the neighbors at that hour, and so on. If subsidiary criteria do not tell the difference between alternative constitutive ends, then the best I can do is to pick a form of exercise and get on with it.

[2] The distinction between instrumental and constitutive ends is formalized by J. L. Ackrill (1980, p. 19). I am also borrowing from a recent article by Scott MacDonald (1991).

The three categories are not mutually exclusive. An end like running two miles could be both final and instrumental, pursued for its own sake as well as for the sake of further ends. Nevertheless, distinguishing among these three kinds of ends is useful. For one thing, the distinction makes it easy to see how we can rationally choose some of our ends. In particular, we can choose instrumental and constitutive ends as means to further ends, and so such ends can be rational in the sense that choosing to pursue them can serve further ends. By the same token, we criticize such choices by asking whether pursuing the chosen end really helps to secure the further end, or whether pursuing it truly constitutes pursuing the further end.

The final end that terminates a chain of justification, though, cannot be justified in the same way we justify the links leading to it. Final ends as such are neither constituents of nor instrumental to further ends. They are pursued for their own sake. Thus, the justification of final ends will be a different kind of story, a story that cannot be told within the confines of an instrumentalist model.

A Fourth Kind of End

Suppose that, for Kate, becoming a surgeon is an end. Perhaps it is an end because Kate thinks becoming a surgeon will be prestigious, in which case becoming a surgeon is an instrumental end. Kate becomes a surgeon in order to do something else, namely, to secure prestige. But maybe, for Kate, becoming a surgeon is an end in itself. How could a career in medicine come to be a final end?

Maybe it happened like this. When Kate was a teenager, she had no idea what she wanted to do with her life, but she knew she wanted to do something. She wanted goals to pursue. In particular, she wanted to settle on a career and thus on the goal or set of goals that a career represents. At some point, she concluded that going to medical school and becoming a surgeon would give her the career she wanted. So she went to school to pursue a career in medicine. She has various reasons to pursue this goal, of course, but she also pursues it as an end in itself, much as I might run just for the sake of being out running.

The interesting point is that Kate's story introduces a fourth kind of end, an end of acquiring settled ends, an end of choosing a career in particular. The goal of choosing a career is what I call a *maieutic* end—an end achieved through a process of coming to have other ends. People sometimes describe Socrates as having taught by the maieutic method (that is, the method of midwifery). The idea is that students already have great stores of knowledge in inchoate form, so the teacher's job is to help students give birth to this latent knowledge. I use the term 'maieutic' to suggest that we give birth to our final ends in the process of achieving maieutic ends.[3] In this case, Kate achieves a maieutic end by coming to have particular career goals. As we said, she settles on a career by deciding to pursue a career in medicine. Thus, just as final ends are the further ends for the sake of which we pursue instrumental and constitutive ends, maieutic ends are the further ends for the sake of which we choose final ends.

The immediate worry here is that there may appear to be an inconsistency in the way the terms are defined. I said we could choose a final end as a way of achieving a maieutic end. On the contrary, one might respond, if Kate chooses a career in medicine as a way of achieving a maieutic end, she must be pursuing that career not as a final end but rather as an instrumental end. This would be a natural response. It may even seem indisputable. However, it misses the distinction between *pursuing* a final end (which by definition we do for its own sake) and *choosing* a final end (which we might do for various reasons). By definition, final ends are pursued for their own sake, not for the sake of maieutic ends. Yet, even if Kate pursues an end purely for its own sake, it can still be true that there was, in Kate's past, a process by which she acquired that end. It can also be true that going through the process (of acquiring the new goal) served ends she had at the time. The supposition that the choice process is a means to an existing end leaves open whether the outcome of the process, the chosen end, will be pursued as a means to the same end. The new end may well be something Kate subsequently pursues for its own sake. The dis-

---

[3] I leave open whether, prior to our choosing them, we already have final ends in inchoate form. This sometimes does appear to be the case, though. There sometimes seems, for example, to be a grain of truth in describing a person as having been born for a particular pursuit.

tinction between reasons for choosing and reasons for pursuing an end thus allows us to speak coherently of choosing a final end for the sake of further ends.

Against the distinction, one might object that when we choose an instrumental or a constitutive end, we necessarily pursue it for the same reason we originally chose it, namely, the further end to which we chose it as a means. Analogously, the objection continues, when we choose a final end we thereby take it to be good in itself. Consequently, our grounds for choosing X specifically as a final end must necessarily be the same as our grounds for pursuing X specifically as a final end—its being good in itself.[4]

This objection is more complicated than it looks. The alleged relation of identity between reasons for choosing and reasons for pursuing an end is by no means analytic. Even if it is true by definition that an instrumental end is both chosen and pursued as a means to a further end, it does not follow that the further end for which we chose it is identical to the further end for which we pursue it. It may be a safe assumption that they will be identical, but it is nevertheless an assumption, one that rests on further assumptions about human psychology. It is an empirical issue whether people tend to pursue ends for the same reasons they originally chose those ends as ends.

Similarly, even though it is true by definition that final ends are pursued for their own sake, it remains an open question whether further purposes were served by the process of coming to have final ends. For example, I may write in part because I love to write, but that supposition leaves open a possibility that other purposes were served by the process of becoming so devoted to writing. Developing that kind of devotion may have been what made it possible for me to get a job at a research-oriented university in the first place. I may even have been aware that good things happen to people who love to write when I began doing the things that led me to develop my taste for writing. My point here is that these are empirical matters. Some might insist that my reasons for choosing to pursue an end simply cannot—cannot possibly—differ from my subsequent reasons for pursuing that end. If that is true at all, though, it is a truth grounded in human psychology rather than in analysis of terms. Let us look more closely, then, at the psychological assump-

---

[4] I thank Scott MacDonald for suggesting this objection.

tions underlying this objection to the distinction between reasons for choosing and reasons for pursuing final ends.

My own understanding is that an act of adopting something as an end often changes our attitude toward it. If so, then it is a mistake to assume that our future grounds for pursuing X will be like our present grounds for adopting X as an end. My student may feel ambivalent about each of the subjects in which she might major, but if she anticipates coming to view the study of philosophy as good in itself, then her anticipation of this new attitude can be grounds for choosing to study philosophy in the first place. Similarly, part of the point of choosing a career is that we want—*and do not yet have*—the set of attitudes that goes with pursuing a particular career in a wholehearted way. We might have reasons to choose an end in part because of reasons we expect to develop for pursuing that end.

Observe, then, how the relation between maieutic and final ends differs from the relation between final and constitutive ends. The end of getting some aerobic exercise is schematic; we cannot do what it tells us to do until we choose a specific way of getting exercise, such as a two-mile jog.[5] Choosing specifics is a necessary preface to achieving the end. This is not how it works, though, when the further end is a maieutic end. Choosing specifics is not merely a preface to achieving a maieutic end. On the contrary, a maieutic end just is a goal of settling on a specific end. In settling on a specific goal and thereby meeting the maieutic end's demand, one is achieving the maieutic end, not merely choosing a specific way of pursuing it.

For example, my attempt to jog two miles constitutes my attempt to get some exercise, but Kate's attempt to become a surgeon does not constitute her attempt to choose a career goal. On the contrary, when Kate goes to medical school in an attempt to become a surgeon, she is not just attempting to choose a career goal. At that point, she has already chosen a career goal, namely, to be a surgeon. In the jogging case, I pursue goal A as a way of pursuing goal B. In the second case, Kate *chooses* goal A as a way of *achieving* goal B. Note that in the jogging case, A is the constitutive end,

---

[5] Constitutive ends can be either specific ways of pursuing a more formal further end (Putting on a suit can be constitutive of being well-dressed) or constituent parts of the further end (Putting on a tie can be a constituent of putting on a suit). See also Scott MacDonald's discussion of ends as specifications (1991, p. 59).

while in the other case, B is the maieutic end. Therefore, even if the relation between A and B were the same in both cases (which it is not), constitutive ends and maieutic ends would still be different, for the two kinds of ends are found at opposite ends of the relation.

We also can see how the relation between maieutic and final ends differs from the relation between final and instrumental ends. When one end is pursued purely for the sake of another end, then the rationale for its pursuit depends on its ongoing relation as a means to the further end. For example, if pursuing a career in medicine is merely a means of securing prestige, and Kate one day loses her desire for prestige, then she also loses her grounds for becoming a surgeon. The rationale for her career depends on the persistence of the further end of securing prestige. In the other scenario, though, the rationale for her career does not depend on the persistence of the teenage end of settling on a career. On the contrary, her evolving set of career goals *replaces* the teenage end with something quite different. As long as Kate is settled in her career as a surgeon, she has attained the goal (of settling on a career) that she had as a teenager, thus eliminating the earlier goal as an item to pursue. For Kate, the maieutic end of settling on a career reemerges (as an item to pursue) only if Kate at some point rejects her career as a surgeon and begins to long for something new.

Some readers might worry that a maieutic end is never really eliminated and that the new end it spawns is subsequently pursued, implicitly if not explicitly, as a means to the maieutic end. When Kate settles on a career, her subsequent pursuits might be motivated by the same concerns that drove her as a teenager to settle on a career. My response is that of course this will be true in some cases; some people, after settling on a career, subsequently pursue their careers as instrumental ends (instrumental to the further end of making money) or constitutive ends (constitutive of the further end of keeping busy). In other words, maieutic ends can give birth not only to final ends but to other kinds of ends as well.[6] But such cases are beside the point. If our task were to explain how instrumental or constitutive ends could be rationally chosen, then such cases would be relevant. Our actual objective, though, is to explain how final ends can be rationally chosen. Accordingly, we need to focus on cases in which the chosen ends are subsequently pursued

[6] I thank Lainie Ross for helping me see this.

as ends in themselves. We need to concentrate on the role maieutic ends play in giving birth to final ends, for it is in that role that maieutic ends are relevant to the puzzle of how final ends can be rationally chosen.

But, a critic might persist, how can we be sure that maieutic ends *ever* give birth to final ends? One could argue that, if the desire to have a career is what leads Kate to choose a career, then that same desire will be the further end for the sake of which she pursues her career. If she chooses a career as a mere means to the further end, then she will pursue the career for the same reason. In response, we need not deny that there can be a value that Kate attaches to having a career that persists through her choice and pursuit of a particular career. To say Kate eliminates "settling on a career" as an end (that is, as an item to pursue) is not to say she ceases to value having a career. We need to distinguish between something being valuable and something being an item to pursue. For example, my car is valuable to me. And if I leave it parked on a hill and the parking brake fails, then it also becomes an item to pursue. The car is valuable to me both before and after I secure it, but it ceases to be an item to pursue after I secure it. Similarly, if Kate already has a career, then having a career may be valuable to her, but it is not an item to pursue; it is an item she already has. In fact, it is not clear that having a career was ever an item to pursue. Before settling on a career, Kate pursued the goal of settling on a career. After settling on a career, Kate pursues her particular career, period; she does not pursue "having a career." And if her career is ever in jeopardy, then *securing* her career may well become an item to pursue. Of course, Kate continues to value having a career even as she pursues one, but this is no reason to doubt that she now has goals, acquired in the course of settling on her particular career, that she pursues for their own sake.

Maieutic ends are not the only kind of end that can be eliminated as an item to pursue, but their elimination has a unique upshot. In the means-end relation between instrumental and final ends, eliminating the further end renders the means pointless; it robs the means of normative significance. In contrast, in the means-end relation between final and maieutic ends, eliminating the further end is an essential part of the process by which final ends acquire their characteristic normative significance.

Maieutic ends are not merely a theoretical postulate. They are real. The drive to find a career or a spouse can be powerful, even painful, and such drives are drives to settle on a particular career or a particular person. Recall what it was like to choose a major subject in college or to choose a career. One way or another, we had to choose something, and, for some of us, not having done so yet was an occasion for considerable anxiety. Some of us had hardly any idea of what we really wanted, but it felt better to settle on some end or other than to let that part of our lives remain a vacuum. Of course, there were institutional and parental pressures as well, and some of us felt only those, but many of us also felt palpable pressure from within.

None of this denies that some people are simply gripped by particular final ends.[7] Perhaps such ends are not acquired by choice. If not, then questions about how they could be rationally chosen are moot. But that does not mean all questions are moot, for we can still ask whether further ends are served by the process of coming to have a final end. Whether ends are deliberately selected from a set of alternatives, my model has something to say. It addresses the question of whether an end's acquisition serves further ends.

That, then, is my theory about how an end, pursued as a genuinely final end, could nevertheless have been rationally chosen. There are ends—I call them maieutic ends—to which a final end could be chosen as a means. In passing, note that although the four kinds of ends are conceptually distinct, the four categories are not mutually exclusive. An end could be final, pursued for its own sake, and at the same time could be instrumental, pursued as a means to some further end. Later, I present three formal models of reflective rationality, the first of which models a maieutic end as a final end and the third of which models a maieutic end as an instrumental end. That an end falls into one category does not preclude it from falling into others.

In the next section, I explain how unchosen ends might serve as parts of a framework for judging a choice of ends. I then consider whether explaining the rational choice of one final end presupposes further and still unexplained final ends. Either way, we have seen how final ends could be rationally chosen, but are "loose ends" inevitable?

[7] The issue came up in discussions with Ruth Marcus and Michael Della Rocca.

THE ROLE OF UNCHOSEN ENDS

Although some of our ends are chosen, some are not. For most of us, the goal of survival is a goal with which we simply find ourselves. Likewise, we want to be good at what we do, and this goal also seems to be unchosen, something we simply have. We want to be competent.[8] We do not need reasons to choose our unchosen ends, since we do not choose them. We simply have them. Even unchosen ends can be rejected, of course, but to rationally reject them, one needs a reason to reject them. Unchosen final ends, therefore, have a certain normative inertia, which means they can be part of a relatively stable frame of reference in terms of which we can evaluate ends we might acquire by choice. Not every pursuit, for instance, would be conducive to survival.

Harry Frankfurt goes a bit farther, holding that fixed ends are a *necessary* part of a normative frame of reference. The problem of choosing ends presupposes a frame of reference against which one assesses one's options, and not all of this framework can be an endogenous product of choice. As Frankfurt puts it, "It is only if his volitional nature is in certain respects already fixed that a person can effectively consider what his final ends should be—what is to be important to him, or what to care about. He will not be in a position to inquire into the question of how he should live unless it is already the case that there are some things about which he cares" (1992, p. 17). Frankfurt has a point. We need a fairly stable frame of reference to get started in assessing prospective ends.

At the same time, the stable foundation need not, as Frankfurt himself notes, "be fixed unalterably" (1992, p. 18). Although I accept Frankfurt's point, three related complications bear mentioning. First, the stable foundation need not be permanently fixed. Indeed, it might be something that has to be left behind. Child-

---

[8] It is not a conceptual truth that human beings desire to be competent, but nor is that desire merely a local phenomenon. Probably, it is conspicuously present in all societies. Robert White (1971) says exploratory and playful behavior in children and even young animals serves to develop competence in dealing with the environment and that a sense of competence is a vital aspect of self-esteem. Sarah Broadie says the joy human beings take in doing things well "is so natural that people set up all sorts of trivial ends in order to have the satisfaction of achieving them correctly" (1991, p. 92).

hood is the foundation for adulthood, but childhood is something we outgrow. Second, in the long run, the foundation might not be fixed independently of choice. Rather, some parts of the foundation (character traits, in particular) might arise and change through a process of habituation driven by ongoing patterns of choice. Third, even when an end is acquired by choice, the process of settling on that end may not be a simple act of will. On the contrary, often we settle on something as an end partly by habituating ourselves toward aiming at it. For instance, we want to have someone to love. This is a maieutic end that we achieve when we come to love particular people and when we accept spending time with them and making them happy as ends worth pursuing for their own sake. But coming to love and be devoted to a person is not a simple act of will but rather a matter of growing into a commitment, step by step.

So, some items come to be pursued as final ends through a process of habituation. Although Kate's character is stable with respect to particular decisions, it is also part of her that, over the long run, she shapes in incremental ways through her choices. If all goes well, she will grow into the career (and the husband) she chose, and the person she becomes will some day find that career (and that husband) intrinsically worthy of her ongoing commitment.

Of course, circumstances help determine whether a prospective end is appropriate. Indeed, circumstances determine whether a particular option even exists. A given activity counts as a prospective career, for example, only if there is a market for that kind of activity. (Does becoming a chess player count as settling on a career?) The nature of maieutic ends also depends on circumstances. For example, settling on a spouse can be a maieutic end only if a certain kind of social structure exists to render that end intelligible. To a large extent, culture dictates both the range of maieutic ends one could have and also the range of final ends whose choice would achieve a given maieutic end.

Another part of a framework for assessing prospective ends is supplied by an aspect of maieutic ends that we have yet to discuss. A maieutic end is an end of bringing ends into existence, of giving oneself ends to pursue. To have ends to pursue is to have something to live for. If we have a single overarching and maybe unchosen maieutic end, I would say it is the end of finding things to live for.[9]

[9] I speak interchangeably of having, finding, getting, or coming to have something to live for.

The various maieutic ends (settling on a major subject in college and then a career, defining ideals, choosing a spouse, finding ways of contributing to the community, and so on) are all species of a generic and overarching maieutic end of finding things to live for, ends to which one can devote oneself. In different words, the end of finding something to live for is the end of acquiring ends in general, the end of having one's life be spent on something rather than nothing.

That does not mean we are always looking for things to live for. Sometimes our existing corpus of ends gives us plenty to do, leaving us with neither the need nor the opportunity to look for more. Sometimes feeding ourselves (or our children) is a serious challenge; it keeps our hands so full that taking time to ask what we are living for is out of the question. To have no time for ends beyond bare survival is to have no need for ends beyond bare survival. But when day-to-day survival becomes too easy to keep us busy, that is when we need something else to aim at, lest we find ourselves with plenty of time to ponder the fact that there is nothing for the sake of which we are surviving.

In effect, insofar as bare survival originally presents itself as a final end, we need to convert it into something else, a form of survival that has instrumental value as well. When we do this, we change survival from something we happen to seek as a matter of descriptive biological fact into something with normative weight— a goal we have reason to seek. In this way, we redeem survival as a goal. But to do this, we need to settle on further ends to which survival can serve as means.[10] The next section incorporates these ideas into a model of reflective rationality. After we have the model in front of us, Chapter 4 will have more to say about how we compare prospective final ends.

A New Model

Means-end conceptions of rationality posit instrumental ends. Sophisticated versions also posit constitutive ends. A means-end conception also posits final ends, which rationally justify instrumental

[10] It seems that some people would rather die than live without goals they consider worth living for. Suicide often might be understood not as a repudiation of the unchosen end of survival but rather as the ultimate confirmation of the intolerability of failing to achieve the maieutic end of finding something to live for.

and constitutive ends. Instrumental or static rationality involves seeking effective means to given ends. The essence of reflective rationality is that, although it involves means-end reasoning, it goes beyond instrumental rationality because it does not take ends as given. Reflectively rational choosers realize that their preference functions change over time and that some changes will serve their current ends better than others. To be reflectively rational is to manage one's changing preference function, to do what one can to become the sort of person one wants to become.

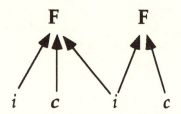

Figure 3.1. The Means-End Conception

In Figure 3.1, F, c, and i stand for final, constitutive, and instrumental ends. An arrow from c to F signifies that pursuing c is a means to F.

There will be as many chains of justification as there are final ends, and instrumental or constitutive ends pass as rational only if they are links within one or more chains, which is to say they serve as means to one or more final ends. The final ends that top the chains, though, are not justified, and final ends as such cannot be justified according to the instrumentalist conception of rational choice. (One might think of the latter as a Humean conception of reason.)

A model of reflective rationality adds the following elements to the means-end conception of rational choice. The point is to embellish the means-end conception rather than to supplant it, in the process showing how even final ends can be subject to rational choice. First, the model posits particular maieutic ends. Insofar as settling on final ends is our way of achieving maieutic ends, the choice is rational if it serves the purpose. Second, we pursue particular maieutic ends (like the end of choosing a career) as constitutive ends relative to the overarching maieutic end of finding something to live for. Getting a career is a way of getting something to live for (see fig. 3.2).

70

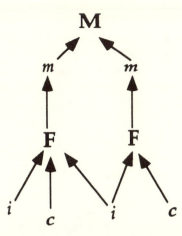

Figure 3.2. The Reflective Model, Taking the Overarching End
as Given

In Figure 3.2, an arrow from i to F signifies that pursuing i is a
means to F. An arrow from F to m signifies that choosing F is a
means to a particular maieutic end m. An arrow from m to M
signifies that pursuing m is a means to the overarching maieutic
end M.

The model that emerges from this has several variations. We will
look at three. In the first version, this is where we stop. We take the
overarching maieutic end as a final end that is simply given. This
first model is noteworthy in two ways. It explains how an end,
pursued for its own sake, could nevertheless be rationally chosen.
Second, the model identifies and characterizes further ends to
which the choice of final ends could be a means. The model takes
at least one final end as given, though, and so from a theoretical
standpoint is not entirely satisfying. It goes beyond the instrumentalist model by showing how even final ends (most of them, at
least) could be rationally chosen, but it shares with instrumentalist
models the property of leaving us with loose ends—terminal ends
not justified within the model.

Judging from the first model, then, it still seems reasonable to
suppose that, as Bernard Williams writes, "There will have to be at
least one reason for which no further reason is given and which
holds itself up" (1985, p. 113).[11] The second model, however, goes

---

[11] Bernard Williams expresses skepticism about the "linear model" of reason-
giving at issue in the cited passage, but his belief that it is impossible for rationales
to go "all the way down" is unwavering.

further. Instead of taking the overarching maieutic end as given, we note that finding reasons to live improves our survival prospects. To whatever extent we care about survival, and to whatever extent finding things to live for strengthens our will to survive and thereby improves our survival prospects, we have a rationale for the overarching end. Finding things to live for is instrumental to the further end of survival. In the second model, we stop here. We take survival as a given final end (see fig. 3.3).

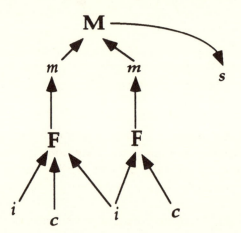

Figure 3.3. The Reflective Model, Taking Survival as Given

In Figure 3.3, an arrow from M to s signifies that pursuing the overarching end M is a means to the end of survival.

Should we take the end of survival as given? Since we are given the end of survival as a matter of biological fact, why not? One problem is that we would still be left with a theoretical loose end, an end accounted for in descriptive biological terms but not in normative terms. There is also a practical reason why we cannot take survival as given. We cannot take it as given because, as a matter of fact, our commitment to the biologically given end of survival is not an all-or-nothing matter. Our commitment is a matter of degree, variable even within persons. The point is not that some people do not have the end of survival. (Even if some people lack the end of survival, this need not affect its normative force for the rest of us.) The more crucial fact is that, even for those of us who have the end of survival, the strength of our will to survive can change. Further, the strength of our will to survive is in part a consequence of our choices.

Accordingly, the third model goes one more step. Survival is a final end with which we begin as a matter of biological fact, but it will be subverted as an end if we cannot we find something that survival is *for*, that is, if we cannot find reasons to live. With some ends, of course, a threat of subversion would not matter. For example, if Ulysses expects the Sirens to subvert his desire for broccoli, he shrugs his shoulders and plans to eat something else. But in contrast, if Ulysses expects the Sirens to subvert his desire to survive, he binds himself to the mast. He wants to survive his encounter with the Sirens no matter how he will feel about survival when the time comes. Therefore, broccoli and survival are different. Unlike a desire for broccoli, the biologically given desire for survival happens to have a certain intransigence. It resists its own extinction. It drives us to find things to live for, as proof against its own subversion.

As we find things to live for, the goal of survival with which we begin as a biological instinct becomes something more than that. It becomes a means to final ends acquired in the process of achieving maieutic ends. And as those new goals insert themselves into our corpus of ends, the goal of bare survival evolves into something else. There comes a time when bare survival is no longer what we are after. By acquiring the final ends that make life instrumentally valuable, we convert bare survival from something we happen to pursue into something we have reason to pursue as part of an increasingly complex hierarchy of ends.[12]

This suggests a circular chain of reasoning (a nonvicious circle, since several and perhaps all of the links have empirical content). Constitutive and instrumental ends are justified as means to final ends. We pursue final ends for their own sake, and the *choice* of final ends is justified as a means of achieving particular maieutic ends. Particular maieutic ends are then justified as constitutive means to the overarching maieutic end of finding something to live

[12] For those with no desire to live in the first place, this argument does not get off the ground unless they have some other desire that can play a similar role in the model. But we are not concerned here with the likelihood that some people's ends cannot be rationally justified in this way. Perhaps some ends cannot be rationally justified at all. Be that as it may, the objective is to show how a final end could be rationally chosen. We do not need to argue that *all* ends are rationally chosen.

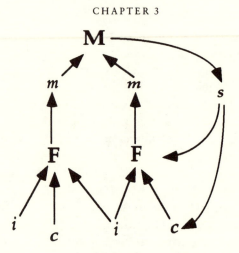

Figure 3.4. The Reflective Model, With No Loose Ends

for. Finding something to live for is instrumentally justified to the extent that, given our psychology, achieving the overarching maieutic end (and thus producing reasons to live) helps us survive. And to close the circle, survival and the implied preservation of the ability to pursue goals has come to be instrumentally justified as a means to the pursuit of final ends (see fig. 3.4).

In this model, survival is a means in the sense of being needed for the sake of other goals. To be an instrumental end, and thus an item to pursue, there must also be something one needs to do to secure it. As I use the terms, being an instrumental end entails being a means, but not vice versa. Survival is not unique in this respect. For example, suppose Tom needs a car in order to attend a concert. If Tom already has a car, though, then having a car is not an item to pursue and thus not an end and thus not an instrumental end, even though it is a means of attending the concert.

We might think there is an easier way to close the circle. That is, we could eliminate maieutic ends from the picture and suppose more simply that survival is justified as a means to our final ends while our final ends are justified by the fact that acquiring those ends gives us reason to live and thereby improves our survival prospects. But how could acquiring final ends improve our survival prospects? We can explain the point of acquiring final ends without reconstructing them as merely instrumental ends (which by hypothesis is not what they are) by saying that in acquiring final ends, we come to have reasons to live. And it is in virtue of giving us reasons to live that acquiring final ends improves our survival prospects. Therefore, the circle cannot close except by way of maieutic ends. Maieutic ends enter the picture even if the name I gave them does not.[13]

Does this mechanism drive the emergence of everyone's corpus of ends? It is hard to say. In any event, the models are not really meant to be descriptive in that sense. They are meant to show how someone, starting even from something as mundane as the survival instinct, could have reason to develop the complicated set of ends that beings like us actually have. The models are also meant to show how each element of an emerging corpus of ends can come to have its own normative force without any end's normative force being simply taken as given. Survival enters the second model as a biological given, but the third model depicts a process by which this biological given eventually becomes something more than that. The third model thus exhibits a striking completeness, since within it there are no loose ends. The chain of justification has a beginning, but it need not come to an end. One might be tempted to ask for a justification of the chain as a whole, but to justify every link is to justify the whole chain. The chain metaphorically represents a series of choices wanting justification in rational choice terms, together with interrelationships that help them justify each other. When one forges the chain in such a way that no link is without justification (that is, no choice is without justification, including basic existentialist choices such as to seek survival or to cultivate ends beyond survival), then no issue of rational choice remains to be represented by the metaphorical chain as a whole.

Even as astute a critic of foundationalism as Bernard Williams joins foundationalists in embracing the least plausible implication

[13] Another way of closing the circle invokes standard instrumental reasons for wanting some of our ends to be final ends. For example, we might be healthier if we eat broccoli as an end in itself—just for the taste—rather than for the sake of our health. (I thank Sara Worley for this point.) Merely acquiring the goal of eating broccoli does not by itself achieve the further end of being healthy, though. The further end persists as an item to pursue, which means the newly acquired end forms an intermediate link in an existing chain. In contrast, maieutic ends are achieved, not merely furthered, by the process of acquiring final ends. Having been achieved, maieutic ends drop away as items to pursue, breaking the circle and leaving the acquired end in the chain's terminal position, which explains how even the link that terminates a chain of ends could have been rationally chosen.

[14] See Williams (1985, pp. 113–17).

of the foundationalist metaphor, namely, the idea that starting points are what subsequently erected edifices must rest upon.[14] We should not be fooled by the metaphor. We should realize that our starting points can be more like launching pads than like architectural foundations. A launching pad serves its purpose by being left behind. Even if we inevitably begin by taking some ends as given, it remains open whether a corpus of ends will always include ends taken as given.

Further, survival is not the only descriptively given end capable of launching the normative rocket. If the primeval desire for survival does not drive a person to develop a corpus of ends, something else might. A desire for happiness also can drive us to find things to live for, because we secure happiness by pursuing ends we care about for their own sake. (If we did not independently care about achieving those ends, then there would be nothing in the achievement to be happy about.) A primeval desire to avoid boredom might have similar consequences.[15] To launch the normative rocket, all we need is some sort of given desire that gives us reasons to find things to live for. I prefer to use survival as an example of such a primeval desire, partly because it is in fact biologically given, partly because it is relatively clear how bare survival could start out as a biologically given final end only to drive the process by which it evolves into a complicated instrumental end, thereby leaving us with no loose (that is, simply given) ends.

Perhaps it is somewhat curious that organisms would have a survival instinct in the first place. The reason why they have it, presumably, is this. Organisms having no instincts other than an instinct to replicate would not be good at replicating and thus would have declining representation in successive generations. The goal of replicating, the ultimate biological given, is better served in organisms who combine or replace that goal with other goals: to survive, to have sex, to eat, and so forth. Obviously, not every organism is guaranteed to have more offspring in virtue of having a complex corpus of ends, but whether the rule has exceptions is not the issue. The issue is whether the probability of replication goes up or down as a corpus of ends becomes complex.

Sociobiological speculation aside, it remains the case that, having posited an initial goal of bare survival, we can see why this goal

---

[15] I thank Harry Frankfurt for this suggestion. See also Frankfurt (1992, p. 12).

would fall away as a driving force in just the way launching pads are supposed to fall away, to be replaced by a set of ends comprising a commitment to survive in a particular way, as a being with a particular hierarchy of ends. In circumstances like ours, to have the thinner goal is to have reason to try to replace it with its thicker analog. (The reason is that the end of bare survival is too thin to sustain itself as a corpus of ends. Unless survival acquires instrumental value, our commitment to it will decay.) It would have been simpler to posit a thicker goal (of surviving in a humanly dignified way, for example, or of having a life filled with happiness) as a biologically given final end, but that would have made the model at once much less interesting and much more controversial.

One might find it odd to model final ends as ends we acquire by conscious choice. Recall, then, that models of reflectively rational choice do not presume we acquire final ends only by conscious choice. We sometimes make choices unintentionally, habituating ourselves toward aiming at an end without realizing that we are doing so. Some of our ends seem simply to captivate us. Nor is anything necessarily wrong with acquiring ends unintentionally. When we find ourselves simply gripped by an end, we have no practical need to formulate a rationale for our ends. (There is a saying: "If it ain't broke, don't fix it.") Nevertheless, there might be a rationale for one's final ends whether one has reason to identify it. Final ends can give us something to live for whether we think of them as serving that purpose.

Thus, the three models have a normative force pertaining not only to ends one acquires by deliberate choice but also to ends by which one is simply gripped. They explain not just how we could come to have final ends but how we could come to have *rationally chosen* final ends, and such an explanation can have justificatory force even when it is not descriptively accurate.[16] For example, if Kate is simply gripped by the end of learning to play jazz guitar, then since she did not choose it at all, she cannot be said to have rationally chosen it either. Nevertheless, we can say her end is rational if the process of adopting it served an end she had at the time and, in particular, if adopting the end gave her something to live for. We can say this even when she neither chooses nor pursues the end with that further purpose in mind.

[16] Alan Nelson (1986) discusses the relation between explanation and justification.

We have seen how final ends could be rationally chosen. In addition, the third model shows that it is not necessary for a chain of ends to terminate in an end that is simply given rather than rationally chosen. Note that these models rely only on the ordinary and well-understood means-end conception of rational choice. The choice of instrumental, constitutive, final, and maieutic ends are all explained as means to further ends. (By definition, the pursuit of final ends cannot be so explained, but even so, the choice of final ends can be.) This shows that the means-end conception of rational choice has the resources to go beyond the instrumentalist model. I do not assume that means-end reasoning is the only kind of rationality there is. Rather, the point of the exercise is to show how even this narrowest of conceptions of rational choice has the resources to explain the rational choice of ends, and further, to do so without leaving loose ends.

Aristotle (*Nicomachean Ethics*, 1112b11–12) said we deliberate not about ends but about ways and means.[17] But I believe we have maieutic ends. And if we deliberate about means to maieutic ends, then by that very fact we deliberate about ends. It is through means-end deliberation with respect to maieutic ends that final ends are brought within the purview of rational choice. To belabor the obvious, though, only choices can fall within the purview of rational choice. Therefore, the intent of this chapter's argument is to show how rationality is conferred on final ends as choices, not as ends per se. Even when there is nothing to say about the rationality of ends as ends, it remains possible to rationally choose final ends in the sense that choosing them can serve further ends.

This chapter's argument does not presume that a person can have more than one genuine final end, but Chapter 4 argues that it is possible and that it can be rational to have a plurality of final ends. Chapter 4 also considers how we compare prospective ends.

---

[17] Aristotle believed that we deliberate about constitutive as well as instrumental means, and some commentators (for example, Terence Irwin in the notes to *Nicomachean Ethics*, 1985, p. 318) suggest that if we deliberate about a constitutive means to a final end, we thereby deliberate about the final end. On the contrary, we may deliberate about whether to run two miles without deliberating about whether to get some exercise. We may deliberate about whether to wear a maroon tie without deliberating about whether to wear a suit. And so on. We do not get to a perspective from which to assess final ends merely by deliberating about constitutive means.

Are some ends better than others? When we have several options (for example, several available career paths), is there a procedure for deciding which alternative is best? Also, when no prospective end emerges as best, is it nevertheless possible to make recognizably rational choices?

Comparing Ends

'Tis not contrary to reason to prefer the destruction
of the world to the scratching of my finger.
David Hume (1978, p. 416; first published 1739)

A RECIPE FOR RATIONAL CHOICE?

CHAPTER 3 gave a formal account of how final ends can be rationally chosen, leaving us with practical questions regarding how to compare ends. Having chosen to become a surgeon, Kate now has ends she can pursue. Still, she had alternatives. She could have tried for a career as an astronaut or a jazz guitarist, which raises a question. Did she make the right choice?

The strange thing is, few people are totally satisfied with their ends. Within an instrumentalist framework, that would be inexplicable, but it is true. People often are dissatisfied not only with the effectiveness of the means at their disposal but they have reservations about their ends as well. Maieutic ends (like choosing a career) can be achieved in various ways (for example, by various career paths) and many people can easily imagine how the process of choosing ends could have gone better. There is a purpose served by the choice of final ends, and some choices serve this purpose better than others.

Unfortunately, as the phenomenon of dissatisfaction suggests, there is no sure way to anticipate how well a given choice will serve its purpose. Even if there were a fail-safe recipe for choosing ends, that is not what we are looking for here. What we seek is not a recipe for choosing ends so much as a characterization of well-chosen ends. Asking what makes some ends better than others is like asking what makes some cakes better than others. It is not like asking for a cake recipe. I have ideas about what to look for when assessing ends, and those ideas can guide action, but the guidance is by heuristic rather than by recipe.

It may be an oversimplification, though, to think of recipes as analogous to algorithms. When a recipe tells us to bake something until it is golden brown, it is not giving us an algorithm.[1] We need to interpret the instruction in light of previous experience, and we may need to repeat the procedure a few times before we fully understand what the recipe is telling us to do. The conditions that support rational endorsement seem quite like recipes so construed. They tell us what to look for, but they are not necessary and sufficient conditions. With experience, we become more aware that countervailing conditions do arise from time to time. And just as there can be more than one way to bake a cake, there can sometimes be other grounds for endorsement.

Consider another analogy.[2] When a stockbroker tells us to buy low and sell high, she has not given us anything resembling an algorithm for portfolio management. Nevertheless, she still has described a perfectly sound criterion of successful portfolio management. This section seeks to identify analogs of the dictum "Buy low; sell high." Such things can guide action, insofar as they give a person a rough idea of what to look for, but they do not add up to a decision procedure.

When comparing prospective career paths, it may be that settling on any one of them would fully satisfy one's maieutic end of settling on a career. So this in itself is no reason to choose one career path over another. Still, there is the overarching end of finding something to live for, and this end is achievable in degrees. Accordingly, we might assess prospective ends in terms of *how much* they would give us to live for. This is a central question when assessing ends. We answer it (if we can answer it at all) in terms that are unavoidably subjective. An end gives us something to live for to the extent that pursuing it makes us feel we are doing something important.

The importance of our pursuits is partly a matter of opinion, of course. But so long as our goals grip us, making us feel our pursuits are worthy, it will not be merely a matter of opinion that our goals give us something to live for; it will be a matter of fact. Although the conviction that our pursuits are important is subjective, it remains a fact that when we have such a conviction, we have something to live for. The sense of importance, or the possibility of

---

[1] The example comes from T. H. Irwin (1993, p. 327).
[2] This one is borrowed from Philip Pettit (1991, p. 166).

developing it, is one thing to look for when assessing prospective ends.

The sense of having something to live for is not a simple function of the importance of the goals being pursued. For example, we might believe ending world hunger is more important than coaching Little League baseball. Yet, we might feel a sense of responsibility and achievement (adding up to a sense of having something to live for) when teaching Little Leaguers to field ground balls, while feeling overwhelmed and frustrated when trying to end world hunger. Coaching Little Leaguers, therefore, might give us more to live for. I do not think one should try to literally maximize the importance of one's pursuits. When one's pursuits become overwhelmingly important, they swallow one's life rather than give it meaning. The sense of importance that best sustains our sense of having reason to live need not be the same as a sense of maximum importance.[3] Nor is the sense of having something to live for a straightforwardly quantitative notion. Sheer multiplication of ends gives us more to live for if we have time for them. But when we take on so many projects that they begin to detract from each other, forcing us to race from one halfhearted pursuit to another, we end up with less to live for rather than more. How much we have to live for has more to do with the wholehearted intensity we bring to our pursuits than with their number.

On the heels of that, we must acknowledge that the sense of importance can be misleading. A grand master might feel chess is important, while others can see that his devotion to chess is stunting his capacity to find things important. He finds chess supremely important partly because his capacity to find anything else important is withering away. His choices shape him in such a way that he becomes someone who is maximally satisfied by the choices he has made. Even so, had he chosen differently, his capacity for satisfaction might have been greater. Therefore, we can question the choices of even a maximally satisfied chess champion if we have reason to think he has less to live for than he could have had.[4] He

[3] I owe this point to Harry Frankfurt. In his words, "A human life may be full of meaning for the person who lives it, even though it has no significant impact upon history or upon the world, and is therefore in that sense quite unimportant" (1992, p. 7).

[4] Chapter 5 levels the same criticism against those, like Thrasymachus, who profess to have no reason to be moral. Being someone who has no reason to be moral can be a great misfortune.

still has something to live for so long as he believes his pursuits are important, but he may have less than he could have had. Perhaps even worse is the thought that if he ever gets tired of chess, he will then have nothing.

We should, no doubt, be cautious about judging the goals of a chess grand master, for the risks associated with single-mindedness do not always materialize.[5] Nor can we assume he would become capable of a more profound satisfaction if we forced him to give up chess. We should not expect people to be shaped in so intimate a way by other people's choices as by their own. We do not have the same psychological push to grow into choices others make for us as we have to grow into choices we make for ourselves. Force of habit and the drive to resolve cognitive dissonance do not attach in the same way to choices made for us by others. So, some cases are hard to judge, and even well-grounded judgments generally do not weigh in favor of using force.

Nevertheless, we do have grounds for judging alternatives, and some cases are easy. Suppose Tom wants to be high on drugs, and views being high as a good in itself. Even so, Tom might reject intoxication as an item to pursue. For one thing, it would compromise his capacities for pursuing goals in general. Tom would have less to live for in part because he would have less to live with. Not only would Tom be less capable of pursuing goals but he foreseeably would be less committed to pursuing goals. So, this is a clear case of a prospective end the pursuit of which would undermine Tom's sense of importance, thereby giving him less to live for.[6] Another point is that we feel our pursuits are important when we believe something or someone depends on us. When others depend on us, we are important to them. That, perhaps more than anything else, confirms that what we do is worth doing (especially when people appreciate our efforts). So, when Tom's drug habit makes it impossible for others to depend on him, it poisons a primary source of his sense of importance.

[5] There is a mathematician named Paul Erdös who has "no wife or children, no job, no hobbies, not even a home, to tie him down. He lives out of a shabby suitcase and a drab orange plastic bag." See Paul Hoffman (1987, p. 60). But Erdös has lived to be seventy-four, and at last notice was publishing fifty papers a year—over a thousand all told. I owe this example to Walter Glannon.

[6] Particular pursuits also can *re*generate our capacity to find things to live for. Undertaking an exercise program, for example, often seems to go hand in hand with rediscovering or reinforcing a sense of purpose.

Thus, our chosen pursuits foreseeably affect our capacities, both for pursuing goals and, more fundamentally, for caring about goals. Further, an end may be incompatible (under actual or expected circumstances) with our other ends and, specifically, with our unchosen end of being good at what we do. Playing jazz guitar is something Kate does for its own sake, but since her friends all describe her playing as intolerable, she realizes the activity will never draw on her talents in a satisfying way. It will never give her a sense of competence, and so it cannot give her the unequivocal sense of importance she can get from practicing medicine. As a surgeon, Kate finds it important not only that her ends be pursued but that she in particular is pursuing them. Her particular talents and positional advantages make her well suited for a career in medicine, and so she finds it fitting to have the ends she has.

Combined with the question of how a prospective end would mesh with our desire to be competent is a question about whether a pursuit will be sufficiently demanding. Kate wants ends she will not be able to meet too easily, for if she meets them too easily, maximal satisfaction will not really be satisfactory. She will not have lived for her goals in a sufficiently intense way. Consider builders of model ships. The end products are things of beauty to the builders. Otherwise, the activity would not be rewarding. Yet, the beauty of the end product is only part of what is rewarding in the activity, for the builders also want the activity to be a delicate and intricate challenge. If such ships took only a moment to assemble, then the point of building them would be lost. The nature of the activity is part of the point of seeking to create the final product.[7] Metaphorically, we want a cup that will not run over too easily, something it takes work to fill. On the other hand, we do not want a cup so big that we find it overwhelming. Challenges can be too small or too big. They have an optimal size, which, by a different route, brings us to our earlier conclusion that we can have reason to cultivate moderate desires (see Chapter 2). When an end strikes us as important, when it is a real challenge but one we are competent to meet, then the end has what seem to be the key ingredients in giving us a sense of having reason to live.

[7] Suppose a person could do much good merely by pressing a button. Harry Frankfurt observes that "A life devoted to bringing about that benefit, in which the only meaningful activity was pressing the button, would be less meaningful than one devoted to a final end that was of smaller value but that could be pursued only by complex and varied activity" (1992, p. 9n).

If none of Kate's alternatives leaps out as the final end whose adoption would give her something to live for, then she must proceed in a more deliberate fashion, asking herself which alternatives are truly feasible, which of them draw well on her particular talents and positional advantages, and so on. If we have a procedure for saying which prospective end will give us the healthiest, most intense, or most enduring sense of having reason to live—so much the better. Suppose, though, that there is no algorithm, and that none of Kate's alternatives grips her. This is not to say the choice does not matter. On the contrary, it may matter a great deal. Kate might be acutely conscious of how different her life will be if she chooses one alternative rather than the other, but the differences between the alternatives may not help her to rank them. Suppose she looks for a decisive reason to choose one end in preference to alternatives, and fails. Even in that case, something eventually emerges as the best she can do. If she cannot afford to wait, or if waiting does not resolve her ambivalence, then at some point the best she can do is pick something and get on with her life, hoping she will grow into that choice and become a person on whom that end acquires a grip. Therefore, it can be rational for Kate to choose an end even when she lacks decisive reasons for choosing that end in preference to alternatives.

This may seem to leave the choice of ends peculiarly underdetermined, but in fact, the same thing happens when we choose mere means to given ends. Suppose Tom wants to buy a car, but none of his prospective purchases emerges as the best means to his end. Still, he sees that it is rational to pick an alternative and get on with it, because even if none of his prospective purchases is clearly best, he eventually reaches a stage when choosing an alternative becomes clearly better than not choosing one. Eventually, it becomes clear that staying on the fence is costing too much, at which point choosing something or other becomes unequivocally rational. There is no general algorithm for rationally choosing final ends. But there is no general algorithm for choosing means to given ends, either, at least not for beings like us. We have no recipe for rational choice.[8]

People sometimes pursue maieutic ends as if they expect to find uniquely suitable means to those ends. People once spoke, for ex-

---

[8] Chapter 2 offered an analogous argument for the rationality of underdetermined choices of means to given ends.

ample, of "looking for Mr. Right." What often is called for, though, is underdetermined choice. When given ends like survival first begin pressing us to find something to live for, that new end is too vague to guide us in ranking alternatives. When we realize this, we begin to understand one of the roles that underdetermined choice plays in a thoroughly rational life plan. Underdetermined choice launches the process of coming to have a thoroughly rational life plan.

It is in the process of choosing ends that a life and thus a corpus of ends becomes a particular framework for ranking alternatives in a nonarbitrary way. As we develop increasingly well-defined images of ourselves and our goals, we develop increasingly concrete criteria for judging whether a prospective end is really something for us in particular to live for. But we do not start our lives with such criteria. Nor are they revealed by reflection. We know only so much about ourselves. And in the beginning, there is only so much to know. As we become too reflective to be sustained by a goal of bare survival, we become reflective enough to choose goals that go beyond bare survival. In time, our corpus of ends conceivably may come to be thoroughly justified, but it cannot start out that way. The process by which a circle of ends completes itself is a process that takes time.

That is one reason why, in abstraction from the context provided by a particular agent's corpus of ends, it is so difficult to say anything concrete about which ends the agent should choose. Still, we have several ways of comparing prospective ends. This section explains why we would be wrong to interpret the question of how to compare prospective ends as a question that can be answered only by giving a recipe for rational choice. We considered examples of the elements of reasoned judgment about prospective ends. We also saw how rational agents might proceed when reasoned judgment is inconclusive, as I think it often is.

THE POSSIBILITY OF DEVOTION

Chapter 3 argued that when we achieve a maieutic end by choosing a final end as an item to pursue, the maieutic end does not persist. Having been achieved, it no longer exists as an item to pursue. If this is right, then one cannot be pursuing a chosen end as a means to the maieutic end, for one no longer has the maieutic end. Final ends are chosen as, but not pursued as, means to maieutic ends. They really do take on a life of their own.

Here is the problem. Although particular maieutic ends do not persist, the overarching maieutic end could.[9] For example, Kate does not keep trying to settle on a career when she has already settled on one, but she may well continue to seek things to live for even though she already has things to live for. The overarching end of finding things to live for cannot be satiated in the way that particular maieutic ends can be.

This undermines my argument that so-called final ends cannot have an ongoing means-end relation to maieutic ends. Final ends replace particular maieutic ends as items to pursue, but they do not replace the overarching maieutic end. And if the overarching maieutic end persists, then we could be pursuing our allegedly final ends not so much for their own sake as for the sake of the one maieutic end that endures. Accordingly, there is some doubt here about whether my model of reflective rationality, intended to explain the choice of final ends, leaves room for final ends at all.

In response, we can admit that the overarching end persists, but it persists only in the sense that, unlike more particular maieutic ends, its satisfaction is essentially a matter of degree. (Having chosen a career in medicine, there may be nothing left to pursue regarding her end of settling on a career, but there will always be more she could do regarding her end of finding things to live for.) And if this is the sense in which the overarching maieutic end endures, there are two things to say. First, even an overarching maieutic end conceivably could be attained and thus not persist as a further end to which purported final ends could serve as mere means. We can envision reaching a point where we already have so much to live for that, if we had an opportunity to take on a new project that would give us a great deal to live for, we should regretfully decline, for our hands are already full. (Unfortunately, it is possible to go beyond this point without knowing it. Fear of not being sufficiently busy seems to drive some people to overload themselves with projects, and the consequent dilution of time and energy leaves them unable to do anything in a wholehearted way. In the end, they have less to live for rather than more.)

[9] I thank David Kelley for noticing this.

I do not want to lean too heavily on this, however, for although such satiation may actually occur, I want to say that even when satiation does not occur, and thus even when the overarching maieutic end persists, an end initially chosen as a means to a maieutic end can still become a final end. Accordingly, the second thing we should say is that even when the overarching end persists in degrees, an end whose choice gives us something to live for can still take on a life of its own. Consider how people become devoted to their chosen ends. When Kate settles on a particular spouse, she can become devoted to him for his sake—devoted to him as a particular person, not just as a convenient occasion for goal-directed activity on her part. If Kate's devotion persists merely as a means of having something or someone to live for, then her devotion should cease as soon as it no longer serves the purpose of giving her something to live for.

So when Kate loses her spouse in a car accident, her devotion to him no longer serves its alleged purpose, which suggests that she should erase her devotion and go back to where she started, with a clean slate and a once-familiar maieutic end of settling on a spouse—on someone to whom she can devote herself. But Kate does not do this. She cannot. Devotion does not work that way. Kate may remember a time when she liked to remark that there are "lots of fish in the sea," but having lost her spouse, the breadth of choice she once perceived will never again present itself in the same way. That part of her life is now empty, but it is not the same emptiness that once could have been filled simply by choosing someone or other as a spouse.

The point of the story is that we can reach a stage when we are heavily invested in the particular ends we have chosen, so heavily invested that the corresponding maieutic ends cannot easily be resurrected as items to pursue. If we cannot live for the sake of the particular ends we have already chosen, we may not be able to live for the sake of substitutes, either. We cannot always wipe the slate clean and seek to choose a final end as if we had not already chosen one. This is part of what underlies the supposition in Chapter 3 that our attitude toward a prospective end typically changes after we adopt it as an end, and thus our grounds for choosing it will not be the same as our subsequent grounds for pursuing it.

Metaphorically speaking, particular compartments in our lives initially are given shape by maieutic ends. These compartments wait to be filled by the choice of final ends. As we choose, the compartments are reshaped by what fills them—by the process of growing into our choices. In time, a once-amorphous shape conforms to a particular chosen end, so that alternative ends that once could have fit into that compartment no longer can. Thus, if the chosen end that once filled a compartment is somehow lost, one might simply be stuck with an empty compartment.[10]

At that stage, it rings false to say one's ongoing devotion to the particular end was a mere means of having or getting something to live for. The truth is that one came to live for the particular end, period. The end has acquired a genuinely independent status, and its status as a final end is not affected by the fact that, in other compartments of one's life, one is still trying to settle on goals to pursue so that one will have more to live for.

We might wonder, why would Kate let herself grow into a commitment so deep that it becomes independent of the end she originally achieved by choosing the particular object of devotion? Why risk becoming so devoted to an end that it takes on a life of its own and becomes a final end? Presumably because that kind of devotion gives Kate more to live for. Kate's career and her spouse give her so very much to live for partly because the depth of her commitment to them has gone beyond considerations of how much they give her to live for.[11]

We also might wonder whether the overarching maieutic end itself is a final end. It could be; the categories are not mutually exclusive. Still, I am inclined to say it is importantly unlike final ends. Kate's final ends guide her choice of means. Although her need to find things to live for pushes her to make choices, that need does not guide her choices in the way her decision to pursue a career as a surgeon guides her subsequent choices. Nor does her end of finding things to live for make her feel she has things to live for in the way her final ends do.

For a similar reason, there is a problem with thinking of happi-

---

[10] Extending the metaphor, we might say compartments have a certain elasticity. A compartment contoured to a particular lost end can return to an approximation of its more loosely defined original shape. Kate can recover the motivation she once had to pursue the maieutic end of settling on a spouse. But it takes time.

[11] For more on the instrumental value of noninstrumental emotional commitment, see Chapter 5, and also Robert Frank (1988).

ness as an end. If my student says she wants to be a professional philosopher, it sounds like she has something to live for. But if she says that all she wants is to be happy, it sounds like finding something to live for is exactly what she needs. Happiness is something she hopes for, but it is not something to live for. She values happiness, yet the fact remains that she will become happy not by adopting happiness as an end, an item to pursue, but only by adopting, pursuing, and achieving other ends, items worth pursuing for their own sake.[12]

For the sake of argument, suppose we say the overarching maieutic end is itself a final end, an unchosen final end. Would that threaten my theory? Not really. The real threat—the threat discussed in this section—consists of the argument that my model leaves no room at all for final ends, and thus it cannot begin to explain how final ends could be rationally chosen. I responded to this threat by showing that the model allows for, and even gives reasons for, the process of coming to view ends as worth pursuing for their own sake.

CAN IT BE RATIONAL TO HAVE MORE THAN ONE FINAL END?

Chapter 1 allowed that morality is arguably categorical; morally speaking, one could have reason to do what is right not because it would serve one's ends but simply because it is right.[13] Alternatively, if one's reason for an action is that it is right, one may be interpreted as having adopted "doing the right thing" as an end. How would the end of doing the right thing, or the end of being moral, fit into our corpus of ends? A monistic conception of rationality commits us to viewing rational choice as essentially unified by a single final end. Such a conception seems to leave us with two alternatives. Either we say being moral is a mere means to this final end or, if we say being moral is itself the final end, we then have to say it is our only final end.

A pluralistic conception of rationality lets us claim that being moral is a final end without having to claim (implausibly) that

[12] I thank Carol Rovane for suggesting both the example and the point it exemplifies.
[13] Chapter 6 pursues this further.

being moral is our only final end. If we have a plurality of ends, we have room for a compartment in our lives for the goal of being moral, alongside our other goals. And the end of being moral could still be a rational choice in the sense of giving us something to live for, just like our other final ends. This section argues that it can be rational to have the kind of plurality of final ends among which the end of being moral might find a place.

A pluralistic conception of final ends has an advantage as a descriptive account of how human beings operate. It helps account for the fact that we do not have an algorithm for making important choices. We lack an algorithm in part because there is no one end with respect to which everything else can be evaluated as a means. This leaves open the possibility that even a final end need not always be decisively important, for irreconcilable conflicts between final ends will be possible. This is something a theory ought to accommodate, however, for it seems to be a fact of life that we sometimes find ourselves in dilemmas in which we elect not to pursue ends that we value highly and for their own sake.

Against this, some would say having more than one final end is impossible, while others would say that, possible or not, having more than one final end is irrational. Jeremy Bentham, for example, thought we could not possibly have more than one final end.[14] Our final end is to maximize pleasure, he held, and such things as the desire to understand or the desire to be a good person must be merely derivative ends, ultimately pursued only as means to the end of maximizing pleasure. Aristotle held that there may be more than one end, but that it would be helpful if in fact there were not. According to W.F.R. Hardie, Aristotle tells us that failing to plan and organize one's life for the attainment of a single end would show lack of practical wisdom (1967, p. 298). Like archers, Aristotle says, our aim would probably be truer if we had a single clearly defined target (*Nicomachean Ethics*, 1094a18–24). Also, as Chapter 2 explained, if we have a plethora of targets, we presumably run the risk of finding ourselves in situations where our goals conflict with each other. So there is an issue here about whether having a variety of occasionally incommensurable goals is worth the price.

Aristotle is surely correct in saying we gain something by regi-

---

[14] For an accessible presentation of Bentham's views, see David Lyons (1991).

menting all our activities under a single end. Presumably, in so regimenting our activities, we can be more organized and less prone to indecision. But that presumed advantage does not entail that having a single end would give us as much to live for as would a plurality of ends. If one wants to hit targets, then there is something to be said for maximizing the accuracy of one's aim with respect to any single target, but there is something to be said for having more targets, too. (If we want to hit targets, then presumably we want opportunities to hit targets, and it is hardly obvious that we give ourselves the optimal number of opportunities to hit targets by having only one target.) In any event, as Hardie notes, "It seems plain that very few men can be said, even roughly, to live their lives under the domination of a single end" (p. 299). If Hardie is right, and I think he is, pluralism is not only possible but, descriptively speaking, it is the rule rather than the exception.[15] And if pluralism is so prevalent, maybe it has a point.

Often (not always but often) we proceed by setting targets and then aiming at them. And utility per se is not the object of our aspirations. Our targets are rather more concrete than that. We look for an apartment in a certain neighborhood, for a roommate who does not smoke, for recordings of Beethoven symphonies, and for a healthy breakfast cereal. We try to lose five pounds, to call our parents once a month, and to keep regular office hours. Our targets are discrete.

Because we operate with a variety of discrete and concrete aspirations, our pursuits tend to fall into separate compartments, differentiated and organized by separate substantive goals. In effect, we compartmentalize our lives.[16] From within those compartments emerge separate domains of rationality. As scholars and researchers, we operate in domains of epistemic rationality, seeking effective means to the substantive goal of learning the truth about particular issues. As colleagues, family members, and so on, we operate within domains of moral rationality, seeking means to the

---

[15] Alternatively, we could frame the issue in terms of the choice between monolithic and aggregate ultimate ends. See Scott MacDonald (1991, pp. 48–53).

[16] The degree of compartmentalization will depend on circumstances, including cultural circumstances, of course, and not every life exhibits the degree of compartmentalization typical among readers of this book. For further discussion, see the section on Eurocentrism in Chapter 10.

substantive ends of doing the right thing or being a good person. And our lives are permeated by domains of prudential rationality, domains in which our substantive ends is to secure our own long-term advantage in one way or another.

All of this is consistent with the very weak version of monism that we get by positing an inclusive ultimate end, to use Scott Mac-Donald's term. An inclusive ultimate end is formal. It is the end of simply living the best possible life. To use my term, it is our global end. As Scott MacDonald explains, "The ideal life will be a coherent overall plan [quite possibly open-ended in various respects] intended to realize the best life" (1991, p. 56). The material corollaries of this final end will be different for different people, since what is the best life for an individual will depend on that person's circumstances, tastes, and talents. This seems eminently plausible, and there is no reason to take issue with it, except to note that having a global end does not imply that one's hierarchy of goals is monistic in any substantive way. If a number of different goals must be achieved in order for a person to be living an ideal life, then we are talking about a plurality of ends, and we do not reduce the plurality of ends to one merely by saying that achieving them would constitute an ideal life. Of course, an ideal life may involve harmonizing and integrating our final ends, which suggests a set of goals that is more than a mere collection. And seeking a contingent harmony (that is, a set of goals that could but probably will not come into conflict) seems healthy, whereas ruling out the bare possibility of disharmony (by rejecting any combination of goals that could ever come into conflict) would leave us with an impoverished set of goals.

We still have a problem, though. Suppose that being moral is part of our global end. And suppose that, by being moral, we have in mind a sort of sacred (that is, "no matter what the cost") commitment to doing what is right. Is that possible? Is it possible for parts of a global end to be sacred? In Hardie's opinion, "If the secondary and inclusive end is the harmonization and integration of primary ends, no primary end can be sacrosanct" (p. 304). Certainly we do not view survival as sacrosanct. On the contrary, there may well be things we would die for. But what about the goal of being honest? Is it not possible that some of our local goals could serve their purposes as means to our global end precisely by being sacrosanct? Such a thing clearly is possible, notwithstanding the fact that there are risks involved in having local goals or self-imposed constraints that one views as sacrosanct.

Here is another possible problem. We may suppose (and later chapters are committed to the view) that to have integrity is to have a kind of internal consistency and a knack of being honest with oneself—in sum, being true to oneself—whereas to be moral requires both integrity and a commitment to be true to others, so to speak. Of interest here is that one might think of a plurality of final ends as inconsistent with integrity, on the grounds that a plurality of final ends would leave us in a position of having to make trade-offs among our most deeply held values.

If anything, the opposite is true. For example, does integrity require that one's goal of learning the truth about a particular issue be reducible to a mere means to a global end? I think not. Isaac Levi apparently would agree, for he says the autonomy of scientific inquiry boils down to the irreducibility of cognitive values to other practical values (1986, p. 17). An intransigent commitment to truth may well be necessary for the attainment of (let's say) happiness, but to admit this is not the same as reducing the commitment to truth to a search for happiness. Indeed, the suggestion here is that a reduction of an irreducible commitment is not even possible.

Likewise, doing the right thing may for some people be an end that is not negotiable in prudential terms. Such an attitude seems to be virtually definitive of integrity. At the same time, having a sacred commitment to doing the right thing (or learning the truth) even at the cost of one's overall happiness may be an important contributor to one's overall happiness. Thus, as we saw with the relation between maieutic ends and the choice of final ends, there can be ends that serve their higher purpose precisely by taking on an importance to us that is independent of the role their choice played in serving that higher purpose.

Monolithic monism implies that moral ends are instrumental to some further end or that being moral is the sole final end. Pluralism lets us say that being moral is something we want for its own sake without having to claim it is the only thing we want for its own sake. Being moral can be its own reward in the same way that successfully pursuing truth can be its own reward. This opens us up to irreconcilable conflicts, but that is life, descriptively speaking, and there are reasons to be glad that we do not live up to the monistic paradigm.

The Inhuman Rationality of Homo economicus

Chapter 3 argued that although final ends are pursued for their own sake, their choice can be a means to what I call maieutic ends. Moreover, a corpus of ends need not have loose ends, ends we must take as given. On the contrary, a corpus of ends can evolve into something of which every member has a rationale. This chapter answers two further questions. First, is there a procedure for choosing among prospective ends? Probably not, but even if there is no such procedure, people still have various commonsense criteria by which they often (if not always) manage to sort out which of their options will give them something to live for, which will grip them with a sense of life's instrumental value. Second, when an agent cannot sort out which prospective end best meets commonsense criteria for choosing among ends, is it nevertheless possible for the agent to make a recognizably rational choice? Yes it is, because, even then, agents can see that their corpus of ends is better served by picking something than by picking nothing. When the best we can do is pick something, hoping to grow into the choice, then choosing to simply pick something and get on with our lives is eminently rational. This chapter also argues that we can have more than one final end and that, at least in principle, being moral can be one of them. Reflective rationality makes room for a plurality of final ends—a plurality of ends one pursues for their own sake and whose acceptance as ends gives one things to live for.

Finally, a comment on how this model of rationality bears on the larger task of developing a conception of characteristically human self-regard, a conception that can help us make sense of our lives as moral agents. The conventional instrumentalist conception of rational choice sometimes is combined with a substantive assumption of mutual unconcern (i.e., that rational agents are immediately concerned with no one's welfare but their own). This combination produces a model of rational agency that has become notorious in the social sciences: Homo economicus. By hypothesis, Homo economicus is purely self-regarding.[17]

[17] This is the Homo economicus model as it enters into the fundamental theorems of welfare economics. Models that incorporate (or claim they could incorporate) other-regarding preferences also are referred to sometimes as Homo economicus, but the term is used here in its narrower sense.

It is commonplace to point out that the Homo economicus model, so defined, does not accurately describe human agents. Like Homo economicus, we have preferences, but unlike Homo economicus, we have preferences directly relating to the welfare of others. Some might regard this as controversial. Psychological egoism is the thesis that all human behavior is purely self-regarding. Responding to obvious counterexamples, defenders of psychological egoism sometimes say we act in apparently other-regarding ways only because we reap so-called "psychic" rewards from helping others. As is well known among philosophers, psychological egoism thus embellished becomes airtight at a cost of becoming literally inconsequential. It does not tell us that soldiers will never give their lives for their countries or that people will never make anonymous donations to charity. It does not predict that Ebenezer Scrooge will never buy Bob Cratchit a Christmas turkey. It offers no testable predictions. Instead, it avoids having false implications by having no implications whatsoever. It merely expresses a determination to stretch the concept of self-regard as far as necessary to fit all behavior, no matter how diverse observed behavior actually turns out to be.[18]

Insofar as there is any real content to the claim that we get psychic rewards from helping others, we can admit that, of course, we tend to feel good about helping others. But this fact does not begin to suggest that our real objective is psychic benefit rather than other people's welfare. On the contrary, there can be no psychic reward for helping others unless we care about others. Imagine Tom helping someone across the street and then saying to her, "Other things equal, I would rather you had been hit by a bus. Unfortunately, helping you is the price I have to pay in order to reap psychic rewards." The fact that we get psychic rewards from helping others *proves* we are directly concerned with the welfare of others. The mark of a purely self-regarding person is not that he really wants to help others but rather that he really does not.[19]

---

[18] Most of the professional economists I know do not make this mistake. They construe psychological egoism not as true but rather as a useful working hypothesis. Not all human action is driven by self-interest; nevertheless, we often arrive at a better understanding of observed behavior by looking for motives of self-interest.

[19] For a classic critique of psychological egoism/hedonism, see Joel Feinberg (1981).

That is the obvious and much celebrated difference between Homo economicus and us.

The less obvious and more interesting difference is that Homo economicus *does not have maieutic ends*. Homo economicus wants to maximize profit; the question of how Homo economicus developed or settled on such an end does not arise. (The end did not develop; it was stipulated.) But whereas Homo economicus deliberates only about alternative means of achieving stipulated ends, we deliberate about ends themselves. We sometimes stop to wonder whether an end like maximizing profit is worth having. We have self-regarding ends, to be sure, but they are not given to us in the same way they are given to Homo economicus. On the contrary, we shape ourselves and our ends as we go. We are the outcomes as well as the makers of our choices.

Admittedly, Homo economicus is a useful model in the social sciences. But we are not Homo economicus, and what is good for us is not the same as what would be good for Homo economicus. Thus, Homo economicus is a poor model of rational choice even when self-interest is all that matters, for even then there is a crucial difference between Homo economicus and beings like us. The difference is this: We need to worry about our goals in a way that Homo economicus does not. Homo economicus does not have to work at maintaining an attitude that his goals are worth living for, but we do.

* CHAPTER 5 *

Reasons for Altruism

We like to flatter ourselves with the false claim to a
more noble motive, . . . but if we look more closely
at our planning and striving, we everywhere
come upon the dear self.
Immanuel Kant (1981, pp. 20–21; first published 1785)

AN ANALYSIS OF OTHER-REGARD

CHAPTERS 3 AND 4 showed how final ends could be rationally chosen. Chapter 4 argued that it can be rational to have a plurality of final ends, leaving us with a theoretical possibility that moral ends could be among our final ends. This chapter takes a more direct approach, explaining why it is rational to have genuinely altruistic concerns and commitments.

According to a well-known version of the instrumental model, rational choice consists of maximizing one's utility, or more precisely, maximizing one's utility subject to a budget constraint. We seek the point of highest utility lying within our limited means. The term 'utility' could mean a lot of different things, but in recent times theorists have often taken the term to mean something related to or even identical to preference satisfaction (and thus utility functions are sometimes called preference functions). To have a preference is to *care*, to want one alternative more than another.

People are self-regarding insofar as they care about their own welfare.[1] People are *purely* self-regarding if they care about no one's welfare other than their own and recognize no constraints on how they treat others beyond those constraints imposed by circumstances: their limited time and income, legal restrictions, and so on. The question is, is it rational—is it *uniquely* rational—to be

---

[1] Insofar as we can distinguish between interests and preferences, welfare is a matter of serving interests rather than satisfying preferences. There is a perfectly natural sense in which many people have preferences the satisfaction of which would not be in their interest.

purely self-regarding? The instrumentalist model does not say. For that matter, neither does the instrumentalist model assume people care about welfare (their own or that of others). The instrumentalist model allows that Hume could prefer the destruction of the world to the scratching of his finger.

The departures from pure self-regard that concern us here come in two varieties. First, we might care about other people, which is to say their welfare enters the picture through our preference functions. Indeed, a desire to help other people often is among our strongest desires. Second, the welfare of others can enter the picture in the form of self-imposed constraints we acknowledge when pursuing our goals. In different words, an otherwise optional course of action may come to be seen as either forbidden or required, depending on how it would affect others. There may be limits to what we are willing to do to others in the course of pursuing our goals.[2]

Insofar as one's other-regard takes the form of caring about other people's welfare, one exhibits *concern*. Insofar as it takes the form of adherence to constraints on what one may do to others, one exhibits *respect*. (The distinction between the two forms of regard for others is probably not so clear-cut in ordinary usage, but this is how I shall use the terms.) We manifest concern for people when we care about how life is treating them (so to speak), whereas we respect people when we care about how *we* are treating them and constrain ourselves accordingly. Note that what motivates one kind of other-regard need not motivate the other. One person may think it out of the question to violate other people's rights and at the same time be unconcerned about other people's welfare.[3] An-

---

[2] People have tried to distinguish between self-regarding and other-regarding actions, separating actions affecting only the agent from actions affecting others as well. (See John Stuart Mill's *On Liberty* [1974; first published 1861], for example.) The distinction is supposed to define a sphere of self-regarding activity with which society may not interfere, but it has proven notoriously difficult to draw, because a person seeking to justify interference with activities she dislikes can always claim she is being *affected* in some way, and thus that the activity is not purely self-regarding. By contrast, the distinction between self-regarding and other-regarding concerns is unproblematic. However hard it is to find important examples of actions that affect only oneself, the distinction between caring about others and caring only about oneself remains sharp.

[3] The distinction between respect and concern does not correspond to a distinction between duties of noninterference and duties to provide positive aid. Ex-

other person may care about feeding the poor and have no qualms about taking other people's money to buy the food. In short, unconcerned people can be principled, and concerned people can be ruthless.

I use the term "altruism" to characterize a kind of action. In particular, an action is altruistic only if it is motivated by regard for others. Expressing concern or respect as a mere means to some other end is not altruistic. The expression is altruistic only if concern or respect for others is what motivates it. (People can act from mixed motives. Robin Hood may undertake a course of action in order to help the poor, make himself look good, and hurt the rich. His action is at once altruistic, self-serving, and vicious.) Whether altruistic action is coextensive with other-regarding action is a terminological matter. Some classify respect for others as altruistic; others would say that to respect others is merely to give them their due, to do what justice requires, and thus cannot count as altruistic.

This definition of altruism leaves open questions about how altruism relates to justice and other essentially moral concepts. There is good reason not to try to settle these questions with definitions. For example, if we elect to stipulate that an act cannot be altruistic unless it goes beyond requirements of justice, then we cannot count ourselves as observing instances of altruism until we settle what justice requires. Someone might wish to define altruism as other-regarding action that goes beyond requirements of justice, but identifying acts as altruistic would then be fraught with difficulties, and pointlessly so. The difficulties would be mere artifacts of a bad definition.

Terminological issues aside, the issue of substance is twofold. We have both concern and respect for others, which raises a question about whether these departures from pure self-regard are rational. This chapter explores reasons for both departures, while acknowledging that some people consider one or the other to be the canonical form of altruism.[4]

---

pressions of concern typically will involve lending aid; yet, out of concern, one might resist one's urge to help a child, knowing that children need to learn to take care of themselves. And expressions of respect typically will involve noninterference; yet, out of respect, one might lend aid to a war veteran.

[4] The people I have polled usually agree that one of the two is the canonical form, but it turns out that they are evenly split on which one it is.

Of course, one account of our reasons for altruism directly follows from the supposition that we have other-regarding preferences. If we prefer on balance to act on our concern for others, then by that very fact we have reasons for altruism. The reasons are not purely self-regarding reasons, to be sure, but they are still reasons, and reasons from our points of view. Therefore, given that we are as we are, altruism sometimes is rational.

It hardly needs to be said, though, that no one would be satisfied with an argument that stopped here. A satisfying account of our reasons for altruism will not take our other-regarding preferences as given. Neither is it enough to offer a purely descriptive account of concern and respect—a biological or psychological or sociological account of what causes us to develop concern and respect for others. Biology and psychology are relevant, but they are not enough. We want an account according to which it is rational for us to have other-regarding preferences in the first place.

The interesting question, then, is this: If we were to abstract from our other-regarding interests and consider the matter from a purely self-regarding perspective, would we have reason from that perspective to affirm our other-regarding interests? This section characterizes altruism as action motivated either by respect or concern for others. The task now is to explain how self-regarding concerns could give people reasons to cultivate concern and respect for others.[5]

Since this chapter aims to rationally ground respect and concern for others, readers may expect me to take for granted that self-regard is the fixed point around which all else must revolve if it is to have a place in rational choice theory's normative universe. That is not the plan. To be sure, self-regard enters the argument as an explanatory tool rather than as the thing to be explained, but that does not mean we can take it for granted. On the contrary, the conclusion toward which previous chapters are driving is this: Hu-

---

[5] It may seem that if the original motivation is self-regarding, then we cannot be talking about genuine altruism. On the contrary, the point of the discussion is to consider whether we can be motivated by reason A to endorse a disposition to be motivated by reason B. (Can one be led by concern for one's health to try to cultivate a liking for vegetables?) Whether the acts motivated by reason B are altruistic depends on the nature of reason B, not reason A. If reason B consists of respect or concern for others, then acts motivated by it are altruistic. It makes no difference whether reason A consists of something else.

man self-regard is a fragile thing. Its fragility is one source of its explanatory power. Although we have a certain amount of respect and concern for ourselves, this amount is not unlimited and it is not fixed. It varies. It is influenced by our choices, and this fact has a direct bearing on how regard for others fits into the lives of self-regarding human agents. The following sections elaborate.

HOMO ECONOMICUS REVISITED

As already mentioned, to be instrumentally rational is to be committed to serving preferences *of* oneself, but one may or may not be committed to serving preferences *regarding* oneself. As Chapter 4 noted, though, when we combine the instrumental model of rationality with a stipulation that rational agents are purely self-regarding, the result is the Homo economicus model of rational agency. The point is worth mentioning again, because the reasons given here to nurture other-regard are reasons for beings like us, not for beings like Homo economicus. The Homo economicus model leaves no room for altruism. The fact that the Homo economicus model assumes pure self-regard, however, is only part of the reason why it leaves no room for altruism. The real problem lies in how the assumption of pure self-regard works when combined with the underlying instrumental model of rationality.

The instrumental model of rationality is static in the sense that it does not provide for rational choice among ends. The instrumental model can be enriched by allowing for the possibility of endogenous preferences (that is, preferences that change in response to choices).[6] This enriched model might explain how we develop our preferences. Even so, something is missing, because a person could have endogenous preferences and still think preference satisfaction is all that matters. For Homo economicus, there remains only one question: How much can I get? We go beyond Homo economicus and develop a truly reflective rationality as we come to see that the quality of our lives is a function not only of what we get but also of what we are.[7] And what we are, no less than what we get, depends on what we choose.

---

[6] Herbert Gintis's (1974) Marxist critique of neoclassical economics rests on the welfare implications of endogenous preferences. See also Peter Hammond (1976) and George A. Akerlof and William T. Dickens (1982).

[7] I thank Jean Hampton for suggesting this way of describing the contrast.

This section's main point is that whether we intend to do so, we develop new preferences as we go, which creates the possibility that beings like ourselves might come to be other-regarding. The next section argues that the same fluidity and capacity for reflecting on our ends that makes possible the cultivation of other-regarding concern also makes it important. There are reasons to embrace and nurture our concern for others, reasons that have to do with what is conducive to our own health, survival, and growth.

REASONS FOR CONCERN

As Thomas Nagel sees it, "Altruistic reasons are parasitic upon self-interested ones; the circumstances in the lives of others which altruism requires us to consider are circumstances which those others already have reason to consider from a self-interested point of view" (1970, p. 16). Altruistic reasons could be parasitic on self-regarding reasons in a second way, insofar as reflective self-regard is the seed from which our regard for others must grow. Or perhaps the last claim is too strong. Respect and concern for others might, for all we know, be the phenotypic expression of a recessive gene. Even so, it remains the case that we do not really give a rationale for other-regarding concerns until we explain how people could abstract from their other-regarding concerns and still find reason from a purely self-regarding perspective to embrace concern for others. Thus, for those who seek to explain how other-regard could be rational, it seems obvious that our other concerns, that is, our self-regarding concerns, must inevitably have explanatory primacy. If we take this approach, it seems we are committed to viewing other-regard as parasitic on self-regard for its rational reconstruction even if not for its literal origin.

However, this is only half of the picture. On closer inspection, the apparently parasitic relationship between other-regard and self-regard turns out to be symbiotic. Insofar as other-regard has to be nurtured, we need self-regarding reasons to initiate the nurturing process. But self-regard is not automatic either. (It may be standard equipment, so to speak, but even standard equipment requires maintenance.) Our interests are not static. They wax and wane and change shape over time, and self-regarding interests are not exempt. An enduring self-regard requires maintenance.

How, then, do we maintain self-regard? Consider that our preference functions are, in effect, a representation of what we have to live for. To enrich the function by cultivating new concerns is to have more to live for. As we increase our potential for happiness, it may become harder to attain our maximum possible happiness, but that is no reason not to expand our potential. New concerns leave us open to the possibility of new frustrations and disappointments, but also to the possibility of deeper and broader satisfaction. And one crucial way to nurture self-regard is to nurture concerns that give us more to live for than we have if we care only about ourselves.

It is rational for beings like us to be peaceful and productive, to try to earn a sense of genuinely belonging in our community. Not many things are more important to us than being able to honestly consider ourselves important parts of a community. When evaluating our goals, we have to ask whether pursuing them is an appropriate way to use our talents, given our circumstances and tastes. We also have to ask how valuable our services would be to others in the various ways in which we could employ our talents.

The latter consideration is not decisive, of course, for if you are bored by computers and feel alive only when philosophizing about morality, then devoting yourself to computer programming might be irrational, even though your programming services are in greater demand. (What might make it irrational is that you would be responding to others at the cost of becoming unresponsive to yourself.) Nevertheless, to create a place for ourselves in society as peaceful and productive members, we must have regard for the interests of others, for serving the interests of others develops and gives value to our own latent productivity. For many of us, being honest and productive members of a community we respect is an end in itself. Even when it is not, it remains that much of what we want from life (and from our communities) comes to us in virtue of our importance to others.[8]

This is not to deny that when personal survival is an urgent concern, it can be quite sufficient to capture our attention. In such cases, we may have no need for other-regarding concerns. Indeed,

---

[8] As Phillip Bricker says, "To be prudent is to effect a reconciliation between oneself and one's world" (1980, p. 401). And, we might add, our world consists in large part of other people.

we may view ourselves as not being able to afford other-regarding concerns. To cultivate additional preferences when our hands are already full is to cultivate frustration. But when circumstances leave us with free time, a more reflective kind of rationality will weigh in favor of trying to develop broader interests. We may begin with a goal of survival, but because we are reflective, we need to cultivate concerns other than survival. As noted in Chapter 3, if there was nothing for the sake of which we were surviving, reflection on this fact would tend to undermine our commitment to survival.

Because we are reflective, it is conducive to survival to have a variety of preferences in addition to a preference for survival, preferences the satisfaction of which gives significance and value to our survival that it otherwise would not have. Paradoxically, it can be healthy to cultivate preferences that can cut against the pursuit of health. Other ends compete for our attention with the end of health, but they also reinforce our concern for our health by giving it instrumental value. Developing concerns beyond the interest we take in ourselves is one way (even if not the only way) of making ourselves and our projects important enough to be worth caring about.

I conclude that we have self-regarding reasons to incorporate (so far as we are able to do so) other-regarding preferences into our utility functions, or, in other words, we have self-regarding reasons to internalize other-regarding concerns. As these new preferences become part of the function, they acquire a certain autonomy, becoming more than mere means to previously given ends. The element of autonomy is crucial. The new preferences must take on lives of their own; we must come to care about them independently of how seeking to satisfy them bears on ends we already had. If they fail to become ends in themselves, then we fail to achieve our purpose in cultivating them, which is to have more to live for. We cultivate a richer set of concerns as a means to a further end, but we cultivate so as to reap new *ends*, not merely new means of serving ends we already have.

That we nurture our emerging ends for the sake of preexisting ends does not stop them from becoming ends we pursue for their own sake. The cultivation *process* is an effective means to existing ends only if the *things being cultivated* are more than that. Our ultimate interest is in having something to live for, being able to devote ourselves to the satisfaction of preferences we judge worthy of satisfaction. Not having other-regarding preferences is costly, for it drastically limits what one has to live for. A person may have no concern for others, but her lack of concern is nothing to envy.[9] Concern for ourselves gives us something to live for. Concern for others as well as ourselves gives us more.

Conc

This section argues that, to the extent that we are reflectively rather than instrumentally rational, we cannot afford the poverty of ends with which pure self-regard would saddle us. Under conditions that leave us time for reflection, we need to have a variety of ongoing concerns with respect to which our survival—our selves—can take on value as a means. When these further ends are in place, survival comes to be more than a biological given; an agent who has further ends not only happens to have the goal of survival but can give reasons why survival is important. As a biologically given end, survival can confer value on our pursuits insofar as they take on value as means to the end of survival, but survival can also come to possess its own value insofar as it comes to be a means to our emerging further ends. Survival thus becomes an end we have reasons to pursue, quite apart from the fact that the end of survival is biologically given. The next three sections turn to the topic of other-regarding respect and to the more general phenomenon of commitment and counterpreferential choice. First, I discuss how our self-imposed constraints (along with our preferences) change over time; later, I discuss why we might want them to change.

THE MECHANISM OF COMMITMENT

My distinction between concern and respect for others is like Amartya Sen's distinction between sympathy and commitment. Sen says that when a person's sense of well-being is psychologically tied to someone else's welfare in the right sort of way, it is a case of sympathy; he says that commitment involves counterpreferential choice. "If the knowledge of torture of others makes you sick, it is

[9] Similarly, Gregory Kavka says, "An immoralist's gloating that it does not pay him to be moral because the satisfactions of morality are not for him [is] like the pathetic boast of a deaf person that he saves money because it does not pay him to buy opera records" (1985, p. 307).

106

a case of sympathy; if it does not make you feel personally worse off, but if you think it is wrong and you are ready to do something to stop it, it is a case of commitment" (1990, p. 31). Whether or not it is best to follow Sen in describing commitment as counter-preferential choice, commitment at the very least involves a different kind of preference than does sympathy.

What I call concern for others seems essentially identical to what Sen calls sympathy.[10] What Sen calls commitment, however, is broader than what I call respect for others. Commitment involves adherence to principles, whereas respect for others involves adherence to principles of a more specific kind, namely, those that specify constraints on what we may do to others in the course of pursuing our goals. This section describes a process by which we can become committed (in Sen's broad sense). Later, I consider why it can be rational to cultivate commitments (in the broad sense) and explore reasons why commitment typically seems to involve the more particular kind of commitment that I call respect for others.

Of course, not everyone sees a need to argue that there are processes by which people develop genuine commitments. Indeed, some people believe we become committed by choosing to be committed and that is all there is to it. Nothing said here is meant to deny that we can simply choose to be committed, but because some people do deny it, this section offers an account of a process by which a person can internalize commitments, thereby making them genuine. This section is addressed mainly to those who are skeptical about whether human commitment is really possible.

Geoffrey Sayre-McCord once proposed a thought experiment in which we imagine we have an opportunity to choose whether we will have a disposition to be moral. "With one hand, say, we might pull a lever that frees us of moral compunction and clears our minds of morality; with the other, we might pull a lever that gives us the will to do what we believe morality demands" (1989, p. 115). Which lever do we have reason to pull, all things considered?

The idea that we could choose a disposition is by no means merely a thought experiment. To borrow Sayre-McCord's metaphor, our actions pull the levers that form our characters. We

---

[10] Amartya Sen (1991, p. 31) considers sympathy to be egoistic, however, on the grounds that sympathetic action is still action done to satisfy one's own preferences. For what it is worth, I disagree. Whether my preferences are egoistic depends on their content, not on the bare fact that I happen to have them.

would not want to pull a lever that would make us act as automatons. Nor can we, for we have no such lever. We would not want to pull a lever that would make us subject to absolute constraints. Nor can we. Again, we have no such lever. But many of us would pull a lever that would strengthen our disposition to be honest, for example, if only we had such a lever.

And in fact, we do. One of the consequences of action is habituation. Because we are creatures of habit, there is a sense in which pulling the lever is possible and a sense in which doing so can be rational. With every action, we have a marginal effect on our own character and on our self-conception. Character is a variable. It is not, however, subject to direct control. Actions that shape character are under our control. Character itself is not. It is neither fixed nor straightforwardly determined by choice. Rather, character is a function of choice. It is shaped by patterns of choice.[11]

Because people are creatures of habit, time eventually leaves a person with the accumulation of dispositions that we think of as a character. We do not face new situations as blank slates. Yet our accumulation of psychological baggage can seem obtrusive at times, leaving us to wonder why we are not blank slates. Why are we creatures of habit to begin with? We evolved as creatures of habit presumably because having routines for coping with repeatedly encountered situations helps us to conserve our cognitive capacities for circumstances that are novel. As Sarah Broadie says, "Habits of doing what is usually desirable are important, not least because at any level they free the agent to reach for special achievement on a higher level" (1991, p. 109). In any event, if the advantage in developing routine responses is real, we need not regret being creatures of habit. However, the price is that, if we are creatures of habit, shaping our characters as we go, then making sure we can live with the changing shape of our accumulation of dispositions will be an ongoing project.

Habituation, then, is a mechanism of commitment. Of course, this is not to say that habits and commitments are the same thing. Kate can be in the habit of checking her mailbox twice a day without being committed to doing so. Likewise, Kate can be committed

[11] Thus, when we interpret Geoffrey Sayre-McCord's (1989) thought experiment as a metaphor for habituation, we reproduce a core insight of Book II of Aristotle's *Nicomachean Ethics*. On the choice of character, see also Roderick Long (1992).

to standing by her husband even if he is arrested for drunk driving, although she has not yet had occasion to make a habit of it. But the fact that habits and commitments are not the same thing does not stop habituation from being one kind of process by which Kate can internalize a commitment to her husband and thereby make it genuine. (Her commitment will then be operative in all kinds of circumstances, even the unprecedented circumstance of his being arrested for drunk driving.)

We might wonder why we pay relatively little conscious attention to the ongoing process of habituation by which we internalize commitments. Why are we so often oblivious to the importance of cultivating good habits? Natural selection builds in a bias—a sometimes unhealthy bias—for the concrete. We have a potential for reflective rationality, but its flowering has not been a precondition of genetic fitness. People are built to worry about things that can draw blood, not about the decay of their characters. The cost of damaging our characters is easily overlooked because it is not reflected in some obvious frustration of our preferences. Rather, it is reflected in something more subtle: changes to the preferences themselves.[12] And so it turns out that when it comes to sorting out what is in our self-interest, we are relatively inept in situations where what is at stake is our character. Our ineptness notwithstanding, however, it remains possible for us to develop and reinforce our commitments, including commitments that embody respect for others. The next two sections offer reasons why we might want to do so.

REASONS FOR COMMITMENT

Earlier, I argued that we have reason to try to enrich our preference functions, for if we develop preferences that go beyond pure self-

[12] Allan Gibbard (1990, p. 276) notes that feelings can induce beliefs whose acceptance has the effect of making the feelings seem reasonable. The beliefs induced, we might add, can amplify our original feelings in the course of giving them a rationale. Some of us, when angry at our spouses, are tempted to dredge up a history of slights suffered at the hands of that person so as to justify our present feelings, and our new beliefs about that person's general inhumanity amplify our original anger to the point where our final blowup is quite spectacular, and only barely intelligible to observers. We need to be careful about our negative feelings, for the beliefs they induce can do lasting damage.

regard, we will have more to live for. Then I explored habituation as a mechanism by which we might internalize self-imposed constraints. This section explains why we might consider some self-imposed constraints worth the price.

There is an important place in our lives for strategic behavior, that is, for seeking effective means to current goals, given how we expect others to act and react. But this important place is not without limits. We want to achieve our goals, to be sure, but we also want to deserve to achieve our goals, and this is not at all like our other goals. (We care about what we are, not only about what we get.) We seek not merely to earn the respect and concern of others; more fundamentally, we seek to earn our own respect and concern. For whatever reason, it is a simple fact that a person of principle inspires more respect than a person driven by mere expedience. Kate may duly note that the object of her attention is herself, but that fact is not enough to guarantee that the object will hold her attention. The motivating power of Kate's self-interest is not without limit and it is not fixed. The more worthy her self is of her interest, the better off she is. Consequently, there is this advantage in having a principled character: We become selves worth struggling for.

Plato took justice to consist of giving each citizen his due, interpreted not as harming enemies and helping friends (Polemarchus's proposal in *Republic*, Book I) but rather as possession of one's own and performance of one's own task (Socrates's proposal in Book IV). Plato tried to argue that, like unjust cities that degenerate into tyranny and civil war, persons whose parts fail to possess their own and do their own job will be at war with themselves. The ultimate point of the argument was to connect justice to rationality (without reducing it to rationality). Few people accept Plato's argument at face value, of course, but even if Plato failed to connect rationality to justice, he did in the course of the argument connect rationality to integrity.

Integrity and justice are analogous insofar as both are species of the genus "giving each part of the whole its due." To have integrity is to be true to oneself, to give each part of oneself its due. To be just is to give each person, each part of the whole society, its due. Plato's argument went awry when he mistook this analogy for a case of identity, which might be one reason why his conclusion about the rationality of being just rings false.[13] But what rings true is that having integrity is rational.

Having integrity is not merely good strategy, a matter of prudence. On the contrary, it is far more important than that. Being a person of integrity may on occasion be wildly imprudent, but that likelihood is not decisive even on prudential grounds. Indeed, the point here is that people who have no commitment to integrity have less to live for, which in the long run tends to undermine their commitment to prudence as well. Although integrity may be incompatible with prudence in exceptional cases, it also rationally justifies prudence in ordinary cases. Integrity rationally justifies prudence because it involves committing oneself to having a self worth caring about.

A person who does not have commitments has little with which to identify himself. What we are is in large part what we stand for. We think of having to make a stand on behalf of our ideals or on behalf of our loved ones as frightening and painful, and it often is. Yet, to make a stand for what we think is right is one of the most self-defining things we can do.

Respect for Others

The reasons offered earlier for cultivating other-regarding concern had to do with the value of enriching our set of goals. Our goals are what we have to live for, and enriching our set of goals gives us more to live for. We do not live for our constraints. Nor would enriching our set of constraints give us more to live for in any direct way, but it does help define *who* we are living for. In effect, our constraints help define what we are living with, what means we can employ while still remaining persons worth living for. De-

[13] Unlike the analogy between integrity and justice, the often-discussed connection between the soul of the state and the soul of the citizen is much more than a matter of analogy. Jonathan Lear (1992) argues that Plato believed not only that the souls of citizens and the soul of the state are like each other but also that the reason they are like each other is because they are outgrowths of each other. The state is the milieu within which children grow up, and so the characters of its adult citizens reflect that milieu. At the same time, the state's ongoing evolution or devolution lies in the hands of its adult citizens, and so reflects the characters of its adult citizens.

fining our constraints is prior to the strategy we formulate and execute within those constraints. It is a prerequisite of prudence.

Why, then, does having a principled character involve respect for others? There is an alternative, namely, that we might accept a suitably demanding set of commitments to ourselves.[14] We might, for example, commit ourselves to achieving excellence in particular endeavors. This means that reasons for commitment per se do not automatically translate into reasons for commitments embodying respect for others. What leads us to develop commitments of an other-regarding nature? Perhaps it is something like this: We want more than to be at peace with ourselves. We also want more than to be liked and respected by others. We want to deserve to be liked and respected. Being a liar can hurt us not only by disrupting our purely internal integrity but also by precluding the kind of honest rapport we want to have with others, and precluding our integration into the larger wholes that would otherwise give us more to live for. As Gerald Postema wisely observes, "To cut oneself off from others is to cut oneself off from oneself, for it is only in the mirror of the souls of others that one finds one's own self, one's character. The pleasures and satisfactions of conversation and intercourse are essential to human life, because they are essential to a sense of one's continuity through a constantly changing external and internal world. . . . Thus, a truly successful strategy of deception effectively cuts oneself off from the community in which alone one can find the confirmation essential to one's own sense of self" (1988, p. 35).

The point is that, human psychology being what it is, respect for others turns out to be part and parcel of having integrity, because integrity has external as well as internal components. Being true to ourselves ordinarily involves presenting ourselves truly to others, but integrity involves not only honestly presenting ourselves to the world but also *integrating* ourselves into the world, achieving a certain fit. We give ourselves more to live for by becoming important parts of something bigger than ourselves. A principled character lets us pursue this wider integration without losing our own identity. People of principled character—those with nothing to hide—can seek integration on their own terms.

[14] Can self-regarding commitments be thought of as moral commitments? See Chapter 8. See also Neera Kapur Badhwar (1993) and Jean Hampton (1993).

We may never quite swallow the conclusion that it is rational to be just, in the sense of giving each person what he or she is due. Yet, it surely is rational to give our own interests their due, and (human psychology being what it is) we have a strong interest in being able to think of ourselves as decent human beings. We identify ourselves largely in terms of what we do, and therefore individual rationality behooves us to do things that can support the kind of self-conception we would like to have. Thus, being a person of integrity rather than an opportunist is rational not merely as a prospective policy (that is, as something that is advantageous in a long-run probabilistic sense); there is also something to be said for it on a case-by-case basis, even when we see in retrospect that we could have lied or cheated without being caught. We desire integrity not only in an internal sense but also in the sense of being integrated into a social structure—functioning well within structures that comprise our environment. We seek real rapport with others, not merely a sham. We want to feel that we belong, and it is our real selves for which we want a sense of belonging, not merely our false facades.

How does that give us reasons to fall on grenades for the sake of our comrades? It may not. Considerations weighing in favor of having a principled character in ordinary cases need not do so in extraordinary cases. Nevertheless, ordinary cases are the crucibles within which characters take shape. It is in the ordinary course of events that we create the characters that we carry into the emergencies. Conversely, in emergencies, we learn something about what we have created. We find out what we are made of, so to speak, and there is a precious dignity in having a character that does not wither away under pressure.

Insofar as we maintain a critical perspective on our ends, it is conceivable that, in an emergency, we will question the concerns and commitments that call on us to fall on a grenade for the sake of our comrades. Depending on how well we have internalized our concerns and commitments, we may find ourselves able to reject them. If we reject our concerns and commitments, though, we cheapen our past as well as our possible future. We reveal ourselves to have been only superficially concerned and committed. Upon being convicted of corrupting the youth, Socrates willingly went to his death, so the legend goes, because his other alternatives were inconsistent with principles by which he had lived to that point.

113

He was seventy years old and his life as a whole would not have been improved by running away to spend his remaining years as an escaped convict.

Our reasons for acting as we do in a given situation stem from concerns we bring with us to that situation. Thus, the rationality of internalizing a given concern does not turn on the consequences of acting on it in a single case. The relevant consequences are those that follow from a certain concern being part of one's life.[15] This is why the task of providing reasons for altruism is first and foremost the task of providing reasons for altruism of the more mundane variety. It is fine to consider whether it can be rational to die for one's comrades, but in truth, the central cases are cases of simply lending a hand in the ordinary course of events. We stop to give people directions. We push their cars out of snowbanks. We hold open doors for people whose hands are full. And we walk away from these mundane encounters feeling grateful for the chance to be helpful.[16]

In nurturing concerns that give us more to live for, we develop concerns that can become more important to us than life itself. In the ordinary course of events, this is a splendid result, but in ex-

[15] Edward F. McClennen (1988) argues that one can be better off as a resolute chooser, that is, a person who can adopt plans and stick to them. For example, suppose Kate wants to buy a television set, but if she does, she will then need to decide whether to watch game shows. Kate's most-preferred option is to buy the television, resolving never to watch game shows. However, she is not sure she can trust herself never to watch game shows, and she would rather not have a television set at all than to end up watching game shows. Subsequently, having bought a television set, how can Kate eschew game shows, if watching them is now her most-preferred option? What difference does it make that she resolved last week when she bought her television never to watch game shows? My theory is that genuine resolve is the sort of thing we can build up over time. Reflectively rational agents can habituate themselves to virtue. Kate is *rational* to build up her capacity for resolve because, as she proves to herself that she can carry out plans calling for resolve, she becomes able to trust herself to make choices that will be optimal if and only if she ignores temptations associated with those choices.

[16] It would be a mistake to say something cannot be altruistic if you really enjoy doing it. This would put the cart before the horse. If you help other people for their sake, you are altruistic whether or not you like having the concern for others that your action expresses. In the *Grounding of the Metaphysics of Morals* (1981; first published 1785), Kant said getting joy out of an action can rob it of moral worth, which seems wrong, but even if he had been right, enjoying an action can affect its moral worth without changing the fact that the action is altruistic.

traordinary situations, concerns worth living for can become concerns worth dying for. We may some day find ourselves in a situation where our other-regarding concerns dictate a course of action that will seriously jeopardize our purely self-regarding interests. The consequences might lead an observer to avoid developing similar commitments and concerns; the observer has not yet internalized those concerns and commitments, and after witnessing their worst-case results, internalizing them may seem unwise if not downright impossible. But for us, when the emergency comes that calls on us to pay the price of having our commitments, we no longer have the option of acting as if our slate of commitments were blank. We received the benefits of integrity by becoming actually committed, and when the emergency comes, we are actually committed.

Gregory Kavka (1985, pp. 307–10) points out that it can be rational to accept a *risk* of death even when it would not be rational to accept *certain* death. And when we develop concerns so deep and genuine that they may some day lead us to willingly give our lives for our comrades or our children, we are accepting a risk, not a certainty. Meanwhile, those concerns give us more to live for. We have no intention of actually dying for them, but if we get unlucky, we may some day find ourselves in a situation in which dying for them is our preferred alternative.

Altruism involves self-sacrifice in exceptional cases, but not as a matter of routine. Altruism involves costs, of course, as does any action, but that an action is costly is not enough to make it a self-sacrifice. Cost-bearing becomes self-sacrificial only when agents deliberately give up something they prefer more for the sake of something they prefer less. Thus, only purely self-regarding agents will view altruism as necessarily self-sacrificial. For agents who have other-regarding concerns, acting on those concerns will be self-sacrificial if it costs too much, and only if it costs too much.

Needless to say, we may regret sacrificing one goal for the sake of another, even when both goals are of a self-regarding nature, and even when we have no doubt that what we give up is less important than what we gain. I may feel anguish when I give up coaching Little League baseball in order to pursue my career in a different city, but the regret I feel when I sacrifice one part of my life for the sake of another is neither necessary nor sufficient to indicate that my choice is a self-sacrifice. However painful it feels, I am not sacrificing myself when I sacrifice a less important goal for the sake of a more important goal. On the contrary, in a world that sometimes requires painful trade-offs, we affirm ourselves and our commitments and our values when we act for the sake of what we consider most important, and this is what altruism often amounts to for other-regarding agents.[17]

That also reveals the limits of rational altruism. For beings who begin with self-regarding ends, it would be irrational to nurture commitments that lead to self-sacrifice as a matter of course. The point is to have more to live for and to meet the prerequisites of prudence. We accomplish this by nurturing respect and concern for family, friends, neighbors, the strangers we meet, and so on. There are forms of respect that, under normal conditions, we can easily afford to extend to the whole world, but we have only so much capacity for genuine concern. If we tried to care about everyone, our lives would be impoverished rather than enriched.

This has implications for morality as well as for rationality. Although I think morality requires us to respect everyone, I do not believe it requires us to care about everyone.[18] This chapter does not argue for that conclusion, of course, but in any event, if morality does require us to care about everyone, then this is one area in which morality and rationality part company.

FROM RATIONAL CHOICE TO MORAL AGENCY

The model of reflective rational choice is, we have seen, rich enough not only to allow for but even to justify the development of

[17] I thank Lainie Ross for helping me work out the connection between altruism and sacrifice. See also Aristotle's discussion of friendship and sacrifice in *Nicomachean Ethics* (1169a).

[18] William A. Galston (1993) distinguishes between progressively more expansive forms of altruism, and he draws attention to the moral cost of altruism in its more expansive incarnations. For example, Galston says, the concern expressed by rescuers of Jewish refugees in Nazi-occupied Europe was an expansive, cosmopolitan form of altruism. Commendable though it was on its face, this cosmopolitan form of altruism often went hand in hand with a failure to express concern for family members thereby put at risk by the rescue effort. The more cosmopolitan form of altruism came at the expense of the more parochial form. More parochial forms of altruism sometimes are not consistent with expressing concern for everyone.

other-regarding concern and respect. In particular, the fragility of self-regard can give us reason to develop concerns and commitments that go beyond self-regard. In the process, we acquire a rationale for our fragile self-regard and thereby make it more robust.

The emergence of these new reasons for action is driven by instrumental reasons, but this does not imply that the new reasons are themselves instrumental reasons. The concern and respect for others that is rationally grounded in reflective self-regard may be of an entirely wholehearted and uncalculating kind. Indeed, that is what we are striving for, for those are the most rewarding concerns a person can have.

Does this mean that concern for others is rationally *required*? I would say not. That concern for others is rationally justifiable does not imply that a lack of concern is unjustifiable. To be sure, most of us are rationally required to nurture other-regarding concerns and commitments, but we are rationally required in virtue of social and psychological circumstances that are not quite universal. People whose survival is immediately secure will be driven to cultivate concerns beyond mere survival.[19] However, being driven to develop concerns beyond survival is not the same as being driven to develop concern for others. Some people have the option of fashioning more ambitious sets of concerns that would be fulfilling yet would still count as purely self-regarding. Even for such people, caring for others remains reasonable, because caring for others remains a particularly effective way of giving oneself more to live for. But it is not uniquely reasonable. Many kinds of commitments and concerns can be motivated by our need to have something to live for; not all of them are other-regarding, and some of them are evil. People commit acts of vandalism for the sake of having something to do. They go to war for the sake of having something to live for.

Be that as it may, the project of showing that altruism is reasonable does not require us to show that altruism is uniquely reasonable. We do not need to prove that failing to care about others would be unreasonable. For most of us, failing to care about others really would be unreasonable, because, for most of us, there are no

[right margin handwritten note] Taking it back....

[19] This claim rests on the argument in Chapter 3 that the goal of bare survival drives us to convert the goal of bare survival into something that has instrumental value within a larger corpus of ends. However, if our will to survive is too weak in the first place, it may not be strong enough to drive us to nurture the further ends that would protect our will to survive against further decay.

self-concerns that could give us as much to live for as we have in virtue of caring for others. Section III argued that we cannot afford to be purely self-regarding, but that may not be true of everyone. There are reasons for altruism, but there also are people for whom those reasons are not compelling. Is the existence of such people a problem? It surely is a practical problem, insofar as the rest of us need to deal with such people. Some readers might feel that the existence of such people is also a problem for my argument; that is, a person might reply to my reasons for altruism by insisting that not everyone has the kind of reasons discussed in this chapter. There are people, sociopaths perhaps, who have no reasons to care about others.

sociopaths

My response is that looking for reasons for everyone is a mistake. If we presume at the outset that our reasons to care about others must be reasons for everyone, the reasons we produce are likely to be reasons for no one. Such reasons are likely to be mere philosophical sleight of hand, a distraction from our real-world concerns. Let us face the fact that our reasons for altruism can be real without being reasons for everyone. We must look for the real reasons, and accept that human societies need to deal with the fact that not everyone has real reasons.

In closing, let me say how this chapter fits into the larger project of identifying connections between rationality and morality. There is a limit to how much other-regard is rational, but whether that opens a gap between rationality and morality is an open question, for there is also a limit to how much other-regard is morally required. This is in part a point about morality leaving room for people to pursue their own projects, but it is also a reminder that the consequences of other-regard are only so good. Whether other-regarding action has better consequences than self-regarding action in a given case is an empirical matter.

Other-regarding action can sometimes seem morally dubious even apart from its immediate consequences in a given case. *Paternalism*, for example, is a form of altruism, an expression of concern for others (for their welfare) that overrides one's respect for others (for their preferences). Altruistic though it might be, paternalism often is objectionable. To give another example, teachers should grade term papers on the basis of what they believe the papers deserve, not on what they believe the authors need. Anyone who has ever graded term papers knows how difficult it can be to ignore one's concern for others, but there are cases in which one is morally required to make the effort. From the viewpoints both of the agent and of those the agent might affect, neither self-regard nor other-regard is intrinsically exalted. A great deal depends on how a concern plays itself out.

In *The Republic*, Socrates concluded that individuals need justice within themselves for more or less the same reasons and with more or less the same urgency as society needs justice within itself. But this did not answer Glaucon's question. Glaucon did not ask whether the individual needs to give each part of himself its due. He did not ask whether society needs to give each part of itself its due. What he asked was whether the individual needs to give each part of society its due. If Thrasymachus neglects to give other people their due, must he at the same time be neglecting to give a part of himself its due?

He might be.[20] Characters like Thrasymachus have reason to act only when doing so will satisfy their purely self-regarding ends. Because almost nothing counts as a reason for Thrasymachus to act (in particular, regard for others cannot move him to act), Thrasymachus's life is impoverished in a certain way. He has fewer reasons to live than the rest of us. (To have fewer reasons to live is not necessarily to have less reason to live, but that will be the tendency.) Thrasymachus lacks a kind of respect and concern for others that could have given him reason to pursue a range of goals. I realize that if Thrasymachus were here, he would laugh at me for saying this, for the range of goals I am talking about would mean nothing to him, but the bottom line remains: Those goals could have enriched his life.

[20] Charles L. Griswold (forthcoming) argues that there is a close connection between justice as an excellence of self and justice as a kind of respect we owe to others, because it is in treating others with concern and respect that we perfect ourselves.

PART II
MORAL AGENCY

*

∗ *Introduction* ∗

PART I began with a means-end conception of rational choice, one that is uncontroversial as far as it goes. And we saw that it can go a long way indeed when combined with empirical assumptions about human psychology. Thin though the means-end conception is, it has enough normative content to motivate the model of humanly rational choice developed in Part I. One purpose in developing this model is to connect an ideal of rationality to human psychology so as to show that human beings have reason to aspire to be rational in that way. A second purpose of the model is to help explain how beings who are rational in that way have reason to be moral.

Regarding the latter purpose, we can think of my model of reflective rationality as a direct response to three theses about the nature of rational choice and its possible connections to morality.

  1. Rationality requires maximizing expected utility, whereas morality requires us to practice a nonprudential kind of self-restraint.
  2. Morality involves pursuing particular kinds of ends, whereas rationality is purely instrumental. It concerns the selection of means only and has nothing to say about ends.
  3. Being moral involves having respect and concern for others, whereas rationality (if it says anything at all about ends) involves being purely self-regarding.

Being rational and being moral involve incompatible constraints, if the first thesis is right, and incompatible goals, if the third thesis is right. The second thesis implies that morality and rationality are tangential to each other. Any connection between them must be purely circumstantial, a matter of what preferences an agent happens to have. Against these theses:

  1. Chapter 2 argued that our purposes often are best served by nonmaximizing strategies pursued within self-imposed constraints.
  2. Chapters 3 and 4 discussed how ends as well as means can be rationally chosen.
  3. Chapter 5 argued that we have reasons to adopt ends that ex-

press concern for others and to pursue those ends (alongside our other ends) within self-imposed constraints, some of which express respect for others.

Now we need to discuss what is involved in being moral. Part I built up to the conclusion that we have reasons to respect and to care for others. To this extent, we have already seen that it is rational for us to act in ways that we intuitively recognize as moral. It would be interesting, though, to see how this informal demonstration bears on formal theory, and vice versa. On what basis are we warranted in judging that it is moral to respect and to care for others? Moreover, unless we become more formal and explicit about the connections between rationality and morality, it might appear that we have no response to a famous objection to the whole project of trying to give reasons to be moral. The project, some have argued, is deeply incoherent. Why? Because it defends being moral as a means to something else, whereas the essence of being moral involves acting with no ulterior purpose in mind. I could ignore this challenge, resting my case on the coherence of what has already been said, but there is much to be learned by meeting the challenge directly, which Chapter 6 undertakes to do.

After explaining why dismissing the "why be moral" question as a conceptual error is itself a conceptual error, Chapter 6 presents a formal framework for analyzing moral theories. Chapter 7 applies that framework to the subject of institutions. Collectively rational constraints (as defined in Chapter 7) are constraints that, as embedded in institutions and social norms, make people in general better off by nonexploitative means. The chapter argues that if moral institutions are collectively rational, then moral institutions give people reasons to be moral.

Chapter 8 incorporates this conception of collective rationality into a theory of moral agency, where the term 'agency' refers to the agency of institutions as well as persons. The theory distinguishes between morality's rules of conduct and rules by which we recognize rules of conduct as moral. It ranges over more than one subject matter, incorporates more than one recognition rule, and is genuinely pluralistic insofar as it adjudicates conflicts among disparate recognition rules without resorting to an overarching principle of adjudication. In a nutshell, moral dualism (as I call it) holds that being moral is a matter of pursuing reflectively rational goals within collectively rational constraints. Chapter 9 defends moral dualism against objections. Chapter 10 then shows how the nine preceding chapters culminate in answers to the "why be moral" question.

CHAPTER 6

Because It's Right

Morality teaches us that, if we look on her only as good
for something else, we never in that case have seen her at
all. She says that she is an end to be desired for her
own sake, and not as a means to something beyond.
Degrade her, and she disappears.
F. H. Bradley (1927, p. 58; first published 1876)

DOES MORAL PHILOSOPHY REST
ON A MISTAKE?

MORALITY CAN BE PAINFULLY demanding, so much so that we sometimes question the wisdom of complying with it. Yet, arguments that we have good reason to be moral are as old as Plato's *Republic* and as new as David Gauthier's *Morals by Agreement*. Indeed, according to H. A. Prichard, making this argument work is the central preoccupation of moral philosophy. But Prichard also believes that to the extent this is true, the whole subject of moral philosophy rests on a mistake (1968a, p. 1; first published 1912).[1]

Prichard is neither the first nor the last person to dismiss an entire discipline as a mistake, of course, but Prichard has an argument that poses a real challenge to moral philosophy, an argument that repays sympathetic analysis. Prichard's article emerges from a particular and peculiar philosophical tradition known as British intuitionism, yet the challenge it poses to moral philosophy is any-

---

[1] At one time, Philippa Foot agreed with Plato that "if justice is not a good to the just man, moralists who recommend it as virtue are perpetrating a fraud" (1978, p. 126). Likewise, David Gauthier says, "The acceptance of duty is truly advantageous" (1986, p. 2). Kurt Baier (1978) and Kai Nielsen (1989) agree that "why be moral" is a legitimate question, although Nielsen's answer is pessimistic. On the other side, H. A. Prichard's view that the question itself is illegitimate is endorsed by J. C. Thornton (1970), Dan W. Brock (1977), and John McDowell (1978), among others. Prichard was not the first to take such a view, either. For example, see Essay II of F. H. Bradley's *Ethical Studies* (1927, first published 1876) or Henry Sidgwick's introduction to *Methods of Ethics* (1962; first published 1907).

thing but parochial. On the contrary, the article has had and continues to have an influence independent of, even in spite of, the intuitionist tradition from which it emerges. For example, it anticipates and to some extent undoubtedly inspires the current antitheory movement in ethics.[2] Nevertheless, although dozens of articles cite Prichard's famous essay, often with approval, it has seldom met with sustained criticism.[3] This chapter reconstructs and criticizes Prichard's argument, then it uses that critique to lay foundations for the larger project of identifying the reasons that beings like us, in situations like ours, have for being moral.

Prichard says we begin to question whether we really ought to do our alleged duty—to keep a promise, for example—when we recognize that doing our duty will not give us what we desire. We then question things we usually accept as duties. We ask if there is any proof that we truly have a duty to act in ways usually called moral. Prichard sees two ways of interpreting this request. We could be asking whether being moral is prudent. Alternatively, we could be asking whether being moral is good in some nonprudential sense—good for others, for example, or intrinsically good quite apart from its consequences (p. 2).[4] The first question is the one that David Gauthier and others inherit from Plato, but Prichard's main target is the second. In any event, he thinks both versions of the question are mistakes, and this chapter looks at each of them in turn.

How can we determine what is moral in the first place? We cannot simply check what is moral. At least, we cannot do so in the same way we can check who is prime minister. Nevertheless, like the words 'prime minister,' the word 'moral' is a word we inherit from an existing language. It comes to us laden with meaning. We can stipulate what we will be referring to when we say "brillig,"

---

[2] Antitheorists characterize (and consequently reject) moral theorizing as an attempt to mechanically deduce all particular moral conclusions from a single universal principle. Robert Louden (1992, chaps. 5 and 6) agrees that any theory fitting that description ought to be rejected, but he argues that the best and historically most prominent moral theories (that is, those of Aristotle and Kant) do not fit the description.

[3] W. D. Falk (1986) accuses Prichard of equivocating between internalist and externalist senses of moral "oughts." The only other substantial critique of Prichard, to my knowledge, is Baier (1978, pp. 231–38).

[4] Except where otherwise noted, page references in this chapter are to Prichard (1968a).

for that is not a term of ordinary language, but there are only so many things we could correctly refer to as eggplant. Like the word 'eggplant,' the word 'moral' is more than a made-up sound. We cannot simply stipulate that it refers to, say, the property of maximizing utility, any more than we could stipulate that the word 'eggplant' refers to rutabagas.

A term's *extension* consists of the set of things to which the term refers. The term 'prime minister' may under certain circumstances have Jean Chrétien as its extension. Even so, we would not want to say Jean Chrétien is the *meaning* of the term 'prime minister.' One implication is that we might not know who is prime minister, despite knowing exactly what the term means. Similarly, even if we settle what the word 'moral' means, we can still be uncertain about which actions are moral.

As it happens, though, we tend to be more sure of the extension of the word 'moral' than we are about its meaning. We have a shared understanding that being moral involves being honest, kind, peaceful, and so on. (I refer to this consensus as commonsense morality.) It may not be part of the meaning of the term 'moral' that honesty is moral, but honesty may be and commonly is understood to be part of the term's extension.

Moreover, the consensus is not only that we should call these things moral, but also that we should *be* these things, which gives us a clue to the word's meaning. When a person refers to an act by saying, "That's immoral," listeners normally understand the speaker to be saying there is reason not to do the act.[5] Further, listeners interpret the speaker as saying something other than that the act will not satisfy an agent's desires. When a person says lying is immoral, listeners normally understand the speaker to mean there is a *special* reason not to lie—special because it is grounded in something other than an appeal to the agent's desires.

This way of understanding the term's use may not fully capture the term's meaning, any more than a set of injunctions to be kind,

---

[5] It seems easier here to speak of wrongness rather than rightness as being associated with special reasons for action. That one course of action involves telling the truth does not imply that one should take that course, but that another course of action involves telling a lie has very clear implications. Roderick Wiltshire (unpublished) argues that wrongness is a natural kind and rightness is not. Rightness is simply the logical complement of wrongness, in the way "non-dog" is the logical complement of "dog."

honest, and peaceful fully covers morality's extension. The conclusion so far is only that moral reasons are understood to appeal to something other than the agent's desires. Moral reasons are *categorical.*[6]

When people argue about what is moral, they may disagree about what constitutes this special kind of reason. Or, they may agree that the property of maximizing pleasure constitutes a special reason for endorsement, but quarrel over which actions (or character traits, or institutions, and so forth) have this property. Even so, when people argue about whether something like affirmative action is moral, they have a shared understanding that it *matters* whether affirmative action is moral. People who argue about what is moral share an understanding that for an act to be morally required is for there to be a special reason to do it. That is why people care about what conclusion they reach regarding whether something like affirmative action is morally required (or forbidden). They understand that whether they have special reasons to support (or resist) the practice goes hand in hand with whether the practice is morally required (or forbidden).

But do we need to prove we have such special reasons? As Prichard sees it, moral philosophy rests on the mistaken assumption that we do—a mistaken assumption that without proof that we have special reasons, we have no basis for saying we *ought* to conform to commonsense morality. Why is this assumption a mistake? Prichard asks us to consider how we would prove that conforming to commonsense morality (which I refer to as being CS-moral) is moral. According to Prichard, there are two ways to try to prove that being CS-moral is moral, and both of them inevitably fail. The first way is to prove that being CS-moral will give us something we want (p. 3). The second way is to prove there is something good (not necessarily for us) either in right action's result or in right action itself. Prichard's objections to these two approaches are as follows.

The first way fails because proving that being CS-moral will give us what we want is beside the point. The demonstration may show that being CS-moral is prudent, but it does not show that being

---

[6] I use the terms 'categorical' and 'deontological' almost interchangeably. An imperative is categorical if it makes no appeal to the agent's interests and desires, and deontological if it makes no appeal to consequences of any kind. Thus, as I use the terms, a categorical imperative is a kind of deontological imperative.

CS-moral is moral. As Prichard puts it, the exercise might convince us that we want to be CS-moral but it cannot convince us that we ought to be (p. 3).[7] To show that being CS-moral is moral, we have to show that we have characteristically moral reasons to be CS-moral, that is, reasons that do more than appeal to our desires.

The second way, according to Prichard, boils down to saying happiness or working for happiness is good and therefore we should work for happiness in general (or if not for happiness, then for whatever the fundamental good happens to be). This answer has an advantage over the first approach, for at least it clearly does more than appeal to our desires. (Even if the act is for our own good only, this at least goes somewhat beyond mere appeal to desires.) But this second way also fails, Prichard says, because it presupposes the view that the rightness of acts has to do with what they accomplish. "The best way to see the failure of this view is to see its failure to correspond to our actual moral convictions. Suppose we ask ourselves whether our sense that we ought to pay our debts or to tell the truth arises from our recognition that in doing so we would be originating something good. . . . We at once and without hesitation would answer No" (pp. 4–5). He says in a later paper that the "fatal objection [to any teleological theory] is that it resolves the moral 'ought' into the non-moral 'ought', representing our being morally bound to do some action as if it were the same thing as the action's being one which we must do if our purpose is to become realized" (1968b, p. 117).[8]

So goes my reconstruction of Prichard's negative argument.[9] In summary, the rightness of keeping a promise, say, does not depend on whether keeping it will have good results at all, let alone on whether keeping it is in the promisor's best interest. Because attempts to prove we ought to do what we believe is right inevitably appeal in one way or another to the goodness of doing what we

[7] And, as Stephen Toulmin (1970, p. 417) adds, making us want to do what we ought to do is not the philosopher's task.

[8] Prichard's point applies to theories grounding rightness in collective prudence as well. So, Prichard's objection not only challenges the Platonic project but most contractarian theories as well. For example, the objection cuts against the view expressed by Baier (1970) that we should be moral because being moral makes us all better off.

[9] Prichard also rejects the idea that an action's rightness lies not in its actual result but rather in its intended result, but present purposes do not require us to address this further argument.

believe is right (p. 2), Prichard concludes that the only place to look for an answer to the question of why we should do what is right is manifestly the wrong place to look. The reductionist urge to ground rightness in something more fundamental is misguided, for rightness neither can be nor needs to be grounded in anything else. The sense of an action's rightness is, in fact, absolutely immediate (p. 7). We see that being CS-moral is moral by direct apprehension, if we see it at all. Trying to *prove* that being CS-moral is moral is a mistake not unlike the epistemological mistake of trying to prove we are awake when we know we are awake by direct apprehension (p. 16). It is an instance of the mistake of seeking a grounding of that which is itself bedrock.

The next two sections respond to Prichard's argument. First, I argue that there is no mistake in asking whether being moral is prudent. Then, I argue that there is no mistake in asking whether it is truly moral to do things like keep promises.

Morality versus Prudence

Prichard concedes that it can be perfectly legitimate to ask why we should perform a certain act when the act is incompletely described in relevant ways. The question becomes illegitimate, in Prichard's view, when the act is described well enough that special reasons to perform the act are, in effect, built into the act's description. For example, it may not be obvious that Kate has reason to give her neighbor a hundred dollars, but it is perfectly obvious that she has reason to *repay a debt to her neighbor* by giving him a hundred dollars (p. 8). Described in this more complete way, the act carries its reason on its sleeve. When an act is described in such a way that asking why we should do it becomes tantamount to asking why we should do what is required, the answer becomes obvious: We should do it because it is required.[10]

Still, an act that is well described in moral terms may remain incompletely described in prudential terms. The question "What's in it for me?" may remain unanswered. We could dismiss the latter question as morally irrelevant, but this would be to ignore the

[10] To call an act right is ambiguous. One might be saying the act is required or that it is permitted. The former sense is more relevant here. I use the terms 'right' and 'required' interchangeably in what follows.

question rather than answer it. Even if Prichard is correct that it is impossible to give an argument why we *morally* ought to do the right thing, this does not foreclose the possibility that philosophers might yet show that it is prudent to do the right thing. Nothing in Prichard's argument cuts against undertaking the Platonic project of showing that being moral is profitable.

Prichard goes on, however, to engage the Platonic project more directly. Prichard says proving that we have a prudential motive to do the right thing would be beside the point. If we are talking about being moral, we are not talking about doing the right thing for prudential reasons. Rather, to be genuinely moral is to do the right thing precisely because it is right. In Prichard's words, "A morally good action is morally good not simply because it is a right action but because it is a right action done because it is right, i.e., from a sense of obligation" (p. 10).[11]

It may seem, as it evidently seemed to Prichard, that the project of reconciling prudence and morality cannot proceed unless this Kantian line of argument is rebutted. This is not so. Even if we grant that being moral involves following a categorical imperative, we remain free to ask whether we are better off following a categorical imperative. And one way or another, the question has an answer. Whether or not moral imperatives are categorical, there remains a fact of the matter concerning whether following moral imperatives is to our advantage. To try to show that being moral turns out to be prudent is not to assume that moral imperatives are prudential imperatives. On the contrary, we can try to prove a conditional of the form "If I want X, then I should be moral" without in any way presuming that moral imperatives have this same conditional form.

If we were asking whether prudence can be a proximate *motive* for being moral and if we took "being moral" to entail "being motivated by a sense of rightness rather than by prudence," then Prichard's objection would be decisive. The very question would be a mistake. The actual question, however, is whether there is an extensional overlap between being moral (and thus being motivated by a sense of rightness) and being prudent, in which case

[11] Perhaps this is why Prichard thought the connection between the sense of rightness and one's reason to be moral has to be "absolutely immediate." If anything intrudes between the two, one will no longer be doing the right thing for the right reason.

Prichard's objection is beside the point.[12] Asking whether doing the right thing is prudent does not presuppose that only prudential answers could move one to do the right thing. It does not presuppose that prudence is even *among* the things that could motivate being moral.

Demonstrating the existence of an extensional overlap need not motivate people to be moral. But really, that was never the point. The point is that even agents committed to doing what is right because it is right might nevertheless wonder whether they would have done anything differently had they been more self-consciously prudent. Moral agents might care about this issue not because they seek a motivation for being moral but rather because they, like Glaucon, sometimes wonder whether they have prudential reasons to *regret* being moral.

In summary, Prichard thinks it is a mistake to try to prove that being moral is for our own good, for the attempt presupposes that whether we ought to be moral depends on whether being moral is prudent. But we need presuppose no such thing. Asking about these things does not commit us to reducing morality or moral motivation to mere prudence. This version of the question is no mistake.

What Do We Do When We Do the Right Thing?

The previous section conceded that we should do what is right because it is right, but it showed that this concession is hardly a conversation stopper. Whether it is prudent to be moral remains an issue. It is perfectly coherent to ask whether we are better off in virtue of being motivated by a sense of rightness. Further, even from the moral point of view, it is not enough to say we should do what is right because it is right. As Prichard would agree, the question we face as moral agents is not about philosophical generalizations but rather about what to do when we get face-to-face with

---

[12] The notion of prudence in question involves acting in one's best interest *simpliciter* rather than acting in one's best interest *because* it is in one's best interest. Otherwise, if we interpret prudence in the latter sense, prudence and morality exhibit a particularly uninteresting kind of incompatibility; the real issue about the overlap between morality and self-interest will inevitably resurface, cast in other terms.

particular situations. And saying we should do what is right would be to miss the point of our asking what we should do. The point is, we need to have concluded that a course of action is right before the incantation "because it's right" can express a reason to undertake that course of action. Naturally, we should do what is right, and we should do so because it is right. But why should we keep promises? Why, in some rare cases, should we break them? Why should we tell the truth? Why, in some rare cases, should we lie instead? What does keeping promises or telling the truth have to do with rightness?

"Why should I do what is morally required?" is the sort of question that wears its moral answer on its sleeve, even if it does not wear its prudential answer on its sleeve. But that is not the same kind of question as "Why should I tell the truth?" Rightness may wear moral motivation on its sleeve, but what rightness patently does not wear on its sleeve is its extension. Indeed, the question of which particular actions are right remains wide open. Prichard has not only left undone the legitimate task of identifying prudential reasons not to regret being moral but he has also left us the more fundamental task of identifying what is moral.

The latter was no accident, of course, for Prichard was, after all, an intuitionist. He says we identify what is moral by intuition.[13]

[13] One could interpret Prichard, qua intuitionist, as being against rationalism in ethics in the same way Michael Oakeshott is against rationalism in politics. That is, we can understand and appreciate ethical traditions only from the inside, by living within them and by knowing their history. Traditions serve purposes that were no part of the intentions of those whose actions created and sustained those traditions. It is hubris to criticize traditions on the grounds that they fail to serve purposes one thinks ought to be served, or that they do not serve their purposes as well as imaginable alternatives. Such criticism is from the outside in, which is not a legitimate critical perspective. Instead, one must get inside the institution and experience the duties it imposes face to face and case by case. See the title essay in Oakeshott (1991). This theme also runs generally through the work of Alasdair MacIntyre. (The thesis that modern moral concepts are holdovers from earlier traditions, in which they had a significance that has since been lost, finds one of its earliest and most concise expressions in G.E.M. Anscombe [1958, pp. 1, 5–8]).

Now, there is some merit in the Anscombe-MacIntyre-Oakeshott line of argument. Nevertheless, moral philosophy is itself a body of traditions and practices. Distancing oneself from the practice of criticizing ethical traditions and viewing that practice with a critical eye amounts to taking an outside-in approach to a central tradition of moral philosophy. Thus, to indulge in such criticism is also

We directly apprehend that something is required. Be this as it may, the question in which we are actually interested is logically prior to this epistemological question. That is, even if we grant that there are occasions on which we directly apprehend that some act X is required, we still want to know what it is about X that triggers our intuitions.[14] Consider this: If we had no idea what triggers our intuitions, what grounds would we have for taking our intuitions seriously?

One might insist that intuitionism is not only an epistemological thesis but also a thesis about what rightness is; a right action simply is an action that directly and immediately strikes us as something we have reason to do. I do not believe Prichard held this ontological thesis, but in any event, if we take intuitionism to be addressing the question of what rightness is, we are taking it to be an alternative *kind* of reductionism rather than an alternative *to* reductionism. It seems more charitable to accept that Prichard's intuitionist epistemology leaves open the ontological question about what properties occasion our intuitions.

Perhaps we learn general principles by generalizing from particular instances. We get face-to-face with particular instances, as Prichard says, and then learn general principles by induction.[15] Even so, the order in which we learn particulars and general principles is not the issue here. Even if we learn particulars first, there

---

tacitly to endorse outside-in criticism. In effect, it involves criticizing philosophy from the outside in by pointing out that philosophy, too, partakes of outside-in criticism. A telling critique will say something interesting about how to distinguish between the use and misuse of outside-in criticism.

[14] Although Prichard's article does not address the issue of what triggers our intuitions, those who worked within the historical intuitionist tradition had a great deal to say about it. The point, though, is not that nothing can be said, but rather that something needs to be said. And when we begin to say what warrants us in intuiting that X is wrong, we begin to leave Prichard's brand of intuitionism behind.

[15] This is one of intuitionism's core insights. Another is that, in forming moral judgments, we draw on tacit knowledge, some of which we are not capable of fully articulating. Similarly, a wine taster may have an astonishing ability to discern when and where the grapes came from, yet the information he or she finds in the wine's taste may be too subtle to put in words. These two ideas—that our knowledge is fundamentally of particulars rather than universals and that much of what we know is incorrigibly inarticulate—are also central tenets of the moral antitheory movement. A reading of Prichard thus is a useful introduction to the antitheory literature.

must be something about particular requirements that makes them requirements. Whether we learn the particulars first, a question inevitably remains regarding what we are seeing in a particular act when we see it as required. What makes promise keeping rather than promise breaking required? And why do we think promise keeping in some exceptional cases is not required after all, and may even be forbidden? What makes those cases different? That we see them differently is not what makes them different. We need to identify what is being seen when some cases of promise keeping are seen as required and others as forbidden or at least not required.

The list of required acts has to be more than a mere list. If membership in the category was determined arbitrarily, then Prichard would be wrong, for in that case membership in the category of required acts would not imply any special reason to do the act. Prichard wants to say that an act being correctly labeled 'required' is itself a good reason to do it, so good we need no other reason. I would not disagree. My point is only that if our intuitions are picking out some things as right and others as wrong, and doing so in a nonarbitrary way, this implies that acts we intuitively identify as right differ in some nonarbitrary way from acts we intuitively identify as wrong. What then is the difference?

One might think this misses the real point, which is that to call an act required is to *state* a special reason to do it. But suppose we *mistakenly* call an act required. In that case, we think we have stated a special reason to do it, whereas in fact there is no such reason to do it. We could say that to *correctly* call an act required is to state a special reason to do it, but then we still need to know (putting the question in different words) what it is in an act that determines whether the label 'required' is correctly attached. If Prichard is correct in saying special reasons for action are entailed by an act's being required, then we cannot label an action 're-quired' (or more precisely, we cannot know we have labeled the action correctly) until we know we have the requisite reasons for attaching the label, that is, that there really are special reasons for doing the act in question. We do not create the special reason merely by (perhaps mistakenly) applying the label.

For an act to be right, there must be a reason why it is right. Prichard's concern that deriving a sense of rightness from something else would run contrary to our actual moral convictions (p. 4) is baseless. Indeed, if there were nothing in the keeping of a promise to ground our judgment that it is right, then the judgment itself would be baseless, which is contrary to our moral convictions if anything is.

Prichard is correct to say we already have a reason to perform an action when we see that it is required. We do not need to know what makes actions required in order to know we ought to do what is required. Still, one can ask what makes required actions required; in which case, we had better have something to say about when there is good reason to see an action as required. To answer questions of that sort, we need a rule of recognition for morals.

A Rule of Recognition for Morals

So far, I have argued against Prichard on two fronts. First, we can have something to say about whether being moral is prudent. Second, we need to have something to say about what makes right actions right in particular cases. It is time to consider what these critical points tell us about the more positive task of constructing a moral theory. My approach is divorced from Prichard's, to be sure, but it is still in part a response to Prichard's challenge to modern moral philosophy. His challenge has stood the test of time even if his own way of responding to it has not.

My approach borrows from H.L.A. Hart. Hart's legal theory distinguishes between primary and secondary legal rules (1961, pp. 89–93). Primary rules comprise what we normally think of as the law. They define our legal rights and obligations. We use secondary rules, especially rules of recognition, to determine what the law is.[16] For example, among the primary rules in my neighborhood is a law saying that the speed limit is thirty miles per hour. The secondary rule by which we recognize the speed limit is: Read the signs. Exceeding speed limits is illegal, but there is no further law obliging us to read signs that post the speed limit. I stay within the speed limit, and the police do not worry about whether I read the signs. Motorists who speed can get a ticket for speeding, but

[16] We speak here primarily of determining the law in an epistemic sense, but in H.L.A. Hart's (1961) theory, secondary rules also determine the law in an ontological sense. For a discussion of the different senses in which secondary rules determine the law, see "Negative and Positive Positivism" in Jules Coleman (1988).

they are not subject to additional penalties for failing to read the signs. In reading the signs, we are following a secondary rule, not a primary rule.

We could think of moral theories in a similar way. For example, utilitarianism's recognition rule is the principle of utility: X is right if and only if X maximizes utility. As it stands, the principle defines a family of moral theories rather than any particular member thereof. The different flavors of utilitarianism are produced by replacing X with a specific subject matter. *Act*-utilitarianism applies the principle of utility to actions themselves. Act-utilitarianism's fully specified recognition rule (an act is right if and only if it maximizes utility) then translates directly into act-utilitarianism's single rule of conduct: Maximize utility. *Rule*-utilitarianism applies the principle of utility to sets of action-guiding rules. The resulting recognition rule states that following a particular set of action-guiding rules is right if and only if following that action guide has more utility than would following any alternative action guide. Of course, the utility-maximizing set of primary rules might boil down to a single rule of conduct that says "Maximize utility." Then again, it might not.

Deontological theories are harder to characterize. We could begin with a generic recognition rule saying X is moral if X is universalizable. Applying the rule to maxims yields a more specific recognition rule (something like: a maxim is moral if acting on it is universalizable), which in turn yields a set of imperatives, reverence toward which is grounded in considerations of universalizability. Perhaps the idea of universalizability does not have enough content to yield determinate imperatives on its own. Deontology may need a second recognition rule formulated in terms of respect for persons as ends in themselves, so that the two rules can converge on a set of concrete imperatives. But that is another story.

A *moral theory* consists of a recognition rule applied to a particular subject matter. Given a subject matter, a rule of recognition for morals specifies grounds for regarding things of that kind as moral. A recognition rule embodies a supporting condition. A supporting condition, as described in Chapter 1, suffices as a basis for endorsement in the absence of countervailing evidence. Formulating recognition rules in terms of supporting conditions rather than attempting to specify necessary and sufficient conditions is one way of acknowledging intuitionist claims that we could never fully articulate all of the considerations relevant to moral judgment. Intuitionists might be right about this, but we can allow for that possibility (without letting it stop us from doing moral theory) by formulating recognition rules in terms of supporting conditions. Supporting conditions suffice to shift the burden of proof while leaving open the possibility of the burden being shifted back again, perhaps by considerations we have yet to articulate.

As an example of a supporting condition, we might say, along the lines of act-utilitarianism, that an act is moral if it maximizes utility, barring countervailing conditions. In two ways, act-utilitarianism properly so-called goes beyond merely offering a supporting condition. First, it denies that there are countervailing conditions, thereby representing the principle of utility as a proper sufficient condition, not just a supporting condition. Second, it says an act is moral *only* if the act maximizes utility, thereby representing the principle of utility not only as sufficient but also as necessary for an act's morality.[17]

Regarding the subject matter of moral theory, we should note that rules of conduct do not exhaust the category of what can be regarded as moral.[18] Acts and rules of conduct are among the subject matters of moral inquiry, to be sure, but so are character traits, social norms, principles, policies, and political institutions. This chapter focuses mainly on the subject of rules of conduct or action guides, but later chapters consider subject matters of other kinds.

Note also that, as with other intellectual endeavors, we need some sense of a subject matter and of questions to which it gives rise before we can have any reason to devise theories about it. Long before we begin to formulate moral theories, we already classify certain issues as moral issues. Roughly speaking, when an issue is crucial to human flourishing in communities, and when human beings can make a difference regarding that issue, we tend to see it as raising moral questions, and thus as a subject calling for moral theory. In this sense, the subject matters of moral inquiry are (at least provisionally) a pretheoretical given.

[17] Samuel Scheffler (1982) defends what he calls a hybrid theory, which departs from act-utilitarianism by holding that maximizing utility is sufficient but not necessary for an act's morality.

[18] As Michael Stocker says, "Good people appreciate the moral world in ways which go beyond simply seeing what is to be done" (1990, p. 114).

The Normative Status of Morality's
Recognition Rules

The next two chapters try to identify rules of recognition for morals. Before we do that, we need to say more about what recognition rules are like. H.L.A. Hart, himself a legal positivist, argued that rules of recognition for law may or may not pick out what is moral when they pick out law. Herein lies a crucial disanalogy between rules of recognition for morals and for laws. Questions about legality are sometimes answered by simply "looking it up." Arguably, we do not need to know we have moral reason to obey a law in order to recognize it as law. Legal positivism is, roughly speaking, the thesis that a recognition rule can correctly pick out a rule of conduct as legal even though the rule is immoral. But there can be no such a thing as moral positivism, since it is manifestly impossible for a rule of recognition to correctly pick out a rule of conduct as moral when it is not moral. It may not be essential to *laws* that they have an inner morality, but we can entertain no such agnosticism about morality itself. A recognition rule must pick out actions as morally required only if there is a morally decisive reason (in the absence of countervailing conditions) to perform them. Only such a recognition rule lets us stop the conversation—as Prichard would want to stop it—on concluding that our recognition rule picks out an action as morally required.

Recognition rules cannot consist of mere appeal to intuition. To say we have intuitions about X would be to ignore rather than address the question of what warrants our intuitive endorsement. If we form intuitions about X on the basis of features of X having no normative significance, then our intuitions have no normative significance either. Similarly, recognition rules cannot consist of mere appeal to authority. To say we were told by a reliable authority that X is right would be to ignore the question of what it is about X that warrants the reliable authority's endorsement. If the authority judges X on the basis of features of X that have no normative significance, then the authority's judgment has no normative significance either.

Neither can a theory's recognition rules consist of rules that are essentially moral rules. To see why, suppose the contrary. In other words, suppose we had to know whether consideration R was

140

moral before we could say whether R could be a reason for endorsing something as moral. In that case, we would need to recognize R as moral before we could recognize it as a reason for endorsement. But if we must first recognize R as moral, then R must first be picked out as moral by the theory's recognition rules before it can enter the theory. Therefore, R cannot be among the theory's recognition rules. To avoid begging the question about how we identify morality's content, a theory's recognition rules must stand above morality. They cannot enter the theory as a part of morality's content.[19]

For a similar reason, we should not try to formulate recognition rules in terms of rights-claims. Some would insist that we have reason to endorse institutions that protect our rights. I would not deny it. Nevertheless, people claim all kinds of different ostensible rights. Merely asserting a claim is not enough to give us reason to regard it as rightful or to endorse institutions that enforce it. If we are to have reason to regard a claim as a genuine moral right, as having a sacrosanct quality lacking in arbitrary legal privileges, then we need some way of distinguishing between pretenders and the real thing. We need a recognition rule for genuine rights. Rights-claims themselves cannot function as recognition rules. Of course, after we recognize a particular rights-claim as a genuine moral right, it can guide our actions. To say that rights-claims are not recognition rules is not to deny that some rights-claims are well grounded and thus have a place among morality's rules of conduct.

In terms of what, then, should recognition rules be formulated? Chapter 1 promised not to ignore the fact that there is something sacrosanct about morality's imperatives. They are imperative independently of how acting on them engages our interests and desires. It also promised to explore the extent to which moral considerations give reasons for action in ordinary ways, ways appealing to interests and desires. Is it possible to honor the spirit of both prom-

---

[19] A realm's fundamental justification is a justification that does not appeal to concepts of that realm (Peter Danielson, 1992, p. 19). Or as Christopher Morris (unpublished, chap. 6; see also Morris, 1988) says, fundamental justification within a domain is justification by reference to standards independent of that domain. If we recognize X as moral by recognizing a reason to endorse X that is not an essentially moral reason, our recognition rule serves its epistemic function by recognizing what Danielson and Morris would call X's fundamental justification.

ises? Yes it is. We keep the first promise by allowing that, at the action-guiding level, moral imperatives can be categorical, making no reference to interests or desires. At the same time, we keep the second promise by allowing that a recognition rule, on the basis of which we identify imperatives as moral in the first place, may well appeal to interests and desires. Certain considerations can give reasons, in ordinary ways, to endorse a rule of conduct as moral even though the rule of conduct itself is unconditional, enjoining us to, say, keep promises whether we have reasons of the ordinary kind to do so.

This leaves us with a tricky question. How can a recognition rule, the normative force of which is not essentially moral, set out reasons to regard something as moral? How can recognizing morality-independent reasons to endorse X support the conclusion that X is moral? Here is one answer. In Part I, means-end efficacy served us surprisingly well as a recognition rule for rational choice. It has the same great advantage here, namely, that it clearly is a reason for endorsement. It is not an open question why means-end efficacy matters to us. We have reason to endorse an effective means to our ends precisely because it is an effective means to our ends. Further inquiry might reveal that an end was simply given to us as a matter of brute biological fact. Nevertheless, if it really is our end, then we have reason to endorse effective means to it. Indeed, we have sufficient reason, barring countervailing conditions (such as conflicting ends or prior commitments that rule out certain means). Moreover, this conclusion does not depend on whether the end is moral. The normative force of means-end efficacy is morality-independent. A normative grounding in means-end efficacy, therefore, does not beg the question.

But how can X's means-end efficacy give us reason to regard X as moral? To answer that question, we need to say more about what it means to regard X as moral. Within the context of this book, the point of doing moral theory at all is to illuminate the concept of morality as it appears in the "why be moral" question. What is being questioned when a person asks "why be moral"? First, when asked in earnest, "why be moral" is a question about something that matters. "Why stand on one foot" is, on its face, an idle question, but "why be moral" is not. Second, the question matters despite the fact that it patently does not presume that being moral

142

matters to people from their first-person singular perspectives. Whether people have first-person singular reasons to be moral is pointedly left open. Thus, the implicit urgency comes from another source.

It stems, I would say, from the fact that morality essentially is something that matters to us from a first-person plural perspective. My endorsement begins to look like characteristically moral endorsement when grounded in the thought not that *I* have reason for endorsement but that *we* have reason for endorsement. While endorsement as rational need not go beyond the first-person singular, endorsement as moral at a minimum goes beyond the first-person singular to the first-person plural.[20]

The next thing to say is that the transcendence of the singular perspective involved in moral endorsement cannot go much farther than this. If moral endorsement involves taking a plural perspective, then we can imagine how being moral could be disadvantageous for you or me and yet we could still have clear reason to endorse being moral. For example, many theorists now think of cooperating in a Prisoner's Dilemma as a paradigm case of being moral.[21] Cooperating in a Prisoner's Dilemma is disadvantageous from an I-perspective, yet it remains rational in the sense of being to our advantage from a we-perspective. It is from a plural perspective that, in a Prisoner's Dilemma, we find something horribly irrational about individual rationality. When you and I each decide not to cooperate, you and I each do as well as possible, and yet *we* do not do as well as possible. However, if being moral was pointless not only from a singular perspective but from a plural perspective

---

[20] The distinction between first-person singular and first-person plural perspectives is borrowed from Gerald Postema (unpublished). Note that this framework leaves open the possibility of our having duties to ourselves. In some situations, taking a singular perspective might be something we would endorse from a plural perspective.

[21] See especially David Gauthier (1986). A Prisoner's Dilemma is a game in which individuals must make separate decisions about whether to contribute to a cooperative enterprise. In essence, the problem is that if an individual contributes, the benefits will be dispersed in such a way that the marginal benefit per unit of contribution is less than one unit to the contributor but more than one unit to the group. See Schmidtz (1991, p. 105). In an obvious sense, people are better off as a group if they contribute but in an equally obvious sense they are better off as individuals if they do not.

as well, then it would be pointless, period. Being moral would be something we would have reason to avoid in ourselves and condemn in others. Being moral, though, is not like that. Being moral need not be rational from a singular perspective, but part of the essence of being moral is that we have reason to endorse it from a plural perspective.

It is because morality is bound up with what we have reason to endorse from a plural perspective that "why be moral" is a pressing question. The "why be moral" question as it comes down to us from Plato is a question about the relation between two kinds of telos—between what matters to us as individuals and what matters to us as a society. Because morality, as we conceive of it and as Plato conceived of it, matters to us from a first-person plural perspective, we have reason to hope it matters to us (or can be made to matter to us) from our first-person singular perspectives as well. If, *per impossible*, morality did not matter from our plural perspectives, then neither would it matter whether morality could be reconciled with our singular perspectives. The fact that we care about whether we have reason to be moral from an I-perspective presupposes that we already care about morality from some other perspective, a we-perspective.

Unfortunately, while the scope of a person's I-perspective is fixed (encompassing the person's own interests and preferences), the we-perspective does not have fixed borders, which makes it hard to describe. It should go without saying, though, that the plural perspective is no mere fiction. It is not for nothing that natural languages have words like "we" and "us" for plural self-reference.

Except where otherwise noted, when I speak of the plural or we-perspective, what I have in mind is not the sort of group perspective you and I might take when we identify ourselves as fellow Mets fans, but rather the perspective we take when we worry about the "why be moral" question. That perspective need not encompass the whole world. If I see that my mowing the lawn will hamper your efforts to write your book, then my taking a we-perspective involves identifying with you as a member of the group of people who will be affected by my mowing the lawn. If I see that mowing the lawn will adversely affect people in a faraway country (because they are waiting anxiously for your book), then my taking a we-perspective involves identifying with them as well. The scope of my we-perspective expands and contracts along with my awareness of whose interests are at stake.[22] This does not mean I should not mow the lawn. We could not live together if we did not allow ourselves the latitude to impinge on each other in various ways. Your latitude may not serve my ends, and mine may not serve yours, but what is relevant from the plural perspective is that our latitude serves our ends. We are better off in virtue of the members of our group having that kind of latitude.

Compare this to the view that Geoffrey Sayre-McCord attributes to David Hume. "The scope of morality will, on Hume's theory, remain bounded by the actual reach of our sympathetic responses. Exactly what that reach is, we might not be able to say, but that it falls short of engaging us equally in the welfare of all sentient beings is clear" (1994, p. 224). I take it as given that we can ask "why be moral" in earnest, and that when we ask the question with the utmost sincerity, we are taking a perspective limited only by the actual reach of our sympathetic responses. That is the perspective I have in mind when I speak of the plural perspective. The scope of that perspective is fluid. With respect to a particular decision, it will include only those who have, in our eyes, a significant stake in the decision, which means it can but generally does not encompass everyone.

This explains how something with morality-independent force can support characteristically moral endorsement. Given that X is subject to moral assessment, a recognition rule for morals picks out X as moral by identifying X as having properties that we have reason to endorse from a plural perspective. When we endorse X as serving our ends from a plural perspective, we endorse it in terms that represent reasons for endorsement independent of whether we label them as moral reasons but which nevertheless are grounds for the kind of endorsement that we call into question when we ask "why be moral."

---

[22] The scope of my plural perspective will not always coincide with the scope of yours, which is one reason why we sometimes disagree about what is moral. Discussing our differences often helps us extend our perspectives in ways that bring them into alignment, though, so disagreement that can be traced to differences in perspectival scope need not be intractable. If you convince Kate that her we-perspective until now has failed to encompass the interests of members of other races, for example, then she will broaden her perspective accordingly. Or if she willfully refuses to do so, then her kind of we-perspective reveals itself to be quite unlike the perspective that I am attributing to people who earnestly ask the "why be moral" question.

The Descriptive Boundaries of Moral Inquiry

This, then, is the normative status of morality's recognition rules. Being recognized as moral has normative force because, when morality's recognition rules pick out X as moral, they do so by recognizing that X has properties we have reason to endorse from a plural perspective.[23]

Consider the following objection. Kate has reason from a plural perspective to endorse Disneyland. "We'll have a lot of fun there. Nearly everyone does," she says to her friends. Yet, although Kate endorses Disneyland from a we-perspective, she is endorsing it not as moral but as amusing, or something like that. To endorse something as moral is to endorse it from a plural perspective, but not everything endorsed from a plural perspective is thereby endorsed as moral.

I agree. Certainly, we should not equate endorsing Disneyland from a plural perspective with endorsing Disneyland as moral. How then should we think of the plural perspective's role in moral theory? From a plural perspective, we do not pick out capital punishment (for example) as moral. Still less do we pick out Disneyland as moral. Instead, we pick out a property that gives us a basis for endorsement if we find that property in something like capital punishment.

Now, if something is a lot of fun for almost everyone, why is that not a property that we have reason to endorse from a plural perspective? Or, if being a lot of fun is such a property, then what distinguishes endorsing something as fun from endorsing it as moral? Earlier, I noted that it is not the task of recognition rules to circumscribe their own subject matter. On the contrary, any theory has to take a subject matter as given. There has to be a subject that gives rise to moral questions before we can have occasion to devise theories to answer those questions. No doubt, our conception of the scope of moral inquiry changes as we gain practical and theoretical wisdom; my point here is only that we have to start somewhere. We begin with an intuitive understanding that subjects giving rise to moral questions include (roughly speaking) things that

[23] Note that this is a characterization of the perspective from which we formulate recognition rules. Whether *being* moral necessarily involves taking a plural perspective is a separate question. (Do morality's rules of conduct include an injunction to take a plural perspective?)

bear on human flourishing in communities, regarding which human action can make a difference. (Let me stress that I am not offering my intuitions as recognition rules for morals. Intuition enters the picture as a source of questions, not as a tool for answering them.) The subject matters of moral inquiry are pretheoretically given, that is, given in the sense of raising moral questions prior to our devising moral theories to answer them.

Accordingly, "X is moral if X is a lot of fun" is not a recognition rule because, when applied to any of the subject matters over which moral theories range, the property of being a lot of fun is not a reason for endorsement from a plural perspective. It is no reason to endorse capital punishment, or promise keeping, or any of the subjects that normally give rise to moral questions. It may be grounds for endorsement when the subject in question is amusement parks, but that would make it a basis for moral endorsement only if amusement parks as such were among the pretheoretically given subject matters of moral inquiry, and they are not. A moral perspective is more specific than a plural perspective not because it is a more narrowly defined perspective but rather because it consists of taking a plural perspective only with respect to issues already defined as moral issues.

Admittedly, a recognition rule like the principle of utility could embody a genuine reason for endorsement from a plural perspective and still fail to exclude Disneyland as a subject for moral assessment. However, it is not incumbent on recognition rules to have the internal resources to limit their subject matters. We test a purported recognition rule not in abstraction but rather as applied to a pretheoretically given subject matter. We test it by asking whether it homes in on a property that, given the subject matter, grounds endorsement from a plural perspective. If we apply the principle of utility to Disneyland, and then afterwards decide that Disneyland is not a legitimate subject of moral inquiry, it would hardly be fair to blame the principle of utility for the misapplication.

We considered how recognition rules distinguish things that are moral from things that are not, given a subject matter with respect to which such questions arise. I have no theory to tell me what the subject matters of moral assessment are. I have only a sense that morality and moral assessment concern things that make it possible for human beings to flourish together. Given this pretheoretical understanding of the general character of the subject matters of moral assessment, amusement parks are not among morality's subject matters, but *institutions* are. Thus, Disneyland is subject to moral assessment not as an amusement park but rather as an institution that has a bearing on whether people flourish within their communities. (Similarly, Michael Jackson is subject to moral assessment not as an entertainer but rather as a person whose choices have an impact both on himself and on many other people.) Likewise, acts, rules of conduct, and character traits are subjects of moral assessment because they make a difference to whether people flourish within communities.

No doubt our intuitive conception of the proper subjects of moral assessment is more complicated than this, and I am not proposing to shed much light on our intuitive and pretheoretical understanding of the descriptive boundaries of moral assessment. It remains that, given an understanding of the subject matters of moral inquiry—of the kinds of things concerning which moral questions arise—we have something about which we can theorize. We can devise a theory about how those questions should be answered and why.

The descriptive boundaries of the subject matters of moral inquiry are given prior to our doing moral theory. They define what we want to have a theory about. Given a predefined subject matter, my proposal is that we capture the normative bite of morality's recognition rules when we say they home in on properties that, with respect to that subject matter, we have reason to endorse from a plural perspective. If amusement parks are not among the subject matters of morality, then morality's recognition rules do not range over amusement parks in the first place, which is why morality's recognition rules cannot pick out Disneyland per se as moral.

IS THE RIGHT PRIOR TO THE GOOD?

One might worry that if we analyze the rightness of acts in terms of the goodness of states of affairs, the concept of rightness loses its turf, so to speak. The concept becomes superfluous, and we may as well dispense with it entirely. But this worry is not well founded. To explain our grounds for identifying an act as right is not to explain rightness away. The explanandum does not disappear merely in virtue of having been explained. In different words, giving an account of an action guide's normative force does not eliminate the need for an action guide. We cannot dispense with talk about what is right because we cannot dispense with talk about what we should do. We can still speak of keeping promises because it is right (or because breaking promises would violate rights).

Only when we ask how we recognize that keeping promises is right (or that breaking promises would violate rights) do we move from questions addressed at the action-guiding level to questions addressed by recognition rules. This is crucial. If one thinks of recognition rules as part of morality's action guide, one is missing the distinction between recognition rules and rules of conduct. To properly address Prichard's objections to teleology, a theory must isolate its teleology at the level of recognition rules, so that the concept of rightness can take on a life of its own at the action-guiding level. When a theory's teleology is embedded in recognition rules, it specifies terms by which we might recognize what is required, in the process leaving agents with an action guide that tells them what is required and which they should follow because doing so is required.

For the sake of example, suppose the principle of utility is morality's recognition rule and that a set of ten commandments against lying, stealing, and so on, are recognized by the principle of utility as morality's rules of conduct. If we thought of the principle of utility as something like morality's ultimate rule of conduct, then we naturally would interpret the ten commandments as rules of thumb—rules that give way to the principle of utility when it is obvious that following them will not maximize utility. A recognition rule, however, is *not* an ultimate rule of conduct. Rather, it identifies morality's rules of conduct, a set of ten commandments in this case, and the ten commandments are thereby certified as the ultimate rules of conduct. Conduct is judged not according to whether it maximizes utility but rather in accordance with whether it follows the ten commandments.

Consider a legal analogy. "Read the signs" may be the rule by which we recognize rules of the road, but if we found ourselves in a situation where obeying a speed limit would somehow prevent us from reading a traffic sign, that would not be enough to make the speed limit give way. It would not even begin to make the speed limit give way. The highway patrol judges our conduct by the rules of the road, and would be properly unimpressed if we said we violated the rules of the road out of commitment to a higher law bidding us to read the signs.

Given that recognition rules are not rules of conduct, ultimate or otherwise, it is entirely possible that some of morality's rules of conduct are deontological (that is, they make no appeal to consequences) even if morality's rule of recognition is teleological.[24] A rule by which we *recognize* deontological imperatives can be teleological without in any way compromising the deontological force of the imperatives thus identified. An imperative may dictate an action without appealing to the action's role in serving the agent's purposes. It may dictate an action without appealing to *anyone's* purposes. But that does not preclude the possibility of the imperative having teleological support. It may serve a purpose to be committed to keeping promises come what may, even though it sometimes happens that keeping a promise serves no purpose. It serves a purpose to keep regular office hours even though some of those hours predictably will be spent waiting in vain for students to drop by. Using the vocabulary of Chapter 2, the point is that keeping promises may help us reach a global optimum whether or not it helps us reach local optima.

A teleological recognition rule, when applied to imperatives, is analogous to a rule of recognition in law; we need it only when pondering whether a particular imperative is moral. Upon recognizing an imperative as moral, we thereby know what we need to know to see that we have a moral reason to follow it. Having settled that the imperative is morally imperative, the rule of recognition has no further role to play. It drops out, leaving us with action-guiding imperatives that may well present themselves to us in deon-

---

[24] At best, Prichard says, the element of truth in the view that rightness is teleologically grounded is that unless we recognize that an act will give rise to something good, we would not recognize that we ought to do it. But, he hastens to add, this does not imply that pain's badness is the reason not to inflict it (1968a, p. 5). This looks like a massive concession, but Prichard mentions it in passing as if it were unimportant. In a footnote, Prichard claims that if pain's badness grounded the wrongness of inflicting it, then inflicting pain on oneself would be just as wrong as inflicting it on others. This does not follow. Suppose two rules of conduct (Do not inflict pain on others; do not inflict pain on yourself) are grounded in the same general principle (Pain is bad). Contra Prichard, the common grounding implies nothing about whether the two rules of conduct are equally stringent.

tological form. In any event, the action-guiding imperative, not the rule of recognition, is what guides action.

A "soft" deontological prohibition is insensitive to consequences in normal cases but it makes exceptions in extraordinary cases. We saw how there could be a teleological grounding for imperatives that are normally insensitive to consequences. In contrast, absolute imperatives (as I defined them) are insensitive to consequences even when the universe is at stake. It also is conceivable, though just barely, that we could have teleological grounds for recognizing an absolute imperative as moral. It might have good consequences to internalize the rule "I will not lie—not even to save the universe," so long as it never actually happens that we need to lie to save the universe. I doubt that there are any teleologically well-grounded absolute rules of conduct, but the idea is not incoherent. The idea that morality is teleological at the level of recognition rules does not preclude the possibility of there being absolutely exceptionless rules of conduct.

There is, of course, a controversy in moral philosophy over whether the right is prior to the good. Some theorists dismiss the idea that morality's recognition rules are teleological; they assume it contradicts their belief that the right is prior to the good. It would be a mistake to dismiss my theory on that basis, though, because my theory is entirely compatible with the view that the right is prior to the good at the *action-guiding* level. We should keep promises because it is right, and at the action-guiding level this is all that needs to be said. But that does not tell us what makes promise keeping right, or even (in cases of doubt) whether promise keeping is right. We judge acts in terms of the right, but when we need to explain what makes an act right, or whether it is right in a doubtful case, we can do so only in terms of the good. Any non-teleological account with normative force would presuppose a conception of the right and thereby beg the question. Accordingly, my position regarding the controversy over the relative priority of the right and the good is (1) the right is prior at the action-guiding level, and (2) the good is prior at the level of recognition rules.[25]

[25] Although John Rawls's official position is that in justice as fairness the right is prior to the good (1971, p. 31), his theory's recognition rule is paradigmatically teleological. We are to recognize a principle as just by asking whether people behind a veil of ignorance would perceive a basic structure informed by the principle as being to their advantage. "The evaluation of principles must proceed in

Recognition rules, which have a teleological spirit, support action guides, parts of which may not.

Prichard thinks that if one understands that keeping a particular promise is required, then by that very fact one recognizes reason to keep it. In that case, pointing out that keeping promises has good consequences would be irrelevant. Prichard is correct about this, and now we can see why. When we already recognize that we are required to keep a promise, pointing out good reasons to keep it is *redundant*. The redundancy of pointing out good reasons to keep a promise, when we already see that keeping it is required, is what makes the good reasons irrelevant.[26] But what if we have not yet recognized that keeping a particular promise is required? In that case, coming to see that breaking the promise would have bad consequences is not redundant at all. In that case it is Prichard's point that is irrelevant, for in that case we are not asking why we should do what is required. Rather, we are asking whether promise-keeping is required in the first place.

One might be troubled by the idea of keeping a promise simply "because it's right." "Because it's right" may seem oddly abrupt as a reason for action. However, it certainly is not peculiar to morality. For example, when a motorist's impatient passenger asks her why she is driving at twenty miles per hour, it would not be peculiar for her to reply by saying "because it's the law." Her passenger now knows why she is driving at twenty miles per hour and might go on to ask how she knows that it is the law. She might answer that she read the speed limit sign. In a more philosophical if still somewhat impatient frame of mind, the passenger might then ask what is the telos of the twenty-miles-per-hour speed limit. What justifies it? The driver may not know. But she still knows the law. Further, if she knows that there is a school in the neighborhood,

---

terms of the general consequences of their public recognition and universal application" (p. 138). This is not the sort of statement one expects to find at the core of a theory in which the right is supposed to be prior to the good. Perhaps what Rawls really wants to say is that the right is prior to the good at the action-guiding level.

[26] Even so, we should not concede to Prichard that pointing out good reasons to keep promises is *always* irrelevant to someone who believes promise keeping is required. Even someone who believes promise keeping is required might be unable to articulate good reasons to keep promises and might learn something from discussion.

then she can add that the school's presence justifies the law (and she can say this even though she has no idea whether the school's presence is what actually moved authorities to impose the speed limit). A conversation about morality might unfold in the same way. Asked why she keeps promises, a person might say "because it's right." She might be asked how she knows keeping promises is right or she might be asked about the telos of promise keeping, but those will be different questions.[27]

In summary, Prichard denies that the good plays a role in determining the right. He infers this from the premise that we keep promises because doing so is right, not because doing so is good. I accept the premise, but the inference is invalid. Of course we should keep promises because it is right, and at the action-guiding level this is all that needs to be said. But this is different from the question of why promise keeping is right, or (in cases of doubt) whether promise keeping is right. To answer the latter questions, we need to formulate good reasons to keep promises. And pointing out that promise keeping is right is to *imply* there are good reasons rather than to *identify* them. Explaining why we ought to do what is right and identifying what is right in the first place are two different tasks.

CONCLUSION

H. A. Prichard argues that the question "why be moral" is fundamentally confused. It turns out, however, that there is no confusion involved in asking the question from a prudential point of view. Asking the question from the prudential point of view does not presuppose any reduction of morality to a system of hypothetical imperatives. On the contrary, we can intelligibly ask if following categorical imperatives is to our advantage. One way or another, the question has an answer.

A recognition rule cannot be constituted in such a way that the

[27] One thing that makes moral reasoning different from legal reasoning is that questions about how we recognize morality are hard to separate from questions about whether we have reason to endorse it. Morality's recognition rules pick out the extension of 'moral' just as the law's recognition rules pick out the extension of 'legal'. Morality's recognition rules, however, pick out X as moral by homing in on properties that, from a plural perspective, give us reason to endorse X.

action guide it picks out is just as likely to lead us to do bad as to do good. Morality's recognition rules cannot be arbitrary with respect to goodness. Otherwise, arbitrarily identifying an act as right will not give us a reason to do it. And the idea that we could identify an act as morally imperative without in the process coming to have a reason to perform it is contrary to the supposition shared by Prichard that we should do what is right because it is right. A recognition rule for right action essentially picks out, as right, actions for which there are good reasons, which is precisely what allows us to conclude, as Prichard wants us to conclude, that to recognize their rightness is to recognize good reason to do them.

We have not explored any particular theory about the content of morality's recognition rules beyond saying they recognize a thing as moral by recognizing reason to endorse it from a plural perspective. That exploration and the job of saying what it implies about the connection between morality and prudence are undertaken in the following chapters. This chapter's burden has been to show why we can safely reject Prichard's conclusion that undertaking the project is a mistake. Further, we can reject his conclusion while allowing that his premises (as I understand them) are not without merit. To preface chapters to come, though, there is no single recognition rule that supports all of morality. Morality comes in parts, one pertaining to personal conduct and another pertaining to institutional structures that regulate personal conduct in a social setting. The two parts derive their support from different sources. Or so I shall argue.

* CHAPTER 7 *

Social Structure and Moral Constraint

> Morality describes the conduct of perfect men, and
> cannot include in its premises circumstances that arise
> from imperfection. That rule which attains to universal
> sway when all men are what they ought to be, must be
> the right rule, must it not?
> *Herbert Spencer (1969, p. 270; first published 1850)*

CAN INSTITUTIONS BE MORAL?

THIS BOOK BEGINS AND ENDS in pursuit of answers to the "why be moral" question. What, if anything, gives people reason to be moral? Within the context of that larger project, this chapter considers whether institutions, like persons, can be moral or immoral. What would make an institution moral? Here is one answer: An institution could be moral in virtue of giving *people* a reason to be moral.

Modern ethical theories are supposed to guide individual action. Yet, the most familiar versions of utilitarianism and deontology seemingly address us as if we lived in a cultural, economic, and political vacuum. When they abstract from the institutional context in which real people operate, these theories are not as helpful as they could be even when it comes to guiding personal conduct, let alone when it comes to assessing institutions. As Philippa Foot says, "When anthropologists or sociologists look at contemporary moral philosophy they must be struck by a fact about it which is indeed remarkable: that morality is not treated as an essentially social phenomenon" (1978, p. 189). This chapter is about morality as a social phenomenon.

An institution, as the term is used here, is a social arrangement that affects people by affecting how they interact. In other words, an institution affects people by affecting how they affect each other. Institutions so conceived—I sometimes refer to them as social structures—include governments and their laws, nongovernmental

155

organizations and their formal rules, and also informal social norms (the norm of leaving tips in restaurants). Institutions can arise in all domains of human interaction. They can be political (democracy), economic (stock markets), cultural (the family), legal (contract law), religious (the Catholic church), and so on.

Chapter 6 argued that recognition rules for morals must be teleological. The rules of conduct we recognize as moral may in some instances have a deontological nature, but our grounds for recognizing them as moral will in any event be teleological. Or so I argued. Maybe I was wrong. Maybe, for a subject like (self-imposed) rules of conduct, the grounds for moral endorsement cannot be explained in teleological terms. Even so, it is relatively uncontroversial that the moral significance of institutions (and of the constraints they impose on us) is bound up with how they function, and in particular with how they affect human beings.

It may seem that this view defines me as a utilitarian. What really separates utilitarians from deontologists, though, is that utilitarians apply a principle of utility not only to institutions but to personal conduct as well. Deontologists do not deny that institutions ought to be good for something. Persons may be ends in themselves, but institutions are not persons. They are not ends in themselves, and deontologists need not view them as such. Institutions can command respect as means to the ends of human agents. Unlike human agents, they cannot command respect as ends in themselves.[1] Their morality must be understood in functional terms.

More specifically, then, what sort of function marks an institution as moral? We could define moral institutions as those that give people a reason to be moral. If we define institutional morality in this way, though, we are merely stipulating that moral institutions give people reasons to be moral. My hope was to do something more interesting—to *empirically* connect the idea of giving people reasons for being moral to more conventional ideas about the nature of morality.

For example, it would be interesting if the conclusion that moral institutions give people a reason to be moral could be derived from the conventional assumption that moral institutions serve the com-

[1] Admittedly, some people treat certain institutions as *authoritative* (see Joseph Raz, 1986). Even if I viewed an institution as commanding my unconditional allegiance, however, I would still respond to questions about the institution's justification (were such questions forced on me) by considering how it functions.

mon good. This chapter attempts that derivation. It will not try to prove that moral institutions serve the common good. However, given that an institution's morality turns on how it functions, what sort of function should we be looking for? What sort of function would give us reason to endorse an institution as moral? Presumably, it would involve affecting people in certain ways, ways that would fall under the general description of serving the common good. This idea may not be suitable as a foundation for all of morality, but it seems a reasonable place to start in assessing the morality of institutions.[2]

In any event, this chapter argues that *if* moral institutions serve the common good, *then* moral institutions give people reasons to be moral. Of course, to make this a testable empirical claim, we need to say more about what it means to serve the common good. In particular, we need to interpret the idea of serving the common good in such a way that it is not undermined by objections like those to which unsophisticated utilitarian theories are vulnerable. For instance, most of us would dismiss any theory that says it can be moral for a judge knowingly to hang an innocent person in order to pacify an angry mob.

The next section explores the concept of serving the common good. Later sections return to the idea that moral institutions give people reasons to be moral, but the connection emerging between institutional morality and giving people reasons to be moral will be empirical, not conceptual, having to do with the particular way in which institutions serve the common good. Later sections discuss alternative theories and argue that some familiar reasons for rejecting utilitarian approaches to the evaluation of *personal conduct* do not weigh against taking a teleological approach to institutions. Although the discussion stops short of proving that moral institutions serve the common good, I hope you will agree that we say something morally significant about an institution—something that matters to us as moral agents—when we say it serves the common good.

---

[2] The distinction between morally permissible and morally required applies to the assessment of actions—what one may do versus what one must do. The act of creating an institution might be permissible or required, but institutions as such are neither. Institutions permit some things and require others, and on that basis we can assess institutions as moral or otherwise, but we do not assess them as permitted or required. Such categories do not apply to institutions as such.

FROM THE CONCEPT TO A CONCEPTION
OF THE COMMON GOOD

The previous section proposed that it is moral for an institution to serve the common good. Before we go any farther, consider how mild a proposal this is. The proposal is not that serving the common good is a necessary condition for institutional morality.[3] I would not without qualification even propose it as a sufficient condition. Instead, serving the common good is proposed here as a supporting condition, something that gives us reason to conclude that an institution is moral, barring countervailing conditions. (A supporting condition is sufficient to shift the burden of proof, but shifting the burden does not preclude further argument or investigation that might shift it back again.) With that caveat in mind, let us make the principle more precise.

Suppose we know that an institution makes literally everyone better off. That typically would be a very solid basis for saying it serves the common good and thus is moral. As a recognition rule, though, this universal benefit test is not very useful. It gives us a basis for endorsing an institution only if we have evidence that the institution is making literally everyone better off, and it is hard to imagine having such evidence. Insofar as we seek to make distinctions—to have grounds for endorsing some real-world institutions but not others—we need to look for something that provides broader, albeit weaker, support.

As an alternative, suppose we know that an institution is making at least half the people within its range of influence better off. Is that any reason to think of the institution as serving the common good and therefore as moral? If it is, then we can declare an institution moral if it makes at least half the people within its range of influence better off, subject to countervailing conditions. In fact, such information, by itself, hardly establishes even a presumption in favor of an institution's morality. We need information about what is happening to those who are not being made better off before we have a solid reason to think of the institution as serving the common good. The principle sets too low a standard.

---

[3] I do think that for an institution to be bad for people in general would be decisive grounds for condemnation, but what follows will not rely on that idea.

Suppose we say, then, that an institution is moral if it makes over half of the people within its range of influence better off and no one worse off.[4] Although this principle gives us a genuine basis for endorsement, as far as it goes, it might set too high a standard to take us very far. An institution (that makes most people better off) might be recognizably moral even though someone somewhere is worse off in some respect. For example, a pattern of generally improving opportunities for workers might be to one person's disadvantage insofar as it forces her to raise wages at her factory, but somehow this seems irrelevant to the morality of an institution that generally improves opportunities for workers.

To accommodate this possibility without opening the door to worsenings of all kinds, we might say it is moral for an institution to make over half the people within its range of influence better off, provided either that it makes no one worse off or else that the process by which it makes a few people worse off is *nonexploitative*. It seems consistent with serving the common good that a few are made worse off. However, if the institution makes the minority worse off as a *method* of making the majority better off, then the institution cannot without torturing the language be said to serve the common good.

For example, imagine a geographically isolated company-owned mining town suddenly quadrupling the price of stagecoach tickets so that low-level employees cannot afford to leave town and thus cannot afford to leave their jobs. This enables the company to lower wages even further, to a point where some workers can make ends meet only by sending their children to work in the salt mines. As a result, the townspeople generally become more prosperous, but some residents wish they had never heard of it. Because the company serves the town by making some townspeople worse off as a means of making others better off, it cannot be said to serve the common good.

To give another example, technological innovation may hurt

[4] One institutional arrangement is *Pareto-superior* relative to an alternative if it would make at least one person better off and no one worse off. I think we would have grounds for endorsing an institution that makes one person better off and no one worse off, but not for saying it serves the common good. The basis for endorsement discussed in the accompanying text is a strengthened version of Pareto-superiority, one that strikes me as more in keeping with the idea of serving the common good.

manufacturers committed to outdated and less productive technologies, at least in the short run. But this is not exploitation, and indeed, it is no reason to reject technological innovation or the background institutions that encourage it. I propose, then, that we have reason to endorse an institution as moral if it serves the common good, where serving the common good involves not only making people in general better off but also making them better off by nonexploitative methods.

As defined here, an exploitative institution makes some worse off as a method of making others better off. However, when an institution empowers us to disarm would-be muggers, its purpose is to make muggers worse off as a method of making others better off. Do we want to say disarming muggers is a form of exploitation? Presumably not. Thus, some refinement is in order. An exploitative institution uses its targets as a resource. More concretely, exploitation makes some people better off in virtue of the *existence* of targets. In contrast, disarming muggers does not make people better off in virtue of the existence of muggers, and therefore is not a form of exploitation.

As a necessary condition for the morality of institutions, a prohibition of exploitation could be controversial. It would be controversial because, if an institution does enough good for enough people, some people would want to endorse the institution as moral whether or not it is exploitative. (Consider, for example, a progressive tax system the intent of which is to make a majority better off at a minority's expense.) But the clause excluding exploitative methods does not function as a necessary condition for institutional morality; it functions as one part of a supporting condition. Making half the people better off becomes a reason for endorsement only in conjunction with a presumption that no one is made worse off, or at least that no one is worse off in virtue of being used as a means of making the majority better off.[5]

---

[5] One could argue that redistributive taxation is nonexploitative if one could argue that it constitutes a nonprejudicial way of spreading risk, for example. Or, one could argue that it makes most taxpayers better off by making society more peaceful, which it does in virtue of reducing the incidence of crimes motivated by envy or by need. Or, one could argue that the system is nonexploitative because it makes its targets worse off as a form of self-defense in the face of threateningly large disparities in economic and hence political power; only incidentally does it use its target as a resource. On the other hand, if a taxation scheme were simply a

When I proposed that an institution is moral if it makes over half the people within its range of influence better off, the point of saying "over half" was to give the recognition rule an air of precision. We should reconsider that position now, because, after all, such precision is artificial. To say "over half" is to impose a peculiar cutoff on our grounds for endorsement. It is peculiar because any precise cutoff whatsoever would be peculiar. Our grounds for moral endorsement are not really so precise, and they are not subject to arbitrary cutoffs. In truth, for an institution to serve the common good is for it to make people in general better off, and there is no number that can appropriately be substituted for the notion of people in general, such that 51 percent means people in general but 49 percent does not. If making 51 percent better off gives us reason to endorse an institution, then making 49 percent better off usually will give us similar reason to endorse it.

There may not be a sharp separation between our having reason to endorse an institution and our not having reason to endorse it. The strength of our reasons for endorsement may instead form a continuum. At one end, an institution benefits no one and there is no reason to endorse it; at the other extreme, an institution genuinely makes everyone better off and there is no reason not to endorse it. As we move toward the latter extreme, we encounter institutions that make more and more people better off and which we have increasingly clear reason to recognize as making people in general better off. A theory that pretends to give us a precise cutoff (between institutions that are recognizably moral and those that are not) is, in most cases, merely pretending. When a theory answers our questions about the morality of real-world institutions by presenting us with spuriously precise cutoffs, it fails to take our questions seriously.[6]

This is not to deny that before we can say whether institutions

---

way for the king to maximize revenue, it would make people in general worse off and would be exploitative to boot. Moral support for the scheme would have to come from some other source.

[6] The objection here is to building precise cutoffs into recognition rules for moral institutions. I have no such objection to institutions themselves imposing arbitrary cutoffs that mark, for example, sixteen years as the age when it becomes legal to drive a car. In that case, the precise legal cutoff is subject to moral assessment, and it might be recognizably moral (that is, it might serve the common good) despite being somewhat arbitrary.

make people better off, we need to know what counts as evidence that people are better off. Better off compared to what? What is the baseline? Should we say that institutions serve the common good if people are better off under them than they would be in a hypothetical state of nature? It is hard to specify a baseline in a nonarbitrary way. There also are problems of moral epistemology; that is, how do we know how well off people would be under counterfactual baseline conditions?

My thought is to look at how people answer such questions in the real world. No one begins by trying to imagine a hypothetical baseline array of institutions. We do not need to know about the state of nature or about how to characterize a hypothetical original position. It is easier and more relevant to ask how people's lives actually change through contact with particular institutions. Does a given institution solve a real problem? It is no easy task to say whether a particular institution solves a real problem, thereby affecting people in a positive way. Nevertheless, we do it all the time. We have fairly sophisticated ways of assessing whether rent controls or agricultural price-support programs, for example, make people in general better off. We do not need to posit arbitrary baselines, either. It is enough to look at people's prospects before and after an institution's emergence, to compare communities with the institution to communities without it, and so on. These comparisons, and others like them, give us baselines, and such baselines are not arbitrary.[7]

In assessing institutions, we use any information we happen to have. Evidence that an institution is making people better off could come in the form of information that people who come in contact with the institution have higher life expectancies or higher average incomes, for example. No such measure would be plausible as an analysis of what it *means* to make people better off. But such measures comprise the kind of information people actually have. Therefore, such measures comprise the kind of information on

---

[7] That is, we look at how institution X functions in its actual context, which means we take the rest of the institutional context as given. We have good reason to use this baseline not only because it tends to be the one baseline regarding which we have actual data but also because it is the baseline with respect to which institution X's functioning is of immediate practical significance. By this method, we can evaluate each part of the institutional array in turn. If (for some reason) we wanted to evaluate everything at once, we would need some other method.

which people must base their decisions about whether to regard an institution as moral. The more specific indexes are surrogates for the idea of making people better off. Or, if you like, they are part of the common good's ostensive definition, in the sense that one way to make people better off, other things equal, is to increase their life expectancy; another way is to increase their income, and so on.

I say it is moral for an institution to make people better off "within its range of influence." We need not require of a moral institution that its range of beneficial influence be coextensive with the world population. However, when saying it is moral for an institution to make people within its range of influence generally better off by nonexploitative methods, I do think of the constraint against exploitation as being universal. A nation can be recognizably moral in virtue of making its citizens better off, so long as it exploits neither citizens nor noncitizens in the process. A hospital can be recognizably moral in virtue of making patients and staff better off, but it would not be moral for a hospital to serve patients by occasionally kidnapping visitors for use as unwilling organ donors.

There is no obstacle to reformulating my proposed recognition rule by substituting more precisely defined evaluative criteria (like measuring impact on general welfare by looking at changes in median income), except that we would be in danger of confusing a measurement with the thing being measured. The substitution would gratuitously invite counterexamples: counterexamples showing that institutions could satisfy such criteria without making people in general better off or that institutions might satisfy such criteria by exploitative methods. The ideas of making people generally better off, and making them better off without exploitation, seem to comprise the bottom line, imprecise though such ideas may be. It is fine to gather information about changes in median income as a way of assessing whether people are better off, so long as it is understood that median income is an imperfect measurement, a measurement we should consider morally important only insofar as it indicates that people in general are being made better off. If we learn that, while median income rose, incomes well above the median did not rise and incomes below the median actually fell, then evidence of rising median income would be no basis for drawing conclusions about whether people in general are better off.

This section proposes that serving the common good, as the

basis for a recognition rule for moral institutions, could be understood as making people in general better off without exploitation. One might feel that this proposal sets too low a standard and that we should settle for nothing less than institutions that make literally everyone better off. Realistically, though, trying to guarantee that an institution's benefits fall on literally everyone would usually make us worse off. If the government said organ transplants were forbidden until such time as hospitals were in a position to satisfy all demands for organ transplants, our prospects would be worse, not better. To make people better off at all, we sometimes have to settle for institutions that make people better off in general.

Conversely, one might think that the caveat concerning exploitation sets too high a standard, or perhaps the wrong kind of standard. If we truly want to make people better off, we should in principle be willing to accept exploitative methods of making people better off. Or, if we are concerned about exploitation, we should endorse institutions that minimize exploitation, even if they do so by exploitative means.

Such arguments might be somewhat plausible if we were talking about a subject matter other than institutions. However, just as we could argue that even deontologists have reason to reject institutions that make people worse off, so, too, can we argue that even utilitarians have reason to reject institutions that use some people as mere means to the ends of others. It is a familiar idea that a prohibition of exploitation is not built into the concept of utility maximization. Indeed, exploitation may well be utility-maximizing in particular cases and in such cases would command endorsement on act-utilitarian grounds. But the results of exploitative institutions are not like the results of exploitative acts. Exploitative institutions, like exploitative acts, can have utility in isolated cases, but an institution is not an isolated event. An institution's effect is a cumulative matter. Whether an institution makes people better off is not a matter of how it functions on a particular day but rather of how it functions over its lifetime. An institution that operates by exploitative methods may have arguably good results on a particular day, but as time passes, the institution's overall record is increasingly likely to reflect the tendency of exploitation to have bad results.

If institutions with the power to act by exploitative methods could be trusted to do so only when the benefits would be great and widespread, the situation might be different. Indeed, we might say such institutions are moral after all. (Note that this would not be a problem for the theory as it stands. It would prove only that it was right to insist that making people better off by nonexploitative means is a supporting condition for institutional morality rather than a necessary condition.) Exploitative institutions, though, tend to be costly in an ongoing way, and those costs tend to get out of control. The power of institutions may be used for good purposes but, in any case, the people who successfully compete for that power will use it for whatever purposes, good or bad, they happen to have. When we institutionalize the power to pursue ends by exploitative means, we create a power that invites abuse. And inviting such abuse does not have a history of making people in general better off.

Therefore, when a conception of serving the common good joins the idea of making people better off to the idea of operating by nonexploitative methods, the latter idea is not merely a bit of deontology arbitrarily grafted onto the theory so as to save it from the worst excesses of utilitarianism. On the contrary, we are talking about institutions, and in that special context, a restriction against exploitation naturally follows from a consideration of how institutions make people better off. In other words, readers who prefer to interpret serving the common good as maximizing utility might find that, when they apply the principle to institutions, they can derive the same restriction on exploitation that is built into my conception of serving the common good. A constraint against exploitation is not derivable from the idea of utility maximization as such, but it is derivable from the idea of utility maximization applied to institutional structure. Creating opportunities to pursue goals by exploitative methods generally does not make people better off. Indeed, limiting opportunities for exploitation is one of the primary methods by which institutions make people in general better off.

As an example of a legal structure that makes people better off by limiting opportunities for exploitation, consider constitutional limits on the scope of democratic decision making. Unrestrained democracy pits shifting majorities against shifting minorities in ways that make shifting majorities better off.[8] But this need not and often would not make most people better off. You could have a

[8] Concerning whether political moves should be constrained by group rights as well as by individual rights, see Will Kymlicka (1989) and Allen Buchanan (1991). See also the interesting exchange between Chandran Kukathas (1992) and Kymlicka (1992).

situation where every democratic *move* makes as many as two out of three people better off, even though every *pair* of moves makes as many as two out of three people worse off.[9] People in general tend to be better off when means of isolating minorities for ad hoc exploitation are unavailable.

As a supporting condition for institutional morality, sufficient to ground endorsement in the absence of countervailing considerations, the idea of serving the common good (in the sense of making people in general better off without exploitation) is not controversial.[10] Had we not been talking specifically about what it means for institutions to serve the common good, though, my interpretation of "serving the common good" would have been different. For example, we would not have had the same rationale for a caveat concerning exploitation.

Had we been trying to formulate a necessary condition for institutional morality, we would have been under more pressure to try to force convergence on a single conception of the general concept of serving the common good. But there is nothing in the idea of a supporting condition to suggest there cannot be families of conceptions each member of which provides a related kind of support for moral endorsement. For example, readers can interpret serving the common good in terms of universal benefit or maximum aggregate utility or Pareto-superiority, for example, or in terms of a precisely quantified version of the idea of making most people better off. I think such interpretations will all support the conclusion that moral institutions give people reasons to be moral.[11]

[9] Proof: Let A, B, and C represent individual voters or classes of voters. Suppose A and B vote in favor of a measure that leaves each of them a dollar richer and C two dollars poorer. Then A and C vote in favor of a measure that leaves A and C each a dollar richer and B two dollars poorer. The pair of majority votes leaves B and C poorer and A richer. (And when we factor in things like lobbying costs, the zero-sum game becomes negative-sum.) Each vote made two out of three voters (or classes of voters) better off, but the pair of votes made two out of three worse off. Moreover, if A has the power to set the agenda for this voting mechanism, the outcome described here is just what we should expect.

[10] There will be more to say about this principle's countervailing conditions when we consider a more complete version of my moral theory. See Chapter 8 on how the two strands of moral dualism fit together and how conflict between them is resolved.

[11] We speak here and throughout this chapter of being moral in the sense of acting in accordance with morality. Whether people internalize moral principles is a separate issue, although inducing people to internalize a moral principle certainly is one way of inducing people to act in accordance with it.

GIVING PEOPLE A REASON TO BE MORAL

Some utilitarians have said that they consider it a mystery why morality would incorporate any constraints beyond a requirement to do whatever maximizes the good.[12] Perhaps they are right to be skeptical, insofar as the subject matter is personal conduct. Be that as it may, there is no mystery why it is moral for institutions to impose constraints on individual action. Moral institutions constrain the good's pursuit because the good is pursued by individuals, and individuals do not pursue the good in an impartial manner. If the good is to be realized, then institutions—legal, political, economic, and cultural institutions—must put individuals in such a position that their pursuit of the good in a predictably partial manner is conducive to the good's production in general.

We can approach the point in terms of game theory. *Parametric* games (like solitaire) involve only one decisionmaker, one player. *Strategic* games (like poker) involve several decisionmakers. A strategic game's outcome depends on how you play, obviously, but also on how others play. Thus, you need to adapt your strategy to the strategies of others, and you must be aware that others are adapting their strategies to yours. Unfortunately, utilitarians sometimes seem to treat morality as if it were the sole player in a parametric game. Utilitarian morality, represented as a player in this game, tries to get what it wants—maximum utility—by simply *telling* human agents to maximize utility. (That is how we could end up with a theory whose single rule of conduct is an injunction to maximize utility.) But this approach makes sense only in parametric games. In the real world, human agents are players, having their own ends, making their own decisions, and being somewhat responsive to the way others are playing. In this strategic environment, simply telling people to maximize utility is not likely to maximize utility.

Whatever an institution's purpose is, it cannot serve its purpose just by telling human agents to serve its purpose. People have purposes of their own. They will not serve the institution's purpose unless doing so serves their purposes, too. Whatever you think of deontology as a moral theory, the descriptive fact remains that

[12] For example, see Shelly Kagan (1989, pp. 121–27). Samuel Scheffler (1982, p. 129) expresses similar skepticism, despite having a theory that departs from utilitarianism in other respects.

people are ends in themselves. As a matter of descriptive fact, people formulate and execute their own plans. Any institution that ignores this descriptive fact is bound to function badly. This section's first point, then, is that insofar as the morality of institutions turns on how they function, the morality of institutions depends on how they affect people's strategic environment.

The next point is that institutions themselves are not agents in the same way that people are agents. This is neither to deny that societies really exist nor to presuppose atomistic individualism. The point is only that, although society is real, it does not have the same properties that its parts have. Society is not an agent. It does not pursue goals. But people do. That is one of the constants of human behavior. Of course, different people have different goals and different ways of pursuing goals. Are their goals other-regarding? Do they pursue goals in a solitary, cooperative, or competitive manner? Statistical norms with respect to these questions may vary from one society to another. What is true of any society, though, is that its members have goals.

Some people might believe some institutions (armies, for example) are agents in a sense. I have no quarrel with this idea. I insist only that institutions and human agents are not the same kind of entity and cannot be said to act in the same way. Institutions act, when they act, by moving people, whereas people act by moving themselves.

Therefore, for morality to serve a purpose as it works through institutions, it must induce the game's genuine players—human agents—to act in ways that serve its purpose. To serve its purpose, morality as it works through institutions must affect the opportunities, incentives, and expectations of individual agents. Here, then, is the connection between the idea that moral institutions serve a purpose and the idea that moral institutions give people reasons to be moral. If moral institutions are those that serve some particular purpose, then moral institutions are those that induce human agents to act in ways that serve that purpose.

This conclusion does not depend on the assumption that the common good is the particular purpose that moral institutions serve. When we add that assumption, though, we get the further conclusion that moral institutions induce human agents to act in ways that serve the common good. Regardless of how we interpret the notion of serving the common good, it remains the case that if moral institutions serve the common good, they do so by inducing human agents to act in ways that serve the common good.

Neither does the conclusion depend on any particular theory of the good for persons. No matter what the good for persons consists of, it remains that institutions serve the common good by putting people in a position to pursue their respective goods peacefully and constructively.[13] Moral institutions impose constraints on individual pursuits in order to reduce the extent to which individual pursuits interfere with each other and to increase the extent to which they support each other.[14] This is what we should look for when trying to find out which institutions make people in general better off.

If we believe institutions should serve the common good and that ought implies can, then we need a conception of the common good such that institutions are capable of serving it. Since institutions work by channeling the activities of human agents, it will be in terms of how they channel human pursuits that institutions serve the common good, if they serve it at all. If an institution induces people to peacefully pursue their own visions of the good, then to this extent it closes the gap between individual and collective rationality.

Admittedly, smaller and more informal social structures— families, community associations, and so on—typically do more than simply let people pursue their visions of the good in peaceful

[13] There is some room here for cultural relativism because the question of which social structures serve the common good in a given culture depends on what is in place and on what is possible. A given social structure might work well in one setting even though trying to put it in place somewhere else would be a disaster. (See Robert D. Cooter [1991] for a story of what happened when central authorities tried to convert clan-controlled highlands of Papua New Guinea to individually controlled private property.) Likewise, a given social structure might function poorly in a particular setting even though, once the damage is done and people have adapted to it, trying to root it out and replace it with something else would be even worse.

[14] Part of the process involves helping individuals to develop, in the first place, visions of the good that they are in a position to pursue peacefully and constructively. William A. Galston says, "The challenge of social policy is not just the manipulation of incentives but also the formation of character" (1991, p. 216). I would not disagree. The point is only that incentive manipulation is one of social policy's main ways of accomplishing anything at all, including the formation of character. For further discussion of the connection between serving the common good and helping agents to develop virtuous characters, see Chapter 8.

solitude. The smaller and more intimate the social structure, the greater the potential for sharing and jointly pursuing a thicker conception of the common good. And one way in which larger and more formal social structures (for example, governments) work to greatest advantage is by nurturing small-scale structures. The larger structure sets out constraints that minimize exploitation within smaller structures. For example, a state might pass laws against child abuse, thereby limiting the autonomy of family structures.[15] The larger structure still leaves smaller structures with a measure of autonomy, though, which enables the smaller structures to help their members jointly pursue thicker conceptions of the good within those constraints.

AN ATTAINABLE PATTERN OF COMPLIANCE

Social regulation is largely a matter of self-regulation. For example, institutions at various levels formally constrain hate speech, but in all but the most oppressive regimes, the governance of speech remains primarily a matter of individual self-regulation, with informal social norms providing a certain amount of feedback. Accordingly, in the real world, there is a compliance problem. We cannot legitimately compare systems in terms of how good they would be if compliance could be taken for granted. The morality of an action guide does not turn on what would happen if everyone followed it. Morality is more this-worldly than that. Morality as it works through institutions does not merely *ask* people to serve the common good; a moral institution gives them *reasons*. Morality plays strategically. What it asks, when it asks through institutions, is calculated to produce the attainable pattern of compliance that best serves its purpose.[16]

An institution serves the common good by providing opportunities for agents to make themselves better off in ways that also make others better off and reducing opportunities to make them-

---

[15] I thank Lainie Ross for this example.

[16] In passing, it is easy to overestimate the effectiveness of the threat of punishment in inducing people to act in mutually advantageous ways. Given a choice between the proverbial carrot and stick, the carrot is often a better approach. People are clever at finding ways of avoiding the stick, but they do not even try to avoid the carrot.

selves better off in ways that makes others worse off. The institution cannot serve the common good by relying on agents to act consistently against their own good. It has to *do what it can* to make it advantageous for people to act in ways that make each other better off.[17] For example, universities recently have been subject to increasing scrutiny concerning how they handle federal grant money. Russell Hardin (1994) says the government is justified in cracking down on universities that use federal funds, earmarked for scientific research, to buy yachts. The tougher regulations are justified on utilitarian grounds even if some of the activities prohibited in the process were themselves utility-maximizing. The government is justified in cracking down because the latitude previously allowed to universities invited abuse. The new regulations limit opportunities to use funds in creative ways that would in some cases have been optimal—yachts, for example, might save money when used as conference sites—but limiting such opportunities goes hand in hand with limiting opportunities for abuse.

This view of how institutions function has the consequence that institutions with a utilitarian moral grounding do not require (and at times might not even allow) people to maximize utility.[18] A socially imposed requirement to maximize utility would be a *util-*

[17] This point does not depend on assumptions about what people are like. For example, if people were incorrigibly pure in their self-regard, this would limit what institutions could do to induce people to make each other better off, but the fact would remain that an institution serves the common good by doing what it can.

[18] Critics of rule-utilitarianism sometimes say the only kind of rules of conduct that could be grounded by the principle of utility are rules of thumb that on close inspection inevitably turn out to be mere shorthand for the principle of utility. This is a mistake. Whether the principle of utility weighs in favor of following a particular set of rules turns on the consequences of following that set of rules, not on whether that set of rules includes (or boils down to) the principle of utility. Would following a set of rules of thumb that boils down to the principle of utility have better consequences than following a set of rules some of which have the status of deontological constraints?

In an institutional context, they normally would not. To my knowledge, this point is best articulated by John Rawls (1955). In the game of baseball, batters get three strikes. It is not relevant that there sometimes might be a lot of utility in giving the hometown hero an extra strike. Within the context of a given inning of baseball, the rules are not answerable to utilitarian calculations, and this insensitivity to matters of utility is teleologically well-grounded. The practice of giving batters exactly three strikes would not serve its purpose if it was merely a rule of thumb, chronically sensitive to utilitarian calculation.

ity-maximizing requirement only on the false assumption that people would try to adhere to it. In the real world, it remains the case that, to be conducive to our flourishing, an institution must above all make room for our efforts on behalf of our own flourishing. If the institution tries to eliminate our efforts on our own behalf and replace them with something else, it will fail. To serve the common good, the institution must neither ignore individual rationality nor try to stamp it out. Rather, the institution must function so that people's strategic responses to the institution (and people's subsequent responses to each other's responses) have the effect of promoting the common good.

There are interesting parallels between rational agents and moral institutions in terms of how they operate in the face of real-world complexity. Earlier, I argued that moral institutions respond to people as they are. Similarly, rational agents respond to themselves as they are. Both are sensitive to their own limitations. As Chapter 2 explained, individuals adopt satisficing strategies in pursuit of particular goals. They impose constraints on local goals so as to bring their various goals into better harmony with each other, thereby making life as a whole go as well as possible. Likewise, moral institutions get the best result not so much by aiming at the best result as by imposing constraints on individual pursuits so as to bring individual pursuits into better harmony with each other. Institutions (libraries, for example) serve the common good by leaving well enough alone—creating opportunities for mutual benefit and then trusting individuals to take advantage of them.

THE PUZZLE ABOUT AGENT-RELATIVE CONSTRAINTS

The previous section explained how institutions can have a moral mandate to serve the common good that does not translate (or collapse) into an unrestricted mandate for ordinary moral agents to maximize utility. Insofar as morality is embedded in social structure, it works to produce a pattern of compliance that actually serves the common good. It treats the motivation to be moral as the scarce resource that it is, as something we cannot take for granted. Moral institutions impose and enforce constraints so that their reliance on pure moral motivation is minimized, although not necessarily eliminated. To give the most obvious example, morality allows us to impose legal constraints on what people can do in their self-interested pursuits. Legal and social sanctions ease the burden on moral motivation by creating prudential constraints, so acts otherwise constrained only by morality come to be constrained by prudence at the same time.[19]

If we can impose prudential constraints that keep people from tearing out each other's throats, though, why not go all the way? Why not impose a legal obligation not merely to abstain from violence but to *minimize* violence? (No society has ever rejected a prohibition of murder in favor of laws requiring murder minimization. Can it be that they are all missing something?) Thomas Nagel, for example, doubts that morality requires agents to be thoroughly impartial, but he finds himself in a quandary. Nagel asks, "How can there be a reason not to twist someone's arm which is not equally a reason to prevent his arm from being twisted by someone else?" (1986, p. 178). The question is not rhetorical. For Nagel, there is a real puzzle here about how there can be a reason to refrain from arm twisting that is not equally a reason to prevent arms from being twisted.

Nagel's question is answerable, though, when considered in an institutional context. First, a structurally embedded constraint against arm twisting may do a better job of preventing arm twisting than would be done by trying to enforce an obligation to prevent arm twisting. Second, suppose that the impartial reason to refrain from arm twisting really is, as Nagel suspects, equally a reason to prevent arms from being twisted. In other words, let us concede to Nagel that the reasons why an institution should not twist arms are also reasons why it should prevent arms from being twisted.

How, then, do institutions prevent arms from being twisted? One way in which institutions prevent arm twisting is by *forbidding* it. Institutions carry out their mandate to prevent harm precisely by imposing constraints against causing harm.[20] In addition, and in conjunction with the general imposition of constraints

---

[19] See also Robert E. Goodin (1992).

[20] In Thomas Nagel's terms, agent-relative constraints require an agent to refrain from causing harm, whereas agent-neutral constraints require an agent to prevent harm (1991, pp. 175–80). What Nagel wonders, in these terms, is whether we can make any sense of agent-relative constraints from an agent-neutral point of view. This section shows that we can, because, using Nagel's terms, legal institutions meet their agent-neutral obligation to minimize arm twisting by imposing agent-relative obligations to refrain from arm twisting.

against causing harm, legal and political institutions give selected citizens the mandate to prevent harm by enforcing laws that forbid causing it.[21]

When a legal constraint against causing harm serves the common good, people have reasons for compliance from a first-person plural perspective. The way in which the constraint serves the common good, though, presumably will involve enforcement mechanisms that give people reasons for compliance from a first person singular perspective. In short, the system gives us first-person plural reasons to endorse it partly by giving us first-person singular reasons to comply with it. (When an institution gives *you and me* first-person singular reasons to act in ways that serve our common good, its having that property thereby gives *us* a first-person plural reason to endorse it as moral.) I think Nagel would agree that an institution that would have good results only on the assumption that people have no plans of their own is not the sort of thing we would endorse if we were considering the matter impartially. Neither, of course, should institutions assume that people are like Homo economicus. On the contrary, a moral institution is one that is fit for people as they actually are.

Of course, moral constraints do not strike us as merely a means to an end, not even the end of serving the common good. They have a deontological feel to them. Nagel (1986, p. 179) thinks a moral theory has to explain the special psychological force of moral constraint, but I think that if the force in question is really a psychological force, then explaining it is a job for psychology, not ethics. A moral theory's job is to take the reality of that force into account. The psychological fact is that most of us are averse to doing evil—to twisting arms. And it serves the common good for institutions to work with rather than against that psychological

[21] As I write this, however, two days of rioting in Los Angeles have left over fifty people dead. The riots began when four police officers were acquitted on charges of excessive use of force, and they were acquitted despite the fact that a videotape was produced showing that they pulled a motorist out of his car and clubbed and kicked him sixty times as he lay on the pavement. (See *New York Times*, May 2, 1992.) There were several levels of formal and informal social structure involved here. At each level, there was potential to serve the common good but also a potential for corruption. As it happened, the worst in the government's executive branch brought out the worst in its judiciary, and the worst in its judiciary brought out the worst in the informal social structure of the community at large.

fact. We do not have the same aversion to failing to prevent harm as we do to causing it. Thus, from a structural viewpoint, positive duties to prevent harm and negative duties not to cause harm are not symmetrical. Social structure has psychologically potent material to work with in inducing compliance with negative duties; it has less to work with in inducing compliance with positive duties. Institutions serve the common good by working mainly with the psychological aversion to causing harm.[22]

RESPONSIBILITY FOR OMISSIONS

The previous section explained how a theoretical endorsement of the prevention of arm twisting might manifest itself, at the action-guiding level, as a stringent prohibition of arm twisting. The argument was not that there are no grounds for requiring people to prevent harm but rather that structurally embedded constraints against causing harm can be grounded in an obligation to prevent harm. We now consider whether structurally embedded obligations to prevent harm can be grounded along with constraints against causing it. This section asks when it serves the common good to enforce a legal responsibility to prevent harm.

How much utility is there in assigning responsibility for omissions? How much utility is there in assigning people more responsibility for each other's lives and correspondingly less responsibility for their own? To be sure, the principle of utility applied directly to acts does not formally endorse irresponsibility. Act-utilitarianism does not allow people to be irresponsible in running their own lives. On the contrary, it ordinarily requires us to be fully responsible for our own lives.

But that is not the point. The point is that to whatever extent Kate takes responsibility for other people as well as herself, those

---

[22] Some would say a distinction between acts and omissions is psychologically important only because of cultural contingency; that is, people are beguiled by false moral theory or false religion into thinking the distinction is important. But the origin and alleged contingency of the distinction's psychological salience is beside the point. I am not saying our tendency to distinguish between acts and omissions is hard-wired; I assume only that it is real. No matter what the origin of this fact about human psychology, it remains significant, and so long as it remains a fact, moral institutions will not ignore it.

people are being encouraged by *Kate's actions* (the actions she takes on their behalf as dictated by act-utilitarianism) to depend on Kate rather than on themselves. Act-utilitarianism usually would not permit Tom to live in such a way that Kate's act-utilitarian commitments require her to support him, but unless Tom, too, is a committed act-utilitarian, that will not stop him from doing it.

Theories often have implications other than the ones they formally acknowledge. A theory can stipulate an action guide and it can stipulate an intended result. But a theory cannot *stipulate* that following its action guide will have its intended result, for that is an empirical matter. So it is with a strategy of maximizing aggregate (or individual) utility. One can say that trying to maximize utility actually tends to maximize utility, but saying it does not make it so. A maximizing strategy may tend to lead to the best possible outcome for beings like us in situations like ours. Then again, it may not. For example, consider that if act-utilitarianism naively assigns responsibility for other people's lives, then by that fact it tempts other people to take less responsibility for their own lives, whether or not it permits other people to succumb to the temptation. Maybe this would be a good thing, on balance, but it is not obviously so. Other things equal, more sophisticated act-utilitarians, and institutions that serve the common good, avoid encouraging us to presume that they are responsible for our welfare.

Legislators considering whether or how to craft good samaritan laws ought to be, and sometimes are, aware of such issues. Whether good samaritan laws serve the common good is an empirical issue. In *The Gift Relationship* (1971), Richard Titmuss presents an excellent example of the kind of argument that takes strategic subtleties into account. Titmuss compares alternative methods (English and American) of procuring supplies of blood. He asks which system best induces healthy donors to step forward. He also asks which system creates the best incentives for donors and procurers to be honest about the quality of the blood. For example, will some donors (more under one system than under the other) conceal the fact that their life-styles put them at risk of having AIDS? In addition, whole blood is highly perishable. Will procurers discard their supply of stored blood when it exceeds its useful shelf life, Titmuss wonders, or will they conceal its age and sell it as if it were fresh? Does market pricing of blood products crowd out the kind of other-regarding individual commitments that organizations like the Red Cross have so effectively marshalled in service of the common good? Titmuss's questions are right to the point.[23] Even if moral agents ought to be good samaritans, as virtually any theory of morality would agree, this leaves open the question of how institutional structures best induce good samaritanism.

Whether institutions should try to compel us to be good samaritans—whether they should compel us to donate blood, for example—depends in part on whether that is the most effective way of inducing people to be good samaritans. There are complicated empirical issues here that need sorting out. By way of general observation, though, it seems relatively easy to argue for positive obligations to children. It seems plausible that people owe special concern and support for children, especially their own children. Moreover, the kind of dependency warned of earlier is, in young children, innocuous, indeed appropriate. Enforcing special responsibilities of adults to their children can hardly be thought to undermine the recipients' sense of personal responsibility.

Philosophers disagree about whether our obligations regarding local crises are different from our obligations regarding distant crises. Insofar as the question pertains specifically to the obligations that would be imposed on us by moral institutions, I think there is a difference. When we turn to distant horizons, the fact that there are emergencies somewhere or other is normal. No good could come from institutions trying to stop people from pursuing their own projects until such time as there are no more emergencies in the world. By contrast, local emergencies are rare enough for most of us that we can respond to them, help restore things to normal, and get on with our lives, having done some good. We do not feel stifled. On the contrary, in such cases, we generally are eager to help. Many philosophers see no important difference between a person starving at our feet and a person starving on an-

---

[23] Richard M. Titmuss extols the virtues of voluntary activity driven by community spirit rather than by market forces. Apparently missing the point, Peter Singer infers from Titmuss's findings that "it is only the intervention of the state which can guarantee that everyone who needs blood will receive it" (1978, p. 212). But this was not Titmuss's conclusion; nor is such a conclusion supported by Titmuss's study. On the contrary, the importance to the community of this voluntary activity weighs as heavily against turning the process over to government as it does against turning the process over to the market.

other continent.[24] But there is a difference, psychologically as well as logistically, and a moral institution will be sensitive to it.[25]

Philosophers often voice a concern that certain conceptions of morality depict our lives and projects as hostages to morality. For example, there is injustice everywhere we turn. Must we spend our lives fighting injustice wherever we find it? (If injustice becomes hard to find, will we have to go looking for it?) On my theory, moral institutions do not try to force people to spend their lives fighting injustice. Institutions may impose a blanket obligation not to contribute to injustice, in part because such an imposition leaves people free to lead productive lives of their own. Moral institutions are relatively circumspect, though, in forcing people to fight injustice, because there comes a point after which forcing people to spend their lives fighting for externally imposed goals can no longer be construed as a way of making them better off. Moral institutions do prevent injustice, but one way in which they effectively prevent injustice is by giving us plenty of room to work peacefully on behalf of causes we really care about.[26]

To put in perspective this conclusion about the scope of positive duties, we should note that structurally embedded moral constraints are not the only kind of moral constraint. Part I argued that reflective individual rationality leads us to go beyond adherence to interpersonal constraints and find causes worth living for. Chapter 8 argues that reflective rationality informs a second strand of morality. This personal strand of morality does not require us to throw our lives away fighting for every just cause under the sun, but it does require us to do something meaningful with our lives. Generally speaking, the slogan "If you're not part of the solution, you're part of the problem" is a false dichotomy. If the problem is real, morality requires us to avoid being part of it, and reflective rationality also requires us to be part of the solution either to that or to some other real problems—to take some aspect of the prob-

[24] For example, see Derek Parfit (1984, p. 125).

[25] Lest this be misunderstood, the idea here is not that the person on the scene always is more obligated than the person who is far away; the faraway person might be in a better position to help. (I thank Jon Zerolnick for this point.) Instead, the idea is that being on the scene makes a difference. The person who is on the scene but can do very little may be obligated to do what she can even though she would not be obligated at all if she were not on the scene.

[26] Of course, as the previous section explained, another way institutions prevent injustice is by enforcing rules against causing it.

lem of making the world a better place to live and make that problem our own. Sometimes, an aspect of the global problem becomes ours to solve because we willingly embrace it as our problem. Other times, our role in the larger scheme reaches out and grabs us rather than the other way around, as when we find we are the only ones at the scene of an accident who can perform cardiopulmonary resuscitation.

To some people, good samaritan laws symbolize solidarity. To other people, such laws symbolize the increasing bureaucratization of human interaction. Those who are driven by symbols will be afraid to let their position be contingent on empirical results. Be that as it may, we must look beyond symbols to the issue of what effect such laws would actually have in a given society. (Symbolic attachments can of course be indirectly relevant insofar as they shape people's reactions to an institution and thereby affect how the institution functions. My point is only that the institution should be assessed in terms of how it functions rather than in terms of what it symbolizes.)

Whether a morally significant distinction can be drawn between acts and omissions and whether institutions should be involved in enforcing positive obligations are issues of perennial philosophical interest. The theory that moral institutions make people in general better off by nonexploitative methods applies in a natural way to these issues and to concrete questions of public policy in general. The theory applies to needle-exchange programs devised to slow the spread of AIDS among drug users. It applies to teenage counseling programs devised to prevent juvenile delinquency. It applies to patent and copyright laws devised to encourage technological innovation. It applies to federal water management practices devised to "make the desert bloom like a rose." It applies to strict liability standards in lawsuits against medical practitioners and manufacturers, to the Federal Deposit Insurance Corporation, and so on. The founders of these social structures were no doubt well-intentioned, but the morality of institutions has nothing to do with the good intentions of those who create them. The morality of institutions turns on whether they affect our behavior in ways that make people in general better off. Not all of them do.[27]

[27] Broadhead and Heckathorn (unpublished) have studied how needle-exchange programs have slowed the spread of AIDS despite being riddled with incentive problems. On the surprising failures of teenage counseling programs

Admittedly, those who create legal and political institutions must make decisions on probabilistic grounds. An apparently successful needle-exchange program, for example, might outlive its usefulness. The short-term benefit might not be worth the long-term cost of creating a bureaucracy that later proves hard to dismantle. Analogously, a computer program can play chess by algorithm, but human chess players need creativity, experience, alertness to unintended consequences, and other skills and virtues that are not algorithmic. People who create institutions need similar skills and virtues.

That said, we should note that this chapter is less about which institutions to *create* and more about which institutions to *respect*.[28] The latter question addresses people as citizens rather than as social engineers, and it is relatively concrete. We need not compare the hypothetical utility under counterfactual assumptions (like the assumption of universal compliance) of all logically possible rules of conduct. To find out which of the social constraints to which we are subject are also moral constraints, we must try to assess the performance, now and in the foreseeable future, of existing social structures.

RIVAL THEORIES

We have looked at the institutional strand of my moral theory. In isolation, this part of my theory might look like a version of rule-

---

intended to help potential delinquents, see Joan McCord (1982). On copyrights laws with respect to intellectual property, see Tom G. Palmer (1989). On the large-scale diversion of water resources from higher-valued to lesser-valued uses and consequent environmental tragedy in California and other western states, see Richard W. Wahl (1989).

[28] The theory can, however, be applied to questions about obligations to participate in attempts to create new and better institutions. See Chapter 9. When people are framing institutions, preexisting constraints might limit their legal or political latitude. Such constraints will serve the common good if they restrain people who otherwise would use that latitude for selfish purposes, or if they restrain people who otherwise would botch their honest but hubristic attempts to devise institutions that serve the common good. If no prior constraints are in place, then framers are, qua framers, answerable only to a mandate to serve the common good (and one of their first jobs might be to ensure that legislators who succeed them will be answerable to more than that).

utilitarianism. Chapter 8 situates the institutional strand of morality within a broader moral theory. Meanwhile, we can admit that institutional morality and rule-utilitarianism begin with somewhat similar recognition rules. However, the principle that X is moral if it makes people in general better off (by nonexploitative methods) is nonmaximizing. It diverges from the principle of utility in another way, too, because it does not claim to be a necessary and sufficient condition for something being moral. As a recognition rule for moral institutions, it claims only to support endorsement. To show that an institution serves the common good is to shift the burden of proof to those who remain unconvinced of the institution's morality.

The two theories, therefore, have somewhat different recognition rules. Further, their respective recognition rules are applied to markedly different subject matters. In John Harsanyi's version of rule-utilitarianism, the principle of utility is used to identify the moral code that would have more expected utility than any other logically possible moral code if followed by all rational and morallymotivated people (1985, p. 44). There are other versions of rule-utilitarianism, but the main point is that rule-utilitarianism is usually thought of as offering a personal action guide (selected from the set of logically possible action guides) to agents who want to be moral. In contrast, institutional morality is about which institutions give agents (who are not assumed to be moral) reasons to act in ways that make each other better off. Agents who do want to be moral are asked to respect and uphold actually existing institutions (not logically possible institutions) that serve the common good in this sense. I resist the rule-utilitarian label mainly because it could lead people to overlook what is distinctive about the institutional strand's subject matter.

My position may be more like Thomas Nagel's insofar as he also sees a need for a theory of institutional morality, one that moderates the demands of the impersonal point of view. Moderation is called for, Nagel seems to say, because the impersonal point of view owes it to the personal point of view to give the latter some room. It would be difficult to follow up this suggestion with anything specific, though, and Nagel, by his own admission, has yet to do so (1991, p. 3). In contrast, I am saying the impersonal point of view owes it to *itself* to give the personal point of view some room. I do not agree that "any system must be justified twice, . . . both from the point of view of what would be impersonally desirable and from the point of view of what can be reasonably demanded of individuals" (1991, p. 31). Expressing my disagreement with Nagel in Nagelian terms, I think a system need only be impersonally justified. The personal perspective is important when it comes to justifying systems only because the fact that people have plans and views of their own has practical implications that bear on what system can be impersonally justified.

My view of institutional morality might seem contractarian, especially to readers who believe (as argued in Schmidtz, 1990a) that contractarian grounds for endorsement are essentially teleological. Contemporary contractarians derive conclusions about the legitimacy of interpersonal constraints by asking whether rational bargainers in a state of nature would agree to accept those constraints. But as David Gauthier rightly remarks, "The genuinely problematic element in a contractarian theory is not the introduction of morality, but the step from hypothetical agreement to actual moral constraint" (1986, p. 9).[29]

Contractarians generally seem to think ethics ought to work like this. First, we find out what people would agree to, which tells us what morality's rules of conduct are. Second, we find out how to make people comply with the (hypothetical) agreement. Edward McClennen says, "I share Gauthier's commitment to a contractarian approach to morality, and I think it is possible to interpret moral principles as principles upon which rational self-interested persons can agree. I also share his view that it is crucial to such a project to show that rational persons will dispose themselves to choose in a cooperative manner" (1988, p. 96). As John Rawls puts it, "Persons in the original position assume that the principles they acknowledge, whatever they are, will be strictly complied with and followed by everyone. Thus, the principles of justice that result are those defining a perfectly just society, given favorable conditions. With the presumption of strict compliance, we arrive at a certain ideal conception" (1971, p. 351).[30] Compliance problems are something we take up later, when we do "nonideal" theory.

[29] See also Christopher Morris (unpublished, chap. 4).

[30] For more on the issue of compliance in contractarian theory, see Jules L. Coleman (1992, chap. 2). Peter Danielson (1992, p. 13) says that Rawls's theory presumes motivational monism, that is, that all agents are motivated in the same way regarding principles of justice. In contrast, David Gauthier's (1986) motiva-

That has to be wrong. The compliance problem is not the second step. It is not something to set aside as a task for so-called nonideal theory, as if the degree of compliance were an exogenous (that is, independently determined) variable that could be dealt with separately. The compliance problem is an integral part of the first step. When one chooses a set of rules, one gets a particular compliance problem and a particular pattern of compliance along with it. Therefore, we cannot begin to know whether instituting a given set of rules will be to our mutual advantage unless we know how bad its associated compliance problem will be. We cannot say whether an agreement is mutually advantageous, and we certainly cannot say that what emerges from it will be *just*, until we know what will emerge from it. And knowing what will emerge from it is a matter of knowing what pattern of compliance will emerge from it.

A given system might be hypothetically advantageous for Kantian noumenal selves (as Rawls [1980] envisions them), but that is no guarantee that the system would be mutually advantageous for flesh-and-blood people. If a system must be genuinely advantageous as a condition of being just, then showing that it would be advantageous for noumenal selves hardly begins to show that it is just. Instead, we need to ask whether a system would induce flesh-and-blood agents to act in mutually advantageous ways.

There will, of course, be some system the worst off members of which are in fact better off than the worst off members would be in any alternative system,[31] and there is no denying that having such a property would be of great moral significance. The point is only that the system having this property will be one that faces its compliance problems squarely. The system that actually makes the worst off as well off as possible will not be even remotely like a regime that tries to enforce a formal principle of distribution like "Distribute so as to make the worst off as well off as possible." The

---

tional dualism posits two kinds of agents, constrained maximizers and straightforward maximizers, motivated in different ways vis-à-vis moral constraints. Danielson welcomes this advance and thinks we should aspire to develop theories that assess interpersonal constraints against a background of full-blown, real-world, motivational pluralism. This chapter could be viewed as an attempt to develop such a theory.

[31] Rawls (1971, p. 302) offers this as a principle of justice for institutions. For a concise but thorough critique of Rawls's theory, set in a broader discussion of the role of intuition in the construction of moral theories, see T.K. Seung (1993).

compliance problems created by trying to enforce such a principle would be a nightmare.

An ideal need not be attainable, but attainable or not, an ideal is essentially an object of aspiration. Theorizing in abstraction from compliance problems gives us a fantasy, perhaps, something pleasing to imagine. But it does not give us an ideal; it does not give us something to which people facing real-world compliance problems have reason to aspire. The fact that an arrangement *would* be ideal in a world of strict compliance gives us not the slightest reason to treat the arrangement as an object of aspiration in the real world. To abstract from compliance problems is to abstract from the fact that the agents on whom we impose the institutions are human.

Toward a More Complete Theory

This chapter's main point is that morality as it works through institutions is not like a sole player in a parametric game. Moral institutions are strategic; they do not issue the kind of commands that would make sense only if compliance could be taken for granted. Their commands are structured so as to produce the best attainable pattern of compliance. Institutions serve the common good by making individual agents willing and able to act in ways that make each other better off.

This conclusion about how institutions serve the common good does not depend on any particular theory of the good for persons. By reconciling rather than repudiating individual interests, institutions give people a chance to pursue their own visions of the good, in peace, in a social setting. Of course, moral institutions repudiate interests that cannot be pursued peacefully, like the interest one might have in being a mugger. In this limited sense, moral institutions are not altogether neutral with respect to conflicting visions of the good, but the kind of neutrality they lack is not one that anyone would defend.

There are many teleological principles, but for institutions, the common good is as plausible a principle as I can think of. If the premise that it is moral for institutions to serve the common good is correct, then a tendency to give people reasons to act in accordance with morality is internal to morality as it works through social structure. If the premise is not correct, this chapter has in any event still made the connection between institutions serving the common good and institutions giving people reasons to act in ways that serve the common good.

This chapter's discussion of institutional morality reveals one facet of an answer to the "why be moral" question. The answer is contingent, to be sure, for an institution can give us reason to be moral only if it is actually in place. Still, a contingent answer is no less an answer for being contingent. Moral social structures (or in any event, social structures that serve the common good) narrow the gap between individual and collective rationality.

This chapter talks about how moral constraints work when they work through institutions. The argument may seem to suggest that moral constraints work *only* through institutions, but I do not believe that. The teleological principle defended in this chapter can tell us something about the moral constraints to which individuals are subject. It cannot tell the whole story, though. My theory, as it stands, exhibits huge gaps where, one might think, morality itself has no such gaps. There will be things we ought to do for the sake of the common good, perhaps, things not required of us by existing institutions. Further, there are moral imperatives other than interpersonal constraints. There are matters of personal integrity, for example. The institutional strand is incomplete as a moral theory in part because there is more to morality than structurally imposed constraints. There are matters of character as well. A more complete theory will combine this chapter's theory about interpersonal constraints with a theory pertaining to personal goals.

Moral Dualism

*We cannot, of course, regard as valid reasonings that
lead to conflicting conclusions: and I therefore
assume as a fundamental postulate of Ethics,
that so far as two methods conflict, one or the other
of them must be modified or rejected.*
Henry Sidgwick (1962, p. 6; first published 1907)

THE FORMAL STRUCTURE OF A MORAL THEORY

PART I of this book argued that reflectively rational beings have reasons to be other-regarding and to have integrity. If the conclusion is true, does that give us an answer to the "why be moral" question? It depends on whether having integrity and having concern and respect for others are ways of being moral. Common sense says they are, which counts for something, but (and this too is common sense) common sense is not infallible. This chapter seeks theoretical grounds for endorsing integrity, other-regard, and other parts of commonsense morality as genuinely moral.

Recall points made in Chapter 6 about the structure of moral theory. According to H.L.A. Hart's (1961) legal theory, primary rules comprise what we normally think of as the law. Secondary rules, especially *rules of recognition*, are rules we use to identify primary rules, that is, to determine what the law is. Moral theories, in a similar way, specify both the elements of an action guide and also a secondary rule by which we recognize those elements as parts of morality's action guide. As it happens, the central project in modern ethics (even more central than the "why be moral" issue) is to formulate a rule of recognition for morals.

Along these lines, Chapter 6 analyzed the structures of utilitarian and deontological theories. This chapter proposes an alternative theory. To be sure, I do not think we will ever have a complete analysis of morality, any more than we will ever have a complete

186

analysis of knowledge. We use such terms in a variety of related ways, and there is no single principle nor any biconditional analysis to which the varying uses can all be reduced. This is not an admission of defeat, though, for the important thing is not to find the one true principle but rather to look for principles that can form a backbone for a useful rule of recognition. Three points are worth highlighting.

1. A Moral Theory Can Range over More Than One Subject Matter.

We devise moral theories to help us answer questions raised by the subject of individual choice and action, of course. Yet, we might also want to assess individual character. Or, we might want to assess the morality of the institutional frameworks within which individuals choose and act and develop their characters. These are distinct subject matters.

2. A Moral Theory Can Incorporate More Than One Recognition Rule.

There is nothing in the nature of morality to indicate that we should aim to answer all questions with a *single* recognition rule, because there is nothing in the nature of recognition rules to suggest there cannot be more than one. Modern ethical inquiry is often interpreted (perhaps less often today than a few years ago) as a search for a single-stranded theory, that is, a single rule of recognition applied to a single subject matter, usually the subject of what moral agents ought to do.[1] Perhaps Kant and Mill intended to promulgate single-stranded theories; they are often taken to have done so by friends and foes alike. In any case, when interpreted this way, their theories can capture no more than a fragment of the truth.

[1] I realize that philosophers sometimes try too hard to distinguish themselves from their predecessors, leading them to caricaturize the history of philosophy as monolithically moving in one direction, a direction which is different from the one they themselves propose. I do think the convention within modern moral philosophy is to assume that the correct moral theory will be single-stranded, but I say this without meaning to slight moral philosophy's venerable pluralist tradition.

187

The truth is: Morality is more than one thing. A theory will not give us an accurate picture of morality unless it reflects the fact that morality has more than one strand. Accordingly, I will not try to derive all of morality from a single recognition rule.

I once began a paper by noting that utilitarianism (which says rightness is determined by consequences) and deontology (which says it is not) both express powerful insights into the nature of morality. "On the one hand, doing as much good as one can is surely right. On the other hand, it is also right to keep promises, sometimes even in cases where breaking them has better consequences" (1990b, p. 622). The paper concluded on a grim note. "We have intuitions about morality that seem essentially embedded in theories that contradict each other. Something has to give" (p. 627). At the time, I was stumped by this dilemma, but it has become clear that what can and should give is the assumption that morality is single-stranded. When we come to despair of finding the single property shared by all things moral, we can stop looking for essence and start looking for family resemblance. By abandoning the search for a single-stranded moral theory, we put ourselves in a position to notice that whether rightness is determined solely by consequences might depend on the subject matter.

3. A Moral Theory Can Be Structurally Open-ended.

Utilitarianism and deontology, or single-stranded interpretations thereof, purport to capture the whole truth about morality with a single recognition rule. By the lights of either theory, the other theory is a rival competing for the same turf. The theories are closed systems in the sense that, having incorporated one recognition rule, and claiming to capture the whole of morality with it, they have no room for others.

By contrast, this chapter depicts morality as an open-ended series of structurally parallel strands, each with its own recognition rule, each contributing different threads to morality's action guide. Any particular recognition rule has a naturally limited range, applying only to its own subject matter. No particular recognition rule pretends to capture the whole of morality, and so verifying that they do not do so would not refute the theory.

One might think we ought to be looking for the single recognition rule underlying all of morality, on the grounds that a theory with more than one recognition rule would violate the principle of parsimony. But such an objection oversimplifies the principle of parsimony. The question is not whether a theory is simpler in the beginning, but whether it is simpler in the end. Gracefully admitting the real complexity of morality at the outset can make for a simpler theory in the end. Analogously, when astronomers abandoned the assumption that planetary orbits were circular, having only one focal point, and accepted the reality of elliptical orbits, which have two focal points, their theories became simpler, more elegant, and more powerful.

On my theory, morality has at least two focal points; and it may have more than two. One part of morality focuses on *personal goals* while a second part focuses on the *institutional structures* that regulate the pursuit of personal goals in a social setting. The theory's two parts map a respectable portion of the terrain of morality.[2] They may not map all of it, but the theory is structured so as to allow for that possibility. The two parts do not exclude each other; nor do they preclude the introduction of further parts. If something is missing, the gap can be filled by adding further recognition rules or further subject matters as necessary. Or, more pessimistically, if we come to believe that some of the knowledge on which moral judgment is based is inevitably tacit and could never be fully articulated, this need not stop us from pushing the articulation of morality's recognition rules as far as we can, acknowledging the possibility of an inevitably tacit residue by allowing that the theory's recognition rules admit of countervailing conditions.

The Substance of Moral Dualism

The previous section discussed the formal structure of a multi-stranded, open-ended moral theory. Table 8. 1 depicts one way of fleshing out the substance of such a theory.

According to this theory, a goal is moral if pursuing it is individually rational; a constraint is moral if operating within it is collectively rational. The two subject matters do not jointly exhaust the logical space of morality's possible subject matters, of course, but

---

[2] A good theory, like a good map, accurately represents the subject's most important general features. It does not try to capture fine details.

TABLE 8.1
A Multi-Stranded Moral Theory

	Personal Strand	*Interpersonal Strand*
Generic Recognition Rule	Is X individually rational?	Is Y collectively rational?
Subject Matter	X = personal goals	Y = interpersonal constraints
Fully Specified Recognition Rule	A goal is moral if pursuing it is individually rational	A constraint is moral if pursuing goals within it is collectively rational
	(Subject to countervailing conditions)	(subject to countervailing conditions)

ranging over all possible subject matters is not necessarily a prerequisite for comprehensiveness, because a theory ranging over all possible subjects of moral inquiry might exhibit a great deal of redundancy. (In any case, the theory depicted in Table 8.1 could be made more comprehensive by adding further strands, or more simply, by broadening the subject matters of the existing strands.) Putting the two strands together, to be moral is to pursue individually rational goals within collectively rational constraints.

This is roughly the theory with which I began. The form of the theory does not dictate its content, though, and I was not satisfied with the content. More than once, I changed my mind about how the subject matters and recognition rules should be defined. I was not always sure why I was changing my mind, either. What should we expect of a theory? To what questions is a moral theory supposed to give answers?

Barbara Herman writes, "In general, judgment is possible only when the material to be judged is presented in a manner that fits the form of judgment. Moral judgment is not the first step in moral deliberation" (1985, p. 417). In different words, a subject matter must raise moral questions before we ever start devising recognition rules to help us answer them. Herman also seems to be saying that we can, and sometimes must, reconstruct a pretheoretically given subject matter. If a subject matter raises questions that cannot all be answered by a single recognition rule, then we need to simplify and clarify and separate the materials to be judged before we can devise recognition rules to fit them.

If my experience is any indication, Herman is right. I wanted to apply recognition rules only to subjects that make us feel a need for moral theory in the first place. I began with the general idea of assessing the morality of personal goals (What goals should we pursue?) and interpersonal constraints (How should the interests of others constrain our pursuits?). My subsequent search for recognition rules for those two subject matters was guided by objectives that are not easily reconciled. A recognition rule must home in on a property with normative force, one that constitutes reason for endorsement. To complicate matters, as Chapter 6 explained, the property's normative force must be independent of morality.[3] It must give us reasons for endorsement of an ordinary kind, ordinary in the sense of appealing to interests and desires. (If we said we recognize X as moral in virtue of its having the property of being moral, that would be circular. Our method of recognizing what is moral must not presuppose that we already recognize what is moral.) On the other hand, morality is, after all, what a recognition rule is supposed to be recognizing. The rule has to be a basis for endorsing something as moral despite having a normative force that is not essentially moral. The solution, as explained in Chapter 6, was to formulate recognition rules in terms of properties that matter to us from a plural perspective.

By that standard, individual rationality does not make the grade. However, we can reformulate the personal strand's recognition rule in terms of reflective rationality. As discussed in Part I, reflective rationality is means-end rationality informed by a certain psychological profile. For Kate to be reflectively rational is for Kate to understand that the robustness of her self-regard is a variable. Indeed, it is a key variable in her preference function. Accordingly, Kate rationally takes steps to develop and enhance a healthy self-

[3] Because collective rationality, for example, is not an essentially moral concept, it can provide a fundamental justification within the realm of morality and thus can form the backbone of a useful recognition rule for morals, whereas essentially moral concepts like justice, for example, cannot. (As mentioned in Chapter 6, the term 'fundamental justification' is from Christopher Morris [1988] and refers to justification within a domain by reference to standards independent of that domain.)

191

regard.[4] Principally, she takes steps to give her life instrumental value, and one of the best ways of doing that is to make herself valuable to others, to be a force for good in her community, and to be esteemed by others. Personal morality involves having something and *being* something worth living for. In short, a reflectively rational person asks not only "What do I want to get?" but also "What do I want to be?" The former does not wear moral significance on its sleeve; the latter does.[5]

A second modification of the personal strand involves contracting its subject matter so that we are using its recognition rule to assess personal goals only in terms of their self-regarding effects. Some theorists would say that questions about how we treat others and how we treat ourselves, respectively, define the separate domains of morality and prudence. The distinction cannot be quite this simple, though, for matters of prudence often evoke reactions that seemingly have the character of moral judgment. It is an ancient and I think correct view that there are matters of right and wrong involved in how we treat ourselves. People sometimes say, "You owe it to yourself to take better care of yourself," and when people say such things, they usually mean it quite literally. It is not merely a manner of speaking. One may not violate anyone's rights in the process of becoming addicted to "crack" (an extremely potent form of cocaine), but one does waste a life. There is something wrong with wasting a life regardless of whether doing so violates rights.

Perhaps one reason why it is easy to overlook the moral significance of things we do to ourselves is that this significance is obscured by a persistence in the social sciences of an oversimplified conception of self-regard. There are at least two kinds of self-

[4] Being reflectively rational involves treating herself as a project, as something needing work. A reflectively rational person does not take this attitude to extremes, though. As Jean Hampton once said to me, there is a place in a rational person's life for "loafing in moderation." Rational people do not expect themselves always to be operating at maximum capacity.

[5] Jeffrey Olen says a personal code of conduct is a moral code if (and because) "it is based on reflection on my projects and commitments, and because it concerns the good life, not mere prudence or self-interest or whim or unreflective pursuit of pleasure, and because it admits of backsliding, and because it provides the measure against which I judge the worth of my life, and because it encompasses deeply held principles, not mere preferences" (1988, p. 24). See also Robert Louden's argument (1992, chap. 1) that morality is fundamentally self-regarding.

regard. For example, professional athletes sometimes play for pride, sometimes for money. In abstraction, playing for money is neither moral nor immoral. It all depends on how a person goes about it. Playing for pride, though—pushing oneself not just in pursuit of money but also in pursuit of excellence—is a matter of character. The desire not to waste one's potential is commonly seen as intrinsically moral. We recognize a difference between using our talents in a purely instrumental way and wanting to make the most of our talents and opportunities—wanting to make the most of ourselves—as a matter of self-respect, a matter of integrity.

Suppose, though, that we were to ask whether being a mugger is a moral way of using our talents and opportunities. We could argue that being a mugger is not reflectively rational, and therefore is not moral. But even if the argument was sound, it would seem to get the right answer for the wrong reason. To capture the core reason why we cannot endorse being a mugger, we need to talk about how it affects others.[6] To be sure, being a mugger would not shape one's character in a reflectively rational way, but what makes it wrong to be a mugger is not that wise men would find it unfulfilling but rather that it violates interpersonal constraints. For that reason, we are well advised to apply reflective rationality only to the subject of how our pursuits affect ourselves. Aside from obligations to others that derive from obligations to ourselves, the subject of how we ought to treat others is something we leave for the interpersonal strand.

The final changes to the simple theory with which we started concern the interpersonal strand. Institutions affect human behavior, and their effect on human behavior is subject to moral assessment. If an institution makes people in general worse off, that is an utterly decisive reason to reject it. If it makes people in general better off, that need not be a decisive reason to accept it, because there might be countervailing conditions. But although making people in general better off may not be decisive, few would deny that it is presumptively moral for an institution to make people in general better off, especially if it does so by nonexploitative means.[7] Social structures impose constraints on us that regulate

[6] Samuel Scheffler (1992, p. 117) expresses a similar view.

[7] If a constraint is morally justified, does that *entail* that people are morally bound by it? Possibly not. Later in this chapter, I argue that there are cases in which people are not morally bound by morally justified constraints.

how we deal with others, and I propose that we assess those constraints along the lines discussed in Chapter 7. When a constraint works through a social structure in such a way as to make people in general better off by nonexploitative means, that constraint is morally justified. An interpersonal constraint is a moral constraint if it works through social structure in such a way as to serve the common good.

Regarding my interpretation of collective rationality as the interpersonal strand's recognition rule, I decided not to work with the idea of maximizing aggregate utility simply because we do not recognize institutions as maximizing utility. We do not have that kind of information. Or, when we do know that an institution or social norm is maximizing utility, I have no objection to endorsing it on that basis. From a plural perspective, I approve of institutions that maximize utility, barring countervailing conditions. I also approve of institutions that make literally everyone better off, but how often do we have any reason to think of an institution as passing that test? Probably never. And there is no point in developing a supporting condition that does not actually support anything. For the sake of having a *useful* recognition rule, I chose to work with the idea of making people in general better off by nonexploitative methods. The latter idea is something about which we often do have information: impressionistic firsthand information, a priori theoretical evidence, statistical evidence, and so forth.

The substance of *moral dualism* is that our question about what serves as a recognition rule for morals has at least two answers as shown in Table 8.2. One answer is that structurally embedded constraints on personal conduct warrant endorsement if they are collectively rational, in the sense of making people in general better off by nonexploitative means. Another answer is that personal conduct warrants endorsement in terms of its self-regarding effects if it is reflectively rational, in the sense of helping the agent to develop and sustain a psychologically healthy character along lines discussed in Part I, especially Chapter 5. There may be other answers as well.

One recognition rule says that, barring countervailing conditions, X is moral if it is reflectively rational. The other recognition rule says that, barring countervailing conditions, Y is moral if it is collectively rational. The former rule applies to *internal* effects—

TABLE 8.2
Moral Dualism's Two Strands

	Personal Strand	Interpersonal Strand
Generic Recognition Rule	Is X reflectively rational?	Is Y collectively rational?
Subject Matter	X = goals, in terms of how their pursuit affects the agent's character	Y = constraints on conduct as embedded in social structure
Fully Specified Recognition Rule	A goal is moral if pursuing it helps the agent to develop in a reflectively rational way	A constraint on conduct is moral if it works through social structure in a collectively rational way
	(subject to counter-vailing conditions)	(subject to counter-vailing conditions)

how agents affect themselves. The latter rule applies to structurally embedded constraints within which agents choose and act. It concentrates on *external* effects—how agents affect others. One strand focuses on matters of character; the other focuses on how constraints function when externally imposed on people by formal and informal social structures. The interpersonal strand ranges over social structure in general, including all of the cultural, commercial, religious, political, legal, familial, and fraternal institutions and descriptive norms that affect how people deal with each other.[8]

Applying these generic rules to their respective subject matters yields two fully specified rules of recognition. One rule recognizes, as moral, goals that help the agent develop and sustain a reflectively rational character. The other rule recognizes, as moral, constraints that function in a collectively rational way as embedded in social structure. (The following sections discuss countervailing

[8] Having said that fraternal social structures are governed by the interpersonal strand, we should add that friendship is a matter of personal morality as well. It is reflectively rational to not only look like a friend but to really be one, for reasons like those discussed in Chapter 5.

conditions.) In plainer words, we owe it to ourselves to nurture a good character, whereas we owe it to others to abide by social norms that serve the common good.

The two recognition rules specify grounds for endorsement the force of which goes beyond any appeal they make to self-interest, but they transcend appeal to self-interest in different ways. Collective rationality goes beyond an appeal to self-interest by being *impartial*. It is about serving the common good rather than serving the interests of the individual agent. Reflective rationality goes beyond an appeal to self-interest by being an *idealization* of self-interest. It is about character and about ends that make life worth living rather than about occurrent desires. Reflective rationality does not essentially require impartiality.[9] Moral dualism thus makes room for agents to pursue their own projects within limits defined by morality's interpersonal constraints, but the point is to make room for an idealization of self-interest rather than for self-interest as such.[10]

The interpersonal strand will be seen by some as a kind of rule-utilitarianism, and I have no objection to that, so long as it is understood how far we stretch the label if and when we label moral dualism's interpersonal strand as rule-utilitarian. First, the interpersonal strand does not purport to be the whole of morality. Second, it does not ask us to search the universe of logically possible sets of action-guiding rules. It does not ask us to adopt the action guide that would lead us to produce more utility than we would produce by following any alternative action guide. It does not ask us to adopt the action guide that would have the most utility if it were adopted by everyone. Instead, it asks us to be aware of existing formal and informal constraints and to respect those that are actually working through social structure in such a way as to make people in general better off by nonexploitative

[9] It may contingently require impartiality, given facts about human psychology.

[10] In this sense, moral dualism is more stringent than the interesting theory defended by Scheffler (1992, p. 100). Within more or less coarse-grained general rules imposed on us by formal and informal social structures, personal morality involves living by principles the dictates of which are more responsive to particular circumstances, but which can be more stringent than the general rules precisely because they can set higher standards for particular agents than it would be rational for social structures to expect people in general to meet. For more on the distinction between rules and principles, see Barbara Herman (1983 and 1985).

means. The interpersonal strand ties moral obligations to the content of existing social structure. (It does not do so blindly, though. It ties only one strand of morality to existing social structure, and that strand ties itself to existing social structures only to the degree that we have reason to endorse them.)

MORALITY'S ULTIMATE FOUNDATION

I used reflective rationality as a basis for a generic recognition rule on the grounds that being reflectively rational serves people's ends (see Chapters 1 through 5). Reflective rationality thus has normative force whether or not we recognize it as moral. Accordingly, as a recognition rule, it does not beg the question. Is reflective rationality something we have reason to endorse from a plural perspective? Not necessarily. It depends on the subject matter. When we look at how people treat themselves, though, and especially at how their pursuits affect their characters, reflective rationality does indeed matter to us from a plural perspective. We do approve of people treating themselves in a reflectively rational way, and for good reason; namely, we care about them. We care about them not just as means to our ends or even each other's ends but as ends in themselves. We try to raise our children to be reflectively rational not only because we care about how they treat others but also because we care about how they treat themselves. We approve of people developing in a reflectively rational way, at least insofar as the question before us concerns how people should treat themselves. As a recognition rule, reflective rationality seems to be on its strongest ground when applied to the subject of how people should treat themselves.

Collective rationality, when applied to the subject of interpersonal constraints in general, threatened to collapse into act-utilitarianism with all its attendant controversy. (If we were obligated to search logical space for constraints to impose on ourselves, we might find it collectively rational to constrain ourselves to do all and only that which maximizes aggregate utility.) Narrowing the subject matter to externally imposed constraints, assessed in terms of how they actually function as embedded in existing social structure, seemed to put my interpretation of collective rationality on stronger ground as a reason for endorsement. Thus was born moral dualism.

Think of it this way. Collectively rational social structures constitute morality as a social phenomenon, a phenomenon that influences behavior from the outside in. Reflectively rational character constitutes morality as a psychological phenomenon. When it influences behavior, it does so from the inside out.[11] As a rough generalization, we can say that, at the action-guiding level, the interpersonal strand is something we discover, whereas the personal strand is something we create. We discover interpersonal morality's action-guiding content by learning how the social structures around us are functioning. We create personal morality's action-guiding content by settling on ends that shape our lives and characters, giving us a sense of having and being something worth living for. Interpersonal morality's constraints are out there, embedded in institutions, whether or not we ever discover them. The content of personal morality's action guide is not similarly independent. It is only after we embrace a reflectively rational goal as our own that it begins to dictate what we should do.

Moral dualism's recognition rules pick out parts of commonsense morality that serve our ends from a plural perspective and thus are not merely "moral as the term is commonly understood" but also are independently shown to warrant endorsement. Reflectively rational character and collectively rational institutions engage us (they command our endorsement) from a first-person plural perspective even when they fail to motivate some of us from a first-person singular perspective, and one of the marks of a moral reason is that it engages us in this way. When applied to suitable subject matters, moral dualism's recognition rules identify parts of commonsense morality as warranting endorsement on grounds that go beyond matters of occurrent desire to concerns crucial to human well-being and to a concept of the good life for human beings living together.[12]

[11] I say "*when* it influences behavior" because it may not. We need not be motivated by the fact that, from a plural perspective, we have reason to endorse reflectively rational character.

[12] Chapter 6 supposed that when an issue is crucial to human flourishing in communities, and when human beings can make a difference regarding that issue, we see it as raising moral questions, and thus as calling for moral theory. Robert Louden accepts this, as far as it goes, but he does not think moral inquiry is

I do not know whether moral dualism's two recognition rules are morality's ultimate foundation. Asking whether they are is like asking Charles Darwin whether the theory of evolution is biology's ultimate foundation. The real question is whether the theory serves the purpose for which it was devised, namely, to illuminate its subject matter. Does the theory of evolution explain the origin of species? Maybe not, but if it does, then it serves its purpose. Does moral dualism identify properties that give us reasons for endorsement from a plural perspective? Maybe not, but if it does, then it serves its purpose.

Moral dualism's recognition rules are fundamental enough to support endorsement, and that is what matters. We could try to reduce matters of character to matters of serving the common good, or vice versa. We could try to reduce both to variations on some third and even more basic theme. We might even succeed. But neither rule's status as a supporting condition depends on whether we can reduce it to something else. When we get to either rule, we get to something that, applied to an appropriate subject matter, supports endorsement. We do not need to reduce either rule to anything more fundamental.

Nor must we look for grounds that are *unique* in supporting endorsement. There are other ways to map the moral terrain. Some may be just as illuminating and just as resistant to counter-examples. So be it. We do not need to discover the terrain's one true map. There are truths about how our choices affect our characters, and there are truths about how well our social structures serve our collective ends; therein lie genuine and related grounds for endorsement. That combination of truths may not comprise our only grounds for endorsing parts of common sense morality as genuinely moral, but the grounds they provide are nonetheless real. Our grounds for endorsement must be real; they need not be uniquely so.

---

limited to subjects that are crucial to our well-being in communities. He writes, "Whatever is within our control is (subject to the usual excusing conditions) a possible object of moral assessment. My natural eye color is not a fact for moral assessment; my diffidence may well be" (1992, p. 20). I would not disagree, but neither would it serve my purpose to insist that moral inquiry's scope is this broad. For my purposes, it does not matter exactly how broad the scope of moral inquiry can be, so long as the subject matters over which moral dualism ranges fall within that scope.

THE TWO STRANDS FORM A UNIFIED THEORY

My aim in the rest of this chapter is to argue that moral dualism's two strands belong together; they are parts of the same theory. First, they help to determine each other's content. Second, they help to determine each other's limits. This section explains how the common good is defined in terms of reflective rationality and, conversely, how reflective rationality as a recognition rule has a countervailing condition defined in terms of collective rationality. The next section explains what happens when moral goals clash with moral constraints.

Chapter 7 defined the common good in terms of making people in general better off. With a single-stranded utilitarian theory of the right, there would not be much else to say. We would be more or less at a dead end, needing to look beyond the theory for a conception of goodness. In contrast, since moral dualism has two distinct recognition rules, they can look to each other rather than beyond the theory. For example, we can look to the personal strand for ideas about what social structure is supposed to accomplish. Specifically, we can define collective rationality as the property of being conducive to the flourishing of people in general as reflectively rational agents. The theory's two strands are therefore connected via their recognition rules, since they each incorporate a conception of rationality, one of which is defined in terms of the other. See Table 8.3.

It does not go both ways. I would not try to define reflective rationality in terms of collective rationality. Reflective rationality does have a kind of definitional link to collective rationality, though, because, as the personal strand's recognition rule, it is subject to countervailing conditions that get their content from the interpersonal strand. Specifically, moral goals must be pursued within moral constraints. Kate's goal of going to medical school and becoming a surgeon may be reflectively rational, but the morality of her goal does not give her license to raise tuition money by fraudulent means. Pursuits that sustain a reflectively rational character are presumptively moral, but the presumption can be reversed by showing that the pursuit has run afoul of collectively rational interpersonal constraints. See Table 8.4.

We have looked at two definitional links between moral dual-

TABLE 8.3
Defining Collective Rationality

	Personal Strand	*Interpersonal Strand*
	helps define →	
Generic Recognition Rule	Is X reflectively rational?	Is Y collectively rational?
Subject Matter	X = goals, in terms of how their pursuit affects the agent's character	Y = constraints on conduct as embedded in social structure
Fully Specified Recognition Rule	A goal is moral if pursuing it helps the agent to develop in a reflectively rational way	A constraint on conduct is moral if it works through social structure in a collectively rational way
	(subject to countervailing conditions)	(subject to countervailing conditions)

ism's recognition rules. By definition, collective rationality involves helping individuals to flourish as reflectively rational beings (Table 8.3). Reflective rationality's countervailing conditions, in turn, are defined in terms of collective rationality (Table 8.4). There are contingent links as well. As Chapter 5 argued, being a reflectively rational agent in a social context involves nurturing respect and concern for others, establishing honest rapport with others, and living peacefully and productively within one's community. It involves becoming an important part of one's community and thereby having more to live for. In these ways, matters of collective rationality enter the personal strand not only (by definition) through reflective rationality's countervailing conditions, but also (contingently) through reflective rationality itself, insofar as caring about the common good is contingently part of being reflectively rational in a social setting.

Contingent links between reflective and collective rationality are

TABLE 8.4
Defining the Personal Strand's Countervailing Conditions

	Personal Strand	Interpersonal Strand
Generic Recognition Rule	Is X reflectively rational? *helps define*	Is Y collectively rational?
Subject Matter	X = goals, in terms of how their pursuit affects the agent's character	Y = constraints on conduct as embedded in social structure
Fully Specified Recognition Rule	A goal is moral if pursuing it helps the agent to develop in a reflectively rational way	A constraint on conduct is moral if it works through social structure in a collectively rational way
	(subject to countervailing conditions) *helps define*	(subject to countervailing conditions)

secured not only by the tendency of reflectively rational agents to want to play a role in a collectively rational community but also (from the other direction) by the fact that collectively rational communities create incentives and opportunities such that individually rational agents, reflective or not, normally have reasons to act in ways that serve the common good. See Table 8.5.

We should not think of either strand as independently specifying a sufficient condition for something being moral. No single strand speaks for morality as a whole. If a goal's choice and subsequent pursuit help Kate to sustain a reflectively rational character, then the goal is moral by the lights of the personal strand. If Kate pursues that goal within constraints imposed by collectively rational social structures, then her pursuit is moral by the lights of the interpersonal strand. To be moral, period, her choice and subsequent pursuit must pass both tests (and maybe other tests as well, if there are further strands of morality bearing on action).

TABLE 8.5
Contingent Links between Moral Goals and Moral Constraints

	Personal Strand	Interpersonal Strand
Generic Recognition Rule	Is X reflectively rational?	Is Y collectively rational?
Subject Matter	X = goals, in terms of how their pursuit affects the agent's character	Y = constraints on conduct as embedded in social structure
Fully Specified Recognition Rule	A goal is moral if pursuing it helps the agent to develop in a reflectively rational way	A constraint on conduct is moral if it works through social structure in a collectively ratioal way
	(subject to countervailing conditions)	(subject to countervailing conditions)

helps define (arrow) *contingent links* (arrow) *helps define* (arrow)

In terms of their action-guiding function, then, the two strands are complementary parts of a unified theory. In concert, they converge on an action guide that says something about both ends and means: One should pursue reflectively rational ends via means permitted by collectively rational social structures. Morally, one seeks to make oneself a better person—a person with more to live for—within constraints imposed by social structures that serve the common good.

THE TWO STRANDS CAN COME INTO CONFLICT

Structurally embedded interpersonal constraints are moral in virtue of normally making people in general better off, and moral agents pursue reflectively rational goals within those constraints.

203

Matters are not always this simple, though. Like reflective rationality as applied to personal goals, collective rationality as applied to interpersonal constraints admits of countervailing conditions. Suppose you have a medical emergency on your hands. You are bleeding badly, and the most straightforward way of getting to a doctor involves parking illegally, on a street where parking laws serve the common good. The previous section's remarks on how the strands intertwine, and its conclusion that they constitute a unified theory, may seem to suggest that they cannot yield conflicting guidance. Are the strands really so neatly woven together?

If we insist that, by definition, there can be no conflict between goals that sustain reflectively rational character and collectively rational constraints, then we have two alternatives. We can say *moral* parking laws incorporate exemptions for bleeding motorists as a matter of course, which seems false (unless we want to say no real-world parking laws are moral). Or we can say that if the laws really are moral, then we must never break them, not even to save our lives, and that, too, seems false.

The theory (and our lives as moral agents) would be simpler if we could insist that moral social constraints never conflict with urgent personal goals. Realistically, however, the harmony between moral goals and structurally embedded moral constraints is contingent rather than necessary. Normally, moral social structures help people flourish as reflectively rational agents. It can sometimes be reflectively rational, though, even for people who appreciate and respect moral social structures, to react in ways that are not "by the book." Moral constraints usually trump moral goals, but there can be exceptions. Municipal parking regulations, for example, have normative force insofar as they constitute an institution that generally serves the ends of human agents. Yet, parking regulations can have this normative force without entailing that individual agents have decisive reasons to conform to those regulations in a given case. The kind of moral force that real-world regulations have, when they have any, cannot preclude the possibility of cases where people have decisive reasons to disregard pertinent regulations and, for example, park illegally in an emergency. Regulations may give reasons for action in a broad range of cases, but it is in the nature of the reasons provided that they will not always be decisive.

It does not follow from this that parking regulations are moral in some cases but not in others. Regulations may tell us to do what turns out to be perverse in a given case, but that does not mean the *regulations* are perverse. On the contrary, if we tried to modify an institutional structure so that it allowed us to do what would serve the common good in the particular case, the resulting modified system of regulations might be decidedly more perverse in other ways. An optimal system occasionally will forbid actions that would have served the common good.[13]

In some cases, constraints embedded in one social structure come into conflict with constraints embedded in some other social structure. Thus, in a medical emergency, a doctor's obligation to obey collectively rational parking laws can come into conflict with the collectively rational constraints embedded in his or her code of professional conduct.[14] Although the two constraints each have moral force, circumstances can still bring them into conflict.[15] They can conflict with each other. They also can conflict with the dictates of morality's personal strand. For example, one's reflectively rational promise to be on time to see one's son perform in a school play can, through no fault of one's own, come into conflict with one's professional obligations or with one's obligation to observe collectively rational traffic laws. (Of course, we can owe it to ourselves or to our families or to our clients and colleagues to do

[13] As Jules Coleman puts a similar point, "Rules are incapable of being perfectly fine-tuned. Sometimes rules will include within their domain cases that fall outside their set of background reasons, and they will exclude others that fall within that set. These characteristics are a function of rule generality. Thus, rules are necessarily under- and over-inclusive with respect to the sets of reasons that support or ground them" (1991, p. 710). See also "Moral Conflict: Reality or Theoretical Artifact?" in Chapter 9.

[14] This example comes from Russell Hardin (1994, p. 213). I have since found a similar example in Kurt Baier (1958, p. 193).

[15] In passing, moral goals can conflict with each other in the sense that Tom achieving his moral goal might be incompatible with Kate achieving hers. Some theorists might balk at this, feeling that moral goals are necessarily *compossible* (that is, they do not preclude each other's achievement), and any theory according to which it can be moral to act in a way that prevents others from achieving moral goals thereby shows itself to be incoherent. However, I think a theory that admits that such conflicts actually occur is merely telling it like it is. For example, there may be several people for whom it is moral to seek to discover penicillin, or the shortest route to the East Indies, or the structure of DNA. They cannot all achieve their goals, but the fact that their goals are not compatible does not make them any less moral. Indeed, it might serve the common good for social structures to strongly encourage people to pursue such goals, the incompatibility notwithstanding.

what we can to avoid circumstances that give rise to conflicts.) Perhaps there are also conflicts best viewed as conflicts between the interpersonal strand and some third strand of morality.

The fact that a given pursuit is reflectively rational is not enough to override constraints that work through social structures to serve the common good. On the other hand, if a reflectively rational pursuit is important enough on its own terms, that can make it a matter of collective rationality as well. After all, collective rationality ultimately is a matter of what makes people better off as reflectively rational agents. In situations of conflict, morality's interpersonal constraints normally trump—they constrain— personal goals, but moral agents should realize that forcing people to ignore overwhelmingly important moral goals is no part of moral social structure's purpose. Acknowledging this, presiding judges within an institutional framework can consider mitigating circumstances on a case-by-case basis. This is how legal structures should work, because a legislature that tried to deal with all possible peculiar cases before they happened would not work as well as a legislature that relies on the judiciary to recognize mitigating circumstances as they arise.

This is also how individual conscience should work. Parking regulations become morally irrelevant, for example, to a person seeking emergency medical attention. More precisely, their *action-guiding function* becomes morally irrelevant. We might appreciate that the regulations have moral force even while realizing that they should not guide our actions in a medical emergency. Under the circumstances, a person of conscience breaks regulations, possibly with a fleeting touch of regret but surely without reluctance.[16] It would not serve the common good and thus would not be moral for social structure to force us to ignore overwhelmingly important personal goals or overwhelmingly important interpersonal constraints embedded in other social structures.

While it is essential to morality's interpersonal constraints that they mesh both with each other and with morality's personal strand in normal cases, interpersonal constraints can clash with each other or with reflective rationality in extreme cases. Just as personal goals must defer to interpersonal constraints in normal

[16] For more on act-evaluations that are not action-guiding, see Michael Stocker (1990, chap. 4).

cases, so interpersonal constraints must defer to personal goals in some extreme cases. Naturally, some constraints are less deferential than others. To make a constraint against mugging give way, a case would have to be truly extraordinary, both in terms of its consequences and in terms of the agent being very sure of the consequences.

AN OVERARCHING PRINCIPLE OF ADJUDICATION

Single-stranded theories have dominated modern moral philosophy in part because of a widespread view that theories incorporating more than one recognition rule inevitably are beset by internal conflict. Moreover, so the story goes, conflicts are resolvable only by some overarching principle of adjudication. The overarching principle will be the theory's real and only fundamental recognition rule. Thus, some theorists would say there is an instability in theories proposing more than one recognition rule. With a little pushing, all such theories collapse into single-stranded theories.

Perhaps enough has been said by now to show why this view is mistaken when it comes to moral dualism.[17] Moral social structures impose constraints that can conflict with reflective rationality, but the two strands can settle their disputes without having to resort to outside arbitration. In most cases, the personal strand defers to the interpersonal strand. Reflectively rational agents have reason to defer to (and perhaps to internalize the constraints imposed by) a collectively rational social structure, insofar as the structure serves their ends from a first-person plural perspective and also insofar as the structure gives them various first-person singular incentives to defer.

In extraordinary cases, however, our reflectively rational goals can become overwhelmingly important. Reflectively rational people have reasons to comply with moral social structures in normal cases, but to comply with moral parking laws in a situation in which one is in danger of bleeding to death would not be reflectively rational. In such cases, the personal strand cannot defer, but the interpersonal

[17] Chapter 9 shows that it also is a mistake to assume there would be less conflict in a theory operating with only one recognition rule. Indeed, there might be more.

207

strand can, and it has good reason to do so. Moral social structures do not try to change us in such a way that we would rather die than double-park. The attempt to command such blind allegiance would not serve the common good.

Therefore, both strands, each on their own ground, agree that in normal cases, reflectively rational goals must be pursued within constraints imposed by collectively rational social structures. Likewise, both strands, each on their own ground, agree that there can be cases in which abiding by collectively rational parking laws would be wrong—neither individually nor collectively rational. If it seems paradoxical to say abiding by collectively rational rules is not always collectively rational, then recall that the collective rationality of laws is a matter of how they function over the course of their existence, and we are now talking about the collective rationality of abiding by moral institutions in abnormal cases.

For example, a rule against shouting in libraries is moral because it makes people generally better off by nonexploitative means. The constraint makes people better off in virtue of how it channels behavior in normal cases. The constraint does not spell out what people should do in literally every contingency that might arise. Library patrons generally are better off with simple norms, and the fact that they are generally better off with simple norms is what gives simple norms their moral force. Shouting in a library might be reflectively or even collectively rational in a given case, but that by itself is not enough to undermine the moral standing of a prohibition that (in virtue of making it possible for patrons to count on peace and quiet) remains collectively rational as an ongoing norm.

If you notice smoke pouring from the ventilator shaft, though, the situation has deviated so far from the norm that normal constraints no longer apply. And it is obvious that they no longer apply. When smoke is pouring from the ventilator shaft, the background conditions that give the norm its ongoing utility, and thus its moral force, can no longer be taken as given. The norm's moral force is predicated on the ongoing existence of the library and its patrons, but their ongoing existence is now the issue. When the library begins to look more like a death trap than like a quiet place to do research, disturbing fellow patrons becomes morally okay. The personal strand dictates violating the constraint against disturbing fellow patrons, and the interpersonal strand does not demand compliance (or even permit it, given that different norms apply in emergencies).

Note that there is no direct appeal here to the plural perspecitve as an overarching moral principle. Instead, as in normal cases, the plural perspective is the perspective from which we identify reasons for endorsement; it is not itself a reason for endorsement. Having identified collective rationality as grounds for endorsing social structures as moral, we conclude that a rule against disturbing fellow patrons, grounded in considerations of collective rationality, reaches its natural limit when the building is on fire. The only kind of rule against disturbing library patrons that could be considered collectively rational is a rule that is understood not to apply when you notice smoke pouring from the ventilator shaft.[18]

Likewise, it would run counter to interpersonal morality for a government to hire police officers to run down and handcuff people who double-park in a desperate attempt to avoid bleeding to death. This is so even when laws forbidding double-parking are moral. This is how moral dualism explains the occurrence and resolution of moral conflict. There is no need—there is not even room—for an overarching principle of adjudication.

Moral dualism's two strands provide the source of each other's countervailing conditions. Conflict between the two strands is the source of the personal strand's countervailing conditions in normal cases, and it is the source of the interpersonal strand's countervailing conditions in abnormal cases. See Table 8.6. The latter point is the puzzle's final piece; we have characterized the theory's recognition rules, its subject matters, and now its main countervailing conditions as well. Reflective rationality is defined exogenously, along lines discussed in Part I. Collective rationality is defined in terms of reflective rationality. Personal morality's limits are defined in normal cases by the constraints of interpersonal morality. And interpersonal morality's limits are likewise defined in abnormal cases by considerations of reflective rationality so overwhelmingly important that obeying a moral constraint would defeat the constraint's purpose, which is to help people flourish as reflectively rational beings in a social context.

[18] I thank Geoff Sayre-McCord for especially helpful discussions of this and related points.

TABLE 8.6
Defining the Interpersonal Strand's Countervailing Conditions

	Personal Strand	Interpersonal Strand
Generic Recognition Rule	Is X reflectively rational?	Is Y collectively rational?
Subject Matter	X = goals, in terms of how their pursuit affects the agent's character	Y = constraints on conduct as embedded in social structure
Fully Specified Recognition Rule	A goal is moral if pursuing it helps the agent to develop in a reflectively rational way	A constraint on conduct is moral if it works through social structure in a collectively rational way
	(subject to countervailing conditions)	(subject to countervailing conditions)

(Between the first row cells: "helps define" arrow. Between the Fully Specified Recognition Rule cells: "contingent links" circular arrows. Below: "helps define" crossing arrows.)

In passing, it can be obvious what to do when the library is on fire, or when one needs to double-park to save one's life, but it is not always obvious how to resolve conflicts. We saw that the two strands can conflict, and that they can resolve conflicts without outside arbitration, but it is also true that morality does not give us precisely articulated rules of conduct. That lack of precisely articulated guidance can be especially daunting in cases where morality's strands conflict. Real-world moral agents need to exercise judgment.

Chapter 2 argued that there can be underdetermined rational choice—cases in which it is rational to simply pick something and get on with one's life. Similarly, there may be cases of underdetermined moral agency—cases in which we cannot avoid violating one collectively rational constraint or another, or cases of such unique importance that we are not sure whether we are really bound by constraints that in normal cases are collectively rational. There is no handy rule by which we discern the bright line between emergency and nonemergency cases. Indeed, the bright line may not exist; the boundary between the two categories may instead be a sort of gray area in which there is no definite answer, never mind a definite procedure for identifying the answer. If there are cases in which it never becomes clear which course of action is morally best or morally required, then we have no choice but to pick something and get on with our lives as moral agents.

The other thing to say, again picking up on an earlier theme, is that legislators create bright lines when framing laws, and it can be moral for them to do so. For the sake of argument, suppose we abstract from morally justified constraints imposed on us by institutions. Imagine that, in this abstract situation, there is no definitive moral answer to the question of what we should do when we need to choose between killing one person and letting five people die. Even so, legislators can make sure the question has a definitive, albeit arbitrary, *legal* answer. An arbitrarily drawn bright legal line might then present itself to us as a morally justified constraint, justified because it serves the common good to have some bright line or other rather than none. Thus, not all moral constraints are timeless. They can be born with changing laws and social norms, and they can pass away.

CONCLUSIONS

This chapter's most important conclusions, and those in which I have the most confidence, were stated near the beginning. First, a moral theory can range over more than one subject matter. Second, a moral theory can incorporate more than one recognition rule. Third, a theory can be structurally open-ended, constituted by strands that leave room for adding further strands or for accepting that some of our moral knowledge may be irremediably inarticulate.

I then gave a substantive example of a two-stranded theory. The previous chapter adapts a constrained, nonmaximizing variant of the principle of utility to the task of assessing interpersonal constraints in terms of how they function when embedded in social structure. This chapter adapts a eudaimonist conception of ratio-

211

nality to the task of evaluating personal goals in terms of how they affect the agent. Moral dualism is the theory or partial theory that emerges when we apply this pair of principles to their respective subject matters.

We considered how conflict between the strands is resolved using conceptual resources internal to the two strands, thus showing how the two strands weave together to form a unified whole in the absence of an overarching principle of adjudication. Since the ultimate objective is to examine the degree to which being moral is coextensive with being rational, I isolated these two strands of morality in part because they have particularly interesting connections to rationality. The analysis permits the theory to be open-ended, which lets us explore the reconciliation of rationality and morality without first needing to produce an all-encompassing account of morality. Those who want to make the analysis of morality more complete can add other subject matters and apply other recognition rules, as necessary.[19]

At the action-guiding level, the content of moral dualism is not especially novel.[20] If it was really novel, that probably would be a good reason to reject it. The formal structure, though, is novel, or so it seems to me. It is a new way of doing moral theory. Also novel, I think, is the idea of identifying morality's interpersonal constraints in terms of how they actually function as embedded in existing social structures. Chapter 9 considers some of the more obvious objections to moral dualism. Among other things, it argues that moral dualism can accommodate the intuition that some of morality's demands are deontological in nature.

[19] If we do need a third strand, though, moral dualism's two strands conceivably might not be part of the most effective way of dividing the moral terrain into three parts. Incompleteness per se would not be a reason to abandon the two strands, but the emergence of a simpler alternative would be.

[20] In terms of substantive content, it may be near the truth to say moral dualism combines a Humean theory of justice with an Aristotelian theory of virtue.

CHAPTER 9

Objections and Replies

OF WHAT SORT OF PROOF IS MORAL DUALISM SUSCEPTIBLE?

A RECOGNITION RULE, when applied to an appropriate subject matter, embodies a sufficient condition for morality (barring countervailing conditions). Sometimes, though, I worry that there might not be *any* sufficient conditions. There are practical restrictions on what can count as a moral theory, and it may not be possible for a theory to operate within those practical restrictions and still be true. For example, there are only so many rules that beings like us could use as recognition rules for morals. Within that set of usable rules, there may await discovery a recognition rule that could never lead us astray. Another possibility, a disturbing one, is that they might all have counterexamples.

Attempts to construct counterexamples to moral theories usually consist not of showing that a theory is false but rather that it is controversial, that it diverges from commonsense morality. Having controversial implications is not as decisive a defect as having false implications, for even true theories have controversial implications. Nevertheless, to show that a theory is counterintuitive is to at least put a certain dialectical pressure on it. Other things equal, it would be better if the implications of one's theory were uncontroversially true.[1]

On the one hand, a proposed recognition rule for morals ought to support commonsense morality, more or less. If it does not—if it picks out a set of things having almost no overlap with commonsense morality—then it is not recognizing morality in any ordinary sense of the term. On the other hand, the rule must have a certain way of picking out elements of commonsense morality as moral,

---

[1] We have not discussed obligations to animals. Given the resources of moral dualism, it is easy to explain why we owe it to ourselves and to each other to respect our environment, but the question of what, if anything, we owe to animals is more difficult. I do not have an answer.

namely, by recognizing reasons to endorse them. The recognition rule has to support common sense, not just regurgitate it.

None of this is meant to suggest that there is a canonical form of commonsense morality. Commonsense morality varies from one culture to another. The dictates of either strand of moral dualism could vary from one culture to another, too. For example, a structurally embedded constraint that works well in one culture might not work well in another.

Of course, in any culture, some of commonsense morality's rules of conduct may be grounded in neither collective nor individual rationality nor in anything else. If so, then those commonsense rules of conduct do not warrant moral endorsement. And if parts of commonsense morality do not warrant endorsement as moral, then in that respect we have no reason to take those parts of commonsense morality seriously. A divergence between common sense and moral dualism in such a case would not weigh against moral dualism. Therefore, moral dualism leaves plenty of room to be critical of commonsense morality. According to moral dualism, the test of a thing's morality consists not in whether it coincides with commonsense intuition but rather in whether it is collectively or reflectively (depending on the subject matter) rational.

There may not be any way to prove that moral dualism is accurate or complete as a specification of our reasons for endorsement from a plural perspective. Indeed, it is not clear that much of anything can be proven at the level of moral foundations. "Of What Sort of Proof the Principle of Utility is Susceptible" is the title of Chapter 4 of Mill's *Utilitarianism* (1979; first published 1861). The fallacy-riddled proof that follows is prefaced by a remark that first principles cannot be proven, at least not by deductive argument. Simple observation might support first principles in some domains of inquiry, Mill says, but strictly speaking, "questions of ultimate ends do not admit of proof" (p. 34). Mill evidently had no illusions about the soundness of his argument, which leaves us to wonder why he bothered to offer it. Perhaps he felt obliged to try to give his theory a foundation in indubitable truth, even though he knew that the attempt would be futile. In any event, there is a lesson here for anyone, like myself, wanting to say something about morality's recognition rules.

The lesson is that we do not have to proceed, à la Descartes, by rejecting whatever we cannot prove true beyond all doubt. It is fine to begin with a subject matter that raises what we take to be moral questions and with an honest conjecture about how to answer them. The claim that we ought to reject what is not indubitably certain is itself a conjecture about proper scientific methodology, a conjecture that is hardly beyond reasonable doubt. Therefore, the Cartesian method of hyperbolic doubt fails to pass its own test.

Having formulated a conjecture, we have something to test against objections; we can reject it if it should prove untenable. This chapter tests moral dualism, in a trial by counterexample, as a conjecture about the nature of morality. The possible counterexamples I discuss are largely independent of each other. Accordingly, the different sections of this chapter are more or less self-contained. There is no particular thread of argument running through them.

To begin, one might see moral dualism as failing to find a place for deontological intuitions, and on that basis construct counterexamples illustrating moral dualism's counterintuitive implications. ("Imagine the town sheriff is urged to hang a man whom he knows to be innocent. According to moral dualism, the sheriff has to assess the rule against hanging the innocent by asking whether it serves the common good." You know the story.) The simplest response, also the most controversial, would have been to say, "So much the worse for deontology. Moral dualism ought not to fly in the face of common sense, but it has no obligation to mesh with rival theories." The trouble with this response, though, is that some deontological intuitions are rooted in common sense as well as in deontological theory. A second kind of response would involve making the theory more complete by applying a deontological recognition rule to a third subject matter (maxims, perhaps) to create a third strand. A third response, the one I favor, is proposed in the next section.

HOW TO ACCOMMODATE DEONTOLOGICAL INTUITIONS

Chapter 8 accused modern ethical theories of capturing only a fragment of the truth. I do not purport to have captured the whole truth myself. But at least moral dualism leaves room for its own incompleteness. Unlike standard versions of utilitarianism and deontology, it can accommodate more than one strand. If necessary, it can accommodate more than two. What would it take to make room for deontological intuitions? Do we need a third strand of morality, generated by applying a principle of universalizability to constraints one might legislate for oneself as a member of a kingdom of ends?

Probably not. Universalizability is a standard of rightness rather than a standard of goodness, so in that respect it is not on a par with collective or reflective rationality. It has a sometimes powerful claim on us as a standard of rightness precisely because it is well grounded. It is grounded in two ways. One kind of support for our commitment to universalizability derives from our commitment to collective rationality as grounds for endorsement (or criticism). This is why people take "What if everybody did that?" to be an important question. This aspect of our concern for universalizability points to real or imagined consequences—consequences of a kind that bear on our collective interests and thus fall within the province of the interpersonal strand.

Our commitment to universalizability has a second kind of support as well, which is why deontology is not a form of consequentialism. This second aspect of our commitment is grounded in personal integrity, where having integrity involves being true to ourselves and thus to our principles. (To test one's integrity is to test one's commitment to one's principles.) To say one should be willing to universalize the maxim of one's action is to say one should be willing to let one's actions stand as an example for others, which is a matter of principle in the most literal way. Like the notion of virtue, the notion of universalizability is not really action-guiding; it lacks the kind of content it would need to guide action. But matters of principle are matters of integrity, and matters of integrity are matters of virtue. So the second part of commonsense morality's commitment to universalizability falls within the domain of the personal strand, having to do with developing one's own character in such a way as to earn one's self-respect. This accords not only with common sense, but with much of the spirit of Kant's defense of deontology as well.

If these two proposals fail to exhaust the extent of our commitment to universalizability, then we may need a third strand to capture the residue of deontological intuition. But as far as I can see, the two strands of moral dualism combine to capture what is worth capturing in the commonsense commitment to universalizability. The theory as it stands may be incomplete in various ways, but it seems not guilty of a failure to capture deontology's most important insights.

People sometimes debate whether morality's imperatives are categorical or hypothetical. Some people say we are conscripts in the army of moral duty, while others say we have reason to be moral only if being moral appeals to our own interests and desires. Sometimes participants in the debate seem to talk past each other. One side says, "Morality does not tell us to keep our promises *if we want to*. It tells to keep our promises, period." The other side says, "But why should I listen? If keeping promises doesn't appeal to my interests and desires, then what other reason for keeping them could count as a reason for me?" Yet, it seems obvious that the form and substance of moral imperatives quite often is categorical. To take an example from moral dualism's interpersonal strand, a sign may say, "No Parking" rather than "If You Care about the Common Good, Park Somewhere Else." The imperative embedded in the morally justified parking rule is categorical. However, even when the form and substance of a moral imperative are categorical, the motivation to obey it can be hypothetical. A motorist may say, "It is illegal for me to park here. Indeed, parking here is categorically illegal in the sense that it is illegal whether or not I care about the common good. But as a matter of fact, I don't care, and I have no intention of obeying that law unless doing so is in my interest."

This is not to say moral motivation is *necessarily* hypothetical. As a reason for action, "because it's right" is not mine in the way my interests and desires are mine; however, it can become a reason for me if my existing interests and desires give me reason to try to internalize that new kind of reason for action (for example, if that is the kind of person I desire to be). If I am thereby motivated to internalize "because it's right" as a reason for action, then recognizing something as right will subsequently motivate me, whether or not doing what is right in a given situation has any further instrumental appeal to my interests and desires.

The "why be moral" question as interpreted here presupposes that morality has a point from a plural perspective. It is from a plural perspective that moral imperatives essentially have a point, which explains how moral imperatives can be, from a singular perspective, categorical. Precisely because being moral has a point from a plural perspective, it has an imperative force that is not contingent on whether being moral appeals to interests and desires we have from a singular perspective. We are indeed conscripts in the army of moral duty, notwithstanding the fact that, to become morally motivated, we have to volunteer.[2]

Like the notion of universalizability, the notion of virtue has a place in this theory. Also like universalizability, virtue's place is within the theory's existing strands. Virtue is an ordinary language term. It covers a variety of items related by family resemblance, and we cannot expect a philosophical analysis to track the evolving extension of the ordinary language term. Nevertheless, we capture the main reasons why common sense recognizes virtues as moral when we analyze the virtuous person as a person of reflectively rational disposition, self-disciplined by habitual recognition of collectively rational interpersonal constraints. By the same token, norms of praising and esteeming traits we call virtues are recognizable as moral insofar as such patterns of endorsement are collectively rational social structures, and also insofar as the endorsements themselves exemplify such virtues as magnanimity or fairness.

Of course, as noted earlier, constraints can work through social structures in collectively rational ways without having good results every time. Likewise, character traits we think of as virtuous occasionally lead to collectively irrational acts. Journalists protect the confidentiality of their sources, lawyers seek acquittal even for clients who privately admit guilt, priests do not report crimes confessed to them by parishioners, and so on. When virtuous people internalize these forms of discretion and loyalty, we should not be surprised if their subsequent actions occasionally turn out to be neither individually nor collectively rational.

MORALITY IN AN INSTITUTIONAL VACUUM

Letting the interpersonal strand range over social structure has the advantage of preventing the strand's impositions from being all-consuming in the way act-utilitarianism is all-consuming. It also has the advantage of yielding a recognition rule that turns on con-

---

[2] I owe this way of putting the point to Tamer Francis.

ditions that really matter in a concrete way. In contrast, when Thomas Nagel says the moral status of action-guiding principles depends on "some judgment about the collective result of everyone's following the principles" (1991, p. 41), we are left wondering why Nagel thinks it matters. What difference does it make, here and now, what the collective result would be in the imaginary case in which everyone follows the principles? Further, as Nagel is aware, it is hard to know exactly what we are being asked to imagine. For example, are we supposed to imagine a world in which everyone has an incentive to follow the principles, or are we supposed to imagine a world in which everyone follows principles despite having no incentive to do so?

When moral dualism asks whether social structures make us generally better off, it is not asking us to imagine a world that is unlike our own. Moral dualism asks people to notice how social structures around them are actually functioning. The question may not be easy, but at least it is relevant and relatively concrete. One might be tempted to think that there is not much social structure of any kind in an inner-city ghetto, and certainly not much that is making people better off. Nevertheless, over the last few centuries, life expectancy, especially that of the relatively poor, has risen by several decades, not as a consequence of changes in the gene pool but rather as a result of changes in society. In that respect, and in many others, a ghetto is not a state of nature. To learn what morality's interpersonal strand requires of people living in ghettos, or anywhere else, we look to social structures that are really there and really making people in general better off. What really is there, and making people better off, changes from place to place and time to time, but it remains the thing to look for.[3]

[3] If we do not know whether a social structure is making people in general better off, are we obligated to research the issue? Put it this way. First, there is a matter of objective rightness. Regarding traffic laws, we are obligated to stay within speed limits. We do not have an additional obligation to read the signs so that we know what the speed limits are; simply staying within the limits is enough. Similarly, we are not obligated to know which laws are morally justified; simply operating within their limits is enough. Second, there is a matter of being subjectively justified. As a matter of reflectively rational respect for others and for moral social structures, we make a good-faith effort to be aware of what moral social structures require. If in a particular situation we find we are less confident than we ought to be about our action's objective rightness, we may need to do some research.

Those who think of moral agents as atoms in the void may be disturbed by the idea that what morality demands of (or offers to) a person depends on the person's social context. They may be disturbed by the idea that morality cannot be fully understood (and indeed would have a different character) outside the social matrix in which a key part of morality is essentially embedded. Some readers have expressed such concerns by asking me to suppose no social structures are in place to make people willing and able to serve the common good. The interpersonal strand is oddly incomplete and oddly contingent on its face, they say, because it leaves us subject to no interpersonal constraints except those imposed on us by social structure. What about situations, real or imagined, where there is no social structure? In a state of nature, is everything permissible?

No, for two reasons. First, there remain matters of reflective rationality: matters of character. Even in the state of nature, we are subject to self-imposed constraints generated by the personal strand. The personal strand of morality can be demanding in a state of nature as well as in civil society.[4] Second, the absence of *formal* social structure does not imply an absence of all social structure. For example, as the apparatus of the state breaks down throughout central Europe, interactions within and between groups increasingly are governed by norms that no government has formally ratified. Informal norms are changing shape in ways that radically differ from one country to another, with radically different consequences.

Thus, the interpersonal strand is more complete than it looks, for its subject matter is not limited to formal social structures of civil society. It ranges over social structure in general, not just the sort of institutions that conjure up images of large gray buildings fronted by Roman columns. Even in the state of nature, there will be interpersonal relations. For example, if neither of us has yet attacked the other, then there is an informal but real and precious relation of nonaggression between us. Insofar as that relation con-

---

[4] Picking up on a thought from Chapter 3, if one has no time for ends beyond survival, this will undercut the motivational force of ends beyond survival. Nevertheless, although personal morality's motivational force is contingent, there will, even in a state of nature, still be moral issues of the kind discussed in Chapter 5, issues of integrity and questions about whether we are worthy of our own self-interest.

stitutes a social pattern that serves our common good, there is a moral constraint against disturbing it, according to my theory.

What about situations lacking even de facto social structures? What if we lack even the Lockean state of nature's uneasy truce? What if we find ourselves in the middle of a Hobbesian war? If there is not even an informal pattern of observing the peace on the part of others, then on what basis could one owe peace to them? If other people show no hesitation in firing the first shot, how could we owe it to them not to shoot back? Might we owe it to ourselves not to shoot back? Perhaps. In the Hobbesian jungle, where the other person has already fired the first shot, not shooting back is a matter of reflective self-regard if it is a matter of morality at all.

Looking at the situation in terms of the interpersonal strand, though, it remains the case that, if for some reason I attack you, then the state of nonaggression we previously enjoyed no longer exists, which means you are no longer bound by it. If my attack observes no constraints, then you may defend yourself by whatever methods you prefer. (In civil society, this is not true, for in civil society we have structures in place that serve the common good if and when they take such matters out of your hands.) If you cannot bring about the existence or preservation of a relation of nonaggression, then you are not bound by it either.[5]

Is it possible that morality's interpersonal strand could permit you to launch a preemptive first strike, destroying or subduing potential aggressors before they can fire the first shot? Presumably not. As long as no one has in fact fired the first shot, the structure of de facto peace is in place, forbidding anyone, including you, from firing the first shot. In the real world, of course, the facts of the case may not be neat and tidy. For example, it not always clear whether the other party has already broken the peace. If you turn around and see your neighbor, with whom you have just had a heated argument, pointing a gun at your head, it seems reasonable to assume that war has already broken out, even though your neighbor has not yet pulled the trigger. In that case, you can shoot

[5] What if Kate shot first and you shot back, and now the war has begun in earnest? Does that mean the two of you are now on a moral par, since neither of you is under any obligation to preserve a nonexistent peace? No. If Kate fired first, then Kate is the one who failed to meet a moral obligation, notwithstanding the fact that her failure had the consequence of obliterating the structure that imposed the obligation.

first, reasonably believing that it is not you who is breaking the peace. You might be wrong, though. Your neighbor might be aiming over your shoulder at a rabid animal that is about to attack you. In that case, you have misinterpreted the situation, for the structure of de facto peace that served your common good was in fact still in place, obligating you to hold your fire. You cannot be blamed for breaking the peace, for you had good reason to believe it had already been broken. Nevertheless, this story illustrates the point that one cannot in good conscience launch a preemptive first strike without hard evidence that the other party is already committed to firing the first shot.

In a state of nature, no formal social structures are in place to maintain law and order. We have to admit that the bare observation that truce is morally required may not *motivate* those who do not recognize peaceful commerce as being in their personal interest.[6] To voice this as an objection, though, would be to misunder-

---

[6] In passing, it is interesting that Thomas Hobbes considered it a law of nature (his third law) that one should keep covenants (*Leviathan*, 1962, chap. 15). Why would an alleged egoist like Hobbes think this? Is the third law a mere counsel of self-interest? Or, should we read the third law as positing nonegoistic moral obligation sui generis? Consider a Hobbesian alternative. In the state of nature, we grant for argument's sake, there is a Hobbesian right of nature, which rules out obligations that can interfere with self-preservation. Thus, where one cannot trust others to keep agreements, one is not required to keep them oneself. But what about when keeping contracts is safe? For instance, suppose your partner has already performed as agreed. Or suppose an enforcer exists who will catch her if she reneges, but will not catch you if you renege. Should you keep your end of the contract? Yes, because by hypothesis it is safe to keep the contract, so the kind of danger that could defeat your obligation has not materialized. This is why a contractual obligation, if it exists, is not overridden by the imperative to preserve oneself.

What explains the existence of the obligation in the first place? Hobbes suggests that it goes against self-interest to breach a contract when the other party's performance has been ensured by the sovereign, but this is hardly a necessary truth. Even if it were true, it is not even the right *kind* of explanation of a contract's moral force. For one thing, it obviously does not even address the question of whether one *ought* to breach contracts if and when it is in one's interest to do so.

To explain the obligation itself, we would do better to suppose that the Hobbesian right of nature, in addition to precluding the existence of *obligations* that would interfere with self-preservation, also precludes the existence of *rights* that would interfere with self-preservation. To renege when compliance is safe is to do something warlike in an otherwise peaceful setting. One is morally constrained by

stand how motivation enters the picture. A social structure's morality does not turn on whether it motivates literally everyone to keep the peace. Rather, its morality turns on how it compares to available alternatives in terms of motivating people in general to keep the peace. For example, if people are prepared to shoot back, that creates an incentive not to shoot first.[7] In the state of nature, that may be the best that people can do to keep the peace. If the truce generally improves opportunities for people to flourish as reflectively rational beings, and generally improves opportunities in a nonexploitative way, then according to moral dualism, it obliges would-be model citizens and would-be exploiters alike, whether or not it motivates a particular person in a particular case.

Kurt Baier believes that, since morality is a cooperative enterprise, there is nothing to say about our reasons to be moral when others are not being moral. He asks rhetorically "Why should I be moral *when no one else is*?" (1978, p. 250). This is a different question from the question of why a person should be moral when everyone else is being moral. Baier (p. 251) urges us to be clear about which question we are asking. He believes there can be no answer to the first question (p. 250).

I disagree in two ways. First, there can be reason to comply with personal morality regardless of whether other people are being immoral. The personal strand has normative force even if no one else is moved by it. Second, regarding interpersonal morality, Baier's rhetorical question suggests that when other people fail to be moral, morality stays the same but "I" stop having reasons to take it seriously. In other words, morality's interpersonal constraints remain constant while our reasons to comply with those constraints vary. However, moral dualism tells us that the constraints themselves vary. When everyone else stops cooperating, there is no longer a pattern of cooperation in place, and therefore there is no social structure obligating us to cooperate. Analogously, morality requires one not to shoot first, because as long as no one shoots first, there is a de facto peace that serves the common good. In that

---

social structures conducive to self-preservation, and one is constrained even when one judges that the prospective gains are worth the risk. Therefore, we have no right to renege on contracts when keeping them would be safe. (For an alternative explanation of the obligation to keep covenants, see Gauthier, 1986, chap. 6.)

[7] Christopher Morris (unpublished, chap. 6) discusses several mechanisms by which groups maintain social control without resorting to state intervention.

respect, and at least for the moment, interpersonal constraints are in place. But when other people start shooting, interpersonal morality does not forbid shooting back, because in that case there is, by hypothesis, no structure of de facto peace, and therefore no peace to be disturbed when we return fire.

Now, there may be an obligation to try to bring moral social structures into existence, but what would be the source of such an obligation? At first glance, it seems that such an obligation would have to come from the personal strand or from some third strand; it could not come from the interpersonal strand. Why not? Because, from the perspective of the interpersonal strand, we cannot be obligated to bring a structure into existence by the structure itself, for the structure and the obligations it would impose do not yet exist. However, we should not assume that the interpersonal strand is silent on obligations to bring better social structures into existence, because such obligations can be embedded in already existing structures. For example, suppose there already exists a grass-roots movement to make the armed forces more accountable for the environmental impact of their military exercises, and let us suppose that such accountability would serve the common good. If others are doing their part to bring a mutually advantageous and nonexploitative social structure into existence, then there already exists a social pattern that serves the common good, or will if the activities constituting the pattern achieve their end. This can create an obligation to use opportunities to be part of the pattern, carrying our own weight in that mutually advantageous endeavor.

This leaves open questions regarding who is to take the first step. Such questions may not have a general answer. Perhaps no one has a general *interpersonal* obligation to take the first step. (We may as a matter of reflective rationality be committed to occasionally taking the first step, insofar as doing so gives us more to live for.) In any event, if no one in fact takes the first step, then that is that; others do not become obligated to follow suit, either. There is no end to the various steps we could take to make the world a better place, if only we noticed such opportunities and if only we could reasonably believe that others would follow our example. But the supposition that it would be good to take a particular step, combined with the supposition that no one has taken such a step, do not add up to the conclusion that someone has failed to meet a moral obligation.

When trying to bring about social change, we may have recourse to institutions that embody procedures for social change, like electoral processes. If such avenues are unavailable or unsuitable, we may have to work outside the system. If someone like Martin Luther King comes along to take the lead, such a person's leadership can generate an informal grass-roots structure that itself becomes part of our social framework and obligates us to join in the effort to improve our social framework.

Here is a more prosaic example. There is a constraint against littering whether or not rules and conventions against littering have emerged. If other people are not littering, then there is a de facto social structure imposing an interpersonal moral constraint against littering. If others are littering with impunity, then the moral reason not to litter has more to do with how it affects oneself than with how it affects others. It is a matter of reflective rationality. Kate loses respect for people who litter, and if she litters, she then becomes one of the people for whom she loses respect. As others begin trying to put a stop to littering, Kate comes to owe it to them as well as to herself to at least not be part of the problem.[8]

Perhaps the structure of interpersonal obligation can extend even to situations where the interests at stake include anticipated interests of people not yet born. Stable conventions regarding the sensible use of natural resources, for example, are plausibly viewed as social structures that serve the common good by serving the members of each generation in turn.

The upshot of this section is that the interpersonal strand's subject matter is broad—broad enough even to cover relations like truce in the state of nature. The point is not that people hypothetically or tacitly consent to truce but rather that truce serves the common good, and the person who breaks the truce obliterates a social structure that had previously obligated her not to make war against others and others not to make war against her.

Finally, to avoid any misunderstanding about the point of this section, let me stress that I am not using a "state of nature"

---

[8] Typically, the rest of one's group, as a whole, sends mixed signals. There will be patterns of interpersonal constraint, but there will not be universal compliance with those constraints. On the subject of public goods, I argue elsewhere (Schmidtz, 1991, chap. 7) that when faced with mixed signals, one owes it to the group to contribute one's share of total actual contributions. Further contributions might then be required as a matter of reflective self-regard.

thought experiment to determine moral dualism's actual implications in the real world. This section responds to objections presented to me in terms of the state of nature, but moral dualism in no way derives from contemplation of the state of nature or any other hypothetical scenario. Rather, the point of the exercise is to consider whether moral dualism would have counterintuitive implications in limiting cases, such as the case in which social structure decays to the point of becoming a state of nature. Although moral dualism says that one strand of morality is rooted in social structures that function well in the real world, the theory does not preclude our asking what its implications would be under other conditions.

If a constraint would serve the common good in hypothetical circumstances, then we can say that the constraint *would be* moral in those circumstances. However, I am not committing the error (I would consider it an error) of saying that if a constraint *would* serve the common good in hypothetical circumstances, then it *is* a moral constraint in our actual circumstances. By the same token, we can speculate about what a morally perfect society would be like, but the fact that we would be under a particular constraint in a morally perfect society does not imply that we are under any such moral constraint in the real world. Morality's interpersonal constraints come to us through structures that function well in our own societies.

Should a Moral Theory Be a Decision Procedure?

As discussed in Chapter 8, moral dualism's two strands help to flesh each other out when we put them together because the two recognition rules identify each other's countervailing conditions. In that respect, they make each other whole, or nearly so. A unified theory, though, is not the same as a decision procedure. At the action-guiding level, morality inevitably is somewhat rough. Morality's recognition rules are tests of morality within their ranges, but the things they recognize as belonging to morality's action guide cannot be presumed to guide us in an algorithmic fashion.[9]

[9] As Sarah Broadie (1991, p. 60) notes, Aristotle seems to say precise rules of conduct (and also, I would suppose, precise rules of recognition) are not possible.

We touched on this subject near the end of Chapter 8. This section elaborates.

Part I cautioned against looking for an algorithm for rational choice. Similar cautions are warranted here. No decision procedure can be guaranteed to track all and only that which we have reason to endorse as moral. One might suppose this claim depends on a controversial objectivism about morality. Surely, one might think, there must be a procedure simple enough for us to follow in a mechanical fashion and thereby assure ourselves of being subjectively justified. And surely being subjectively justified is all that morality can ask of a person. But as Chapter 1 explained, the idea that a hiker's chosen path is subjectively justified presupposes an objective end toward which the chosen path is subjectively justified as a means. Being subjectively justified is no guarantee against painful failure. No decision procedure is guaranteed to serve our end, whether our end is to help others, to preserve our integrity, or to comply with the rules of moral institutions. The thing about being a moral agent is, we have to exercise judgment. There is no algorithm to interpose between us and our responsibilities.

Personal morality is more about the morally good life than about morally right decisions in particular cases. It goes beyond what one can do in a mechanical way. The interpersonal strand's action guide is more likely to be something we could follow in a relatively mechanical way. However, the set of rules embedded in social structures, some of which are quite informal, will not be fully articulate. The rules are not always clear enough to follow in a mechanical way.

Moreover, however clear the interpersonal strand's rules of conduct may be, following them in a mechanical fashion would still be problematic, because the rules can come into conflict. Chapter 8 explained how there can be times when, in the face of conflict between the two strands, it is right to break the rules of interpersonal morality. But no formula can tell us when such a time has come.

T. H. Irwin (1993, p. 326) says Broadie attributes to Aristotle a more extreme skepticism than he actually professes, a skepticism that involves rejecting general rules altogether. According to Irwin, Aristotle thought general rules were fine, so long as they were not expected to decide every case in algorithmic fashion. I agree. I take issue only with Irwin's interpretation of Broadie. The passages he cites are not convincing as evidence that Broadie takes a more extreme position.

This is true even in simple cases. To know when a parking law that serves the common good qua ongoing social structure has gone beyond its moral mandate, a person needs to have a sense of when circumstances are abnormal, and when the consequences have become overwhelmingly important. We find it obvious that morality does not forbid double-parking in order to save lives. It is obvious not because we looked it up in a recipe book for moral decision making, but rather because we have enough experience to know that, when lives are at stake, parking laws do not have their normal moral authority. Children seem to go through a stage of overestimating the moral authority of social structures, treating rules as absolutes. (At least, they are aghast when other people break them.) As they gain experience, they gain a different perspective on the nature and significance of rules.[10] With luck, they come to appreciate that there can be rules with limited but still genuine moral authority.

Moral conflicts are not experienced as sudden failures of one's algorithm, nor as uncertainty about which algorithm is the right one to use. Utilitarianism in particular, and deontology to a lesser extent, are sometimes interpreted as saying the moral life is a life spent consistently deploying a decision procedure for moral action. However, no one really lives that way, and there is neither moral nor rational reason why anyone should.

My utilitarian colleagues tend to be among the most moral people I know. However, their morality is bound up with their integrity and self-respect, with their respect and concern for others, and with their respect for institutions that serve the common good. Stretching things a bit, we could even say their morality lies in their concern for general welfare. What we cannot say, though, is that their morality lies in their systematic adherence to a utilitarian decision procedure. None of them systematically adheres to any such procedure, and they understand that it would do no good to try.

One further thought about our lack of a decision procedure: People disagree about which institutions serve the common good. Even if everyone were to conscientiously assess institutions by asking whether they serve the common good, this would not guaran-

---

[10] Jeffrey Olen says that doing "the right thing doesn't matter nearly as much as most philosophers seem to think" (1988, p. 117). Honor and decency, rather than following right rules, constitute the heart of being moral (pp. 121–24). Adults may find Olen's claim intuitively plausible, but it seems there is a stage at which children would not. At a certain stage, children are obsessed by rules.

tee consensus. Moral dualism holds that an institution's morality depends on whether it serves the common good, not on whether we agree that it does so. Moral dualism implies that we must frequently decide whether to endorse an institution on the basis of information that is inconclusive, but that implication is not a theoretical flaw. It is a simple fact of life.

MORAL CONFLICT: REALITY OR THEORETICAL ARTIFACT?

Some readers may still suspect that the moral conflict I have described, and which seems to be part of what precludes our developing a decision procedure for moral agency, is not real. It is, one might claim, an artifact gratuitously produced by moral dualism when it postulates more than one recognition rule. Could that be so? Does the possibility of conflict exist only because moral dualism begins with two different recognition rules? As a matter of fact, no. This section shows how conflicts arise within the framework of theories that begin with a single recognition rule.

It would be natural to suppose that if the two strands began with *identical* recognition rules, they could not yield conflicting guidance; there could not be situations where one strand required an action forbidden by the other. But there could. For example, the principle of utility says X is moral if and only if X maximizes utility. If we let X range over personal conduct, taking external as well as internal effects into account, we get a recognition rule identical to that of act-utilitarianism. How would utilitarian social structures come into conflict with utilitarian personal conduct?[11] For one thing, utilitarian social structures are responses to normal cases. They do not anticipate all of the peculiar contingencies a utilitarian agent might face in a particular case. The prohibitions embedded in these structures may rule out actions that would maximize utility in particular cases. But it is unavoidable (and by no means undesirable) that they address general and normal rather than particular and peculiar cases. Because we do not say the rules are conducive to the good in every case, exceptions will not be

[11] Human agents often act on the understanding that their chosen course of action is their best available alternative. Institutions cannot optimize in any similarly straightforward way. Institutions can only induce patterns, some of which may serve the common good. For the sake of argument, though, this section treats as unproblematic the idea of an institution maximizing utility.

counterexamples. A real counterexample would have to show that a constraint works through social structure to produce suboptimal results in general.

The second reason why utilitarian institutions can conflict with act-utilitarian personal morality is more interesting. It has to do with the fact that utilitarian institutions are not formulated with *utilitarian agents* in mind.[12] If utilitarian institutional constraints hinder genuinely utilitarian agents, we should not be at all surprised, for the rules of utilitarian institutions are formulated not to facilitate the projects of utilitarians but rather to channel the projects of primarily self-interested agents in such a way that even the projects of primarily self-interested agents end up making the people around them better off. Municipal parking regulations, for example, have utility not by responding to the rare driver who wants to park in a way that serves the common good but rather by responding to typical drivers looking for convenient parking spots.

By the lights of the principle of utility, the fact that a social structure would maximize utility in some thought experiment involving idealized utilitarian agents is irrelevant. If institutions are going to maximize utility, they will have to work through agents, which means they have to work through real-world agents. They will be constituted not so they *would* have utility, if only agents were willing to serve the common good. Rather, utility-maximizing social structures are the sort of things that actually have utility, and they have their utility in virtue of doing what they can to give agents reasons to act in ways that serve the common good.

The principle of utility as applied to social structure picks out those structures that minimize conflict between the interests of individuals and the interests of the community. But the point is to minimize the conflict for real agents rather than for their idealized utilitarian counterparts.[13] Thus, conflict between utilitarian per-

---

[12] To speak of institutions being formulated in a certain way is not to suggest they are all products of conscious design. Some are products of social evolution. Institutions like the family, say, were not designed at all, and yet we can still ask whether they have utility.

[13] Having said that utilitarian institutions are not formulated with utilitarian agents in mind, we should add that they are not formulated with utilitarian administrators in mind, either. Institutions that have utility in the real world are those least vulnerable to abuse by the people who run them. Of course, this point applies only to social structures that have administrators. Many informal social structures do not, which can be a point in their favor.

sonal morality and utilitarian social structure will be normal rather than exceptional.

So long as we acknowledge that morality can range over more than one subject matter, we must acknowledge that morality's action guide can have different parts and that these parts can come into conflict. The possibility of conflict does not turn on whether morality incorporates more than one recognition rule. Indeed, a utilitarian personal morality often would be more in conflict with a utilitarian interpersonal strand than would the personal strand of moral dualism.

Because moral agents do not act in an institutional vacuum, they are subject to moral constraints embedded in social structure. Because agents are subject to moral constraints embedded in social structure, they do not have unlimited license to act on the basis of their own utilitarian calculations. This is so even if both strands are grounded in the principle of utility.

In passing, we can conclude from this discussion that (unless we can rule out even the bare possibility that morality ranges over more than one subject matter) modern utilitarian theories *do not follow* from the principle of utility. The theory discussed in this section assumes that the principle of utility is the sole recognition rule underlying all of morality. Even so, the action guide that emerged is nothing like the action guides typically proposed by twentieth-century utilitarians. Morality's action guide could not collapse into act-utilitarianism even if *both* strands began with the principle of utility.

Does Moral Dualism Demand Too Much?

There are two reasons to characterize interpersonal constraints embedded in social structure as a subject matter of moral inquiry. First, focusing on that subject helps us devise a theory that directly addresses the morality of institutions and that does not try to say what morality requires of agents in abstraction from their actual social circumstances. According to moral dualism, agents are not obligated by abstract considerations of what rules would maximize utility if they were perfectly enforced or if everyone obeyed them. Rather, agents are obligated to respect existing social structures that are serving the common good in the agent's actual social context.

Second, when we use collective rationality as a recognition rule for that subject matter, the result is that collective rationality constrains agents from the outside in rather than the inside out. Moral dualism is unlike act-utilitarianism in that respect. According to act-utilitarianism, the principle of utility is supposed to be adopted as an action-guiding principle, imposed on one's actions from the inside. Some theorists say that utilitarianism demands too much of moral agents. They might be right; we do not have to settle that here. More to the point, such theorists might also worry that, because moral dualism's interpersonal strand begins with something like the principle of utility, it, too, must be overly demanding.

Moral dualism, however, uses the principle of collective rationality to assess *externally* imposed constraints, and externally imposed interpersonal constraints can be collectively rational only if they are relatively circumspect. Social structures serve the common good not by demanding too much but rather by doing what they can to arrange incentives and opportunities so that people are willing and able to act in ways that make each other better off.

Therefore, moral dualism's picture of the morality of institutionally embedded constraints is not vulnerable to the objection, sometimes brought against utilitarian morality, that it is excessively demanding. Bernard Williams has asked, "How can a man, as a utilitarian agent, come to regard as one satisfaction among others, and a dispensable one, a project or attitude round which he has built his life, just because someone else's projects have so structured the causal scene that that is how the utilitarian sum comes out?" (Smart and Williams 1973, p. 116). I have no answer to Williams's question, and I would not deny that the price of being a utilitarian *agent* may be as high as Williams suspects. The point here, though, is that utilitarian social structures neither ask for nor expect such sacrifice. Rather, they structure the causal scene in a way that minimizes opportunities to sacrifice other people's projects to one's own and creates conditions in which helping other people is rewarding. As Chapter 5 argued, respect and concern for others can be, but need not be, self-sacrificing. Moral structures do what they can to produce conditions in which respect and concern for others is not self-sacrificing.

Utilitarian social structures do not demand that we sacrifice every waking moment of our lives for the common good. Typically, they demand no more than that we seek peaceful and constructive ways of pursuing our own good. Thus, the interpersonal strand is less demanding than the principle of utility applied to personal conduct would be. This is one advantage of working through social structures rather than applying the principle of utility directly to personal conduct. The interpersonal strand does not demand too much.

Does Moral Dualism Demand Enough?

The other side of the coin is that moral dualism's personal strand may not seem demanding enough. The reflective rationality that motivates a search for goals worth living for also tends to motivate respect for the collectively rational social structures that create opportunities for individuals to flourish as reflectively rational agents. As Chapter 5 admitted, though, reflective commitments to oneself could give life meaning without readily translating into a concern for morality's interpersonal constraints. Human psychology being what it is, the desire for meaning has many ways of translating into action. Chapter 4 claimed that if a pursuit makes us feel we are doing something important, then, as a matter of fact, it has given us something to live for. For some people, an isolated life spent collecting stamps can be meaningful. For many people, a desire for meaning translates into a desire to be a force for good in one's community. For others, becoming a mafia assassin gives life meaning. (The mafia is a community of a sort.) It seems I must admit that all of these things *conceivably* could pass as moral so far as morality's personal strand is concerned.

In fact, I do admit this. To be sure, assassinating others would be difficult to reconcile with reflective rationality. Nevertheless, the tendency for personal morality to motivate an appreciation of interpersonal morality is admittedly just that—a tendency. If there are cases in which being an assassin would be reflectively rational, would this refute a theory that proposed reflective rationality as morality's ultimate recognition rule? As a matter of fact, it would, but the theory refuted would not be moral dualism. Admittedly, the personal strand by itself does not demand enough. It does not even address, at least not directly, the issue of what we owe to others. That is why I do not propose it as the whole of morality. Moral dualism says reflective rationality is *among* morality's recognition rules, which is not the same thing. The strand of morality that forbids being a mafia assassin, and forbids it for the right reason, is a different strand.

Having said that the personal strand does not demand enough, though, I do not want anyone to think it is not very demanding within its own range of application. On the contrary, the self-imposed constraints under which reflectively rational agents operate are typically *more* stringent than constraints imposed by collectively rational institutions. Moral institutions typically demand less from people in general than particular people might morally demand from themselves. For example, it may serve the common good for tort law not to hold us responsible for accidents we cause through no fault of our own. Better to leave damages where they lie. Tort law generally does not treat causal responsibility as sufficient for legal responsibility, and probably this is as it should be. Nevertheless, being causally responsible often is enough to make us feel personally responsible. Taking ourselves seriously as moral agents involves taking responsibility for our actions even when responsibility could not rightly be thrust upon us.

Both strands make vital contributions to morality's action guide. Why is there a constraint against being a mugger? Typically, becoming a mugger is one of the most irrational things a person could do, but it is irrational in part because it cuts against *interpersonal* morality and thus (to the extent that one's fellow citizens disapprove of muggers) it cuts one off from one's community. This is so even if one never gets caught, for one would be cut off psychologically even if one's friends and family never noticed that one was cut off. So, it is interesting that even when we are talking about the personal strand, trying to explain why it rules out being a mugger, the interpersonal constraint enters the picture.

Conversely, why is there a constraint against breaking promises? Because breaking promises does not serve the common good? That counts for something, but surely another reason not to break promises has to do with personal integrity. A promise is morally constraining because when people create that sort of bond, they create new ways of making each other better off. But since the structure emerged through the actual consent of the group's members, keeping promises is a matter of integrity as well. We have, if you will, an obligation to ourselves to be as good as our word. It is part and parcel of taking ourselves seriously. Many constraints are grounded in both strands, and we miss aspects of their morality if we look only at one strand. I would not defend either strand as a self-contained moral theory.

The question for moral dualism concerns how well the *combination* of strands tracks commonsense intuition. Where it does not track, we need to look hard at the possibility that our intuitions are ungrounded. If intuition's divergence from my theory proves well-grounded, we will need to identify grounds for the divergence and incorporate them, either in the form of a new recognition rule or a new subject matter (or both). Or, if it turns out that the theory prohibits something whose permissibility is well-grounded, then something in the theory may need to be removed.

Morality in an Immoral Community

The previous section claimed that becoming a mugger typically would be irrational, in part because it would cut against interpersonal morality and thus would cut one off from one's community, at least insofar as one's fellow citizens disapprove of mugging. The fact that the last statement required qualification, though, points to a practical problem and perhaps a theoretical problem as well.

Suppose one's community consists of a street gang that practices drive-by shootings as a form of recreation. The problem is that psychological and social pressures to belong to a larger community do not necessarily give us reasons to be moral. It depends on the nature of the larger community. William Galston says, "If a community is notably imperfect, citizens who shape themselves in its image and devote themselves to its service will undergo a kind of moral deformation" (1991, p. 218). The question is whether moral dualism has the resources to characterize this deformation. An obedient citizen of Nazi Germany complies with all of its social structures, and therefore with all of its moral social structures, too. Is such a citizen above reproach by the lights of moral dualism?

Let me respond by setting aside moral dualism for a moment and considering a different theory. T. M. Scanlon (1982, p. 111) says morality is a set of rules of action that no one could reasonably reject. On this view, justifiability to others is not merely a consequence of being moral; it is the criterion of being moral. Morality so construed connects to rationality in an interesting way;

when we feel others *could* reasonably object to a choice, the feeling counts against the choice's rationality, insofar as such feelings tend to trigger the psychological defense mechanisms that compromise the reliability of our belief-forming processes. This is not an analytic truth. It is a contingent claim about a pervasive feature of human nature. For better or worse, the psychological reality is that we typically want very much to be able to justify ourselves to others. As Scanlon notes, "People are willing to go to considerable lengths, involving quite heavy sacrifices, in order to avoid admitting the unjustifiability of their actions and institutions" (p. 117).

Unfortunately, the psychological reality is that the pressure we actually feel is to justify ourselves to the people around us in whatever terms they actually accept. There is no similar pressure to justify ourselves in terms that no one could reasonably reject. Part of the problem with Scanlon's theory (that morality is a set of rules of action no one could reasonably reject) is that everything seems to turn on how we define 'reasonably'. What makes this theoretical license especially disturbing is that, as long as the people close to us accept our justifications, it is so very easy to dismiss as unreasonable those who reject them.[14]

The desire to "avoid admitting the unjustifiability of their actions" can be crippling when it gets out of control, for it is one of the main reasons why people try to cover up their failings, and why they become dishonest in the process. It is definitely a threat to integrity. Reflectively rational people keep their desire to justify themselves to others under control. But then, why do we care about justifying ourselves to others in the first place? One reason is that being able to justify ourselves to others is a condition of our real selves being part of something bigger than ourselves. And being part of something bigger gives us more to live for. So we have a genuine and explicable stake in being able to justify ourselves publicly. Why not lie when you will not be caught? Because it will compromise the extent and depth of your honest rapport with others, whether or not they ever find out that you lied.

Still, the need to belong that pushes us into communities need not push us into being moral. We might seize on immoral means of insinuating ourselves into a community. We might misrepresent ourselves, for example. Worse still, whether the push to belong

---

[14] I thank Amber Carpenter for helpful discussion.

translates into a push to be moral depends on the nature of the community into which we end up being pushed. Street gangs offer community of a sort. If one's community is evil enough, then the psychological pressure to become part of something bigger than oneself can work against rather than with moral motivation. Our desire to justify ourselves to others is not necessarily a motivation to be moral.

Neither will justifiability to others suffice as a criterion of morality per se. Why not? Because even if it is true that morality is a set of rules of action that we could justify to others, this tells us little about the content of those rules of action. Having been told that morality is a set of rules we could justify to others, we should ask, "Justify ourselves to others? In terms of what?" We cannot say we should be able to justify ourselves to others in *moral* terms; as a claim about morality's content, that would be circular. Scanlon's account of morality may be correct as far as it goes, but to gain a real understanding of morality's content, we need to look beyond it.

That is where moral dualism could be brought in. It sets out conditions that support moral endorsement, thereby setting out conditions in terms of which we can justify ourselves to others. In answer to the question "In terms of what are we supposed to be able to justify ourselves," moral dualism's answer is "In terms of reflective or collective rationality, depending on the subject matter." And saying that being moral is a matter of seeking to be rationally justified in those ways is a noncircular and, I think, quite plausible account of morality and moral motivation. Moral dualism is an alternative to Scanlon's contractualism, but it need not be seen as contradicting it. Indeed, one could read moral dualism as putting some badly needed flesh on the bare bones of Scanlon's proposal.[15]

This brings us back to the issue with which this section began. When a group adopts a policy of "ethnic cleansing" or prescribes drive-by shootings as a way for boys to prove their manhood, does moral dualism provide any basis for criticizing members who internalize and follow such norms? Yes it does. According to moral dualism, for a person whose community is evil, it remains the case

[15] See Samuel Freeman (1991) and William N. Nelson (1990, chap. 5) for interesting suggestions about how to develop and extend T.M. Scanlon's (1982) contractualism.

that being moral involves respecting social structures that, by non-exploitative methods, make people generally better off within their range of influence. If Kate knows that a social structure's range of influence extends beyond her community, then for Kate to have grounds for endorsing the social structure as moral, she must have grounds for endorsing it from a perspective that extends beyond her community in a similar way. Moral dualism formulates recognition rules in accordance with reasons for endorsement from a plural perspective. In formulating recognition rules, though, it does not look to possibly vicious collective ends that may happen to define a particular group. It looks to general notions of means-end rationality that, when applied to appropriate subject matters, give us reasons for endorsement from a perspective encompassing all of those whose interests we know to be at stake.

Chapter 7 suggested that a group cannot be condemned simply on the grounds that its ends are parochial. For example, a family cannot be condemned merely because it gives special attention to its own children. From a more cosmopolitan perspective, encompassing not only the group but also those with whom the group interacts, we can endorse parochial attachments that make people generally better off by nonexploitative methods. Street gangs, though, do not make even their own members generally better off. And their methods are hardly nonexploitative.

We may draw two conclusions about the situation facing people growing up in an immoral community. First, whether the desire to fit into one's community is a reason to be moral is a matter of circumstance. The psychological and social pressures to conform, which generate reasons to be moral in a more hospitable environment, could generate reasons to be the opposite of moral if one is growing up in Hitler's Germany, or Stalin's Soviet Union, or in a ghetto ruled by street gangs. Our need to belong and to justify ourselves to others is only contingently a reason to be moral. This is, I think, simply telling it like it is. Second, although moral motivation is contingent on social circumstance, morality itself is not contingent in the same way, at least not according to moral dualism. What makes people in general better off varies with social circumstance, but social circumstances are invariably assessed according to whether they make people in general better off by non-exploitative means. In the limit, circumstances may approximate an institutional moral vacuum, in which case one's obligations (*within* the immoral group) would be like those discussed earlier.

Is Moral Dualism Radically Incomplete?

Moral dualism has two strands, both teleological, both modern. Although the theory is thoroughly teleological, it still finds, within each strand, a place for threads of deontology. Although it is thoroughly modern, it still finds a place for threads of Aristotelian virtue theory.

The theory as it now stands may appear notably incomplete because it seems to say that we have no obligations to others beyond those imposed on us by morally justified social structures. The subject of what we owe to others is addressed directly by the interpersonal strand and indirectly through the personal strand's implications concerning the internal effects of treating other people well or poorly. Maybe these ways of addressing the issue of what we owe to others are good enough; maybe not. In any event, even in a state of nature, moral dualism has plenty to say about what we owe to others, in terms of interpersonal constraints imposed on us by our social context and also in terms of requirements of integrity and other-regard that we impose on ourselves from within. If the two strands say less than a moral theory ought to say about what we owe to others, then the addition of a third strand (or a reformulation of existing strands) might be in order.

Chapter 1 asked whether new forms of normative force can emerge from humble beginnings in means-end reasoning with respect to given ends. Chapters 2 through 5 argued that self-imposed constraint, moderation of desire and aspiration, critical reflection on one's goals, and concern and respect for others can indeed emerge, rationally emerge, in beings like us. Chapters 6 through 9 argued for a particular conception of morality and of the moral perspective. Chapter 10 asks how reasons to endorse something as moral come to be reasons a particular agent cares about, that is, how embracing those reasons serves a person's ends.

PART III

RECONCILIATION

*

Why Be Moral?

KAVKA'S ANALYTICAL FRAMEWORK

IN ONE OF MY FAVORITE articles on the "why be moral" question, Gregory Kavka (1985) says the project of reconciling morality and self-interest has four dimensions.

1. The *audience* dimension, as the name suggests, concerns the argument's intended audience. Is the argument addressed to philosophy professors? Philosophy students? Western civilization? (Could Western civilization constitute an audience?)

2. The *agent* dimension concerns the class of agents for whom the argument is supposed to reconcile rationality and morality. The audience dimension defines who the argument speaks to, whereas the agent dimension defines who it speaks about. Thus, agent and audience dimensions need not coincide. If I spoke to an audience of philosophy professors about Thrasymachus's reasons to be moral, the extent of the overlap between agent and audience would be an open question.

3. The *social* dimension concerns the social context in which being moral is supposed to be rational. Under what conditions is it rational to be moral? Is being moral supposed to be rational in all circumstances, even when others are not being moral? (If others are trying to exploit me, why not exploit them first if I get the chance?) How about when others are moral but extremely gullible? (Why not exploit them if it is obvious that I will get away with it?)

4. The *object* dimension specifies the kind of thing that is supposed to be rational. Specifically, are we talking about moral acts or about a moral way of life? Are we arguing, case by case, that all moral acts are rational? Or are we arguing that being moral is rational as a way of life, even though particular moral acts may not be?

This chapter looks at several ways of approaching the "why be moral" question, referring to Kavka's analytical framework when it seems most illuminating. The next section briefly explores Kurt

Baier's essentially Hobbesian approach, showing how it achieves universality along the agent dimension by approaching the question from a plural perspective. The following section explores, also very briefly, Alan Gewirth's essentially Kantian way of answering the question from a singular perspective, and it considers how Gewirth's approach handles agent, object, and social dimensions. Two sections recall several of the main arguments of earlier chapters, pulling them together and trying to show how they converge on the "why be moral" question. Finally, I comment on the audience and agent dimensions of my own approach, particularly with regard to whether it applies to members of other cultures.

In Kavka's terms, this book's intended audience consists of people who are reflectively rational, who have the time and inclination to read works of philosophy and to think about their lives in philosophical terms. The book takes its audience to consist not of sociopaths but rather of people who want both to be moral and to be rational, but who sometimes wonder whether this pair of commitments leaves them with a soul divided against itself. The class of agents it speaks about is a bit broader, including not just people who already are reflectively rational but also people with a capacity for reflection and hence a capacity for self-conscious moral agency. Concerning the social dimension, agents have reason to embrace personal morality under virtually all social circumstances, while reasons to embrace interpersonal morality are sensitive to social and personal circumstances. Finally, I agree with Kavka that the reconciliation project's proper object is to show that it is rational to choose morality as a way of life.

Why Should We Be Moral?

Kurt Baier says, "Moralities are systems of principles whose acceptance by everyone as overruling the dictates of self-interest is in the interest of everyone alike, though following the rules of a morality is not of course identical with following self-interest" (1970, p. 437). Baier goes on to say, "The answer to our question 'why should we be moral?' is therefore as follows. We should be moral because being moral is following rules designed to overrule self-interest whenever it is in the interest of everyone alike that everyone should set aside his interest" (p. 438). As Baier stresses, this does not dispel the suspicion that "a person might do better for himself by following enlightened self-interest rather than morality. It is not possible, however, that *everyone* should do better for himself by following enlightened self-interest rather than morality. The best possible life *for everyone* is possible only by everyone's following the rules of morality, that is, rules which quite frequently may require individuals to make genuine sacrifices" (p. 438).

Baier is essentially right. Morality sometimes rules out actions that would be rational from a singular perspective, but from a plural perspective, heeding such constraints is rational—it serves *our* ends in the first-person plural sense. Two caveats are worth mentioning. First, one might infer that we have nothing to say about our reasons to be moral other than that being moral makes us better off as a group. If, from a singular perspective, you do not care about what makes us better off as a group, you do not care, and that is the end of it. However, according to moral dualism, moral social structures have an internal logic that tends to induce even primarily self-interested agents to respond to those structures in mutually advantageous ways. To that extent, people will care, or will at least act as if they care, about what makes us better off as a group.

The second caveat concerns Baier's view that, since morality is a cooperative enterprise, there is nothing to say about our reasons to be moral when others are not being moral. The previous chapter discussed Baier's rhetorical question, "Why should I be moral *when no one else is*?" (1978, p. 250). Baier believes the question has no answer (p. 250). But first, personal morality's demands do not depend on whether other people are moral, and neither do a person's reasons to abide by personal morality. Second, when Baier asks "why be moral when no one else is," he is thinking of morality as requiring cooperation, so that the question really asks why one should cooperate when others are not cooperating. So interpreted, Baier's question makes perfect sense. According to moral dualism, though, whether morality requires cooperation in the first place can depend on whether other people are cooperating. Part of the point of registering this second caveat is to draw attention to its implications for (using Kavka's terms) the reconciliation project's social dimension. By the lights of moral dualism, the project's social dimension is complicated by the fact that interpersonal morality's requirements vary with social context. For rationality to track morality is for it to track different things under different circumstances.

Caveats notwithstanding, it seems to me that Baier has answered the question of why *we* should be moral, namely, that being moral makes us better off as a group. The agent dimension of Baier's project is meant to encompass everyone, but if his argument gives everyone a reason to be moral, the reason it gives is a reason from a plural perspective. Baier's approach seems to leave open whether people have reason, from a singular perspective, to be moral.

WHY SHOULD I BE MORAL?

This section explores reasons to be moral from a singular perspective. One option is to rest our case on the sort of neo-Kantian argument recently defended by Alan Gewirth. The argument has a broad and enduring appeal. We see it also in recent work by Kurt Baier and J. David Velleman.

Velleman says, "A person who profoundly desires others' pain cannot establish a truly coherent personality because he cannot wholeheartedly desire his own pain and hence cannot make his stance toward others coherent with his stance toward himself" (1989, p. 306n). Likewise, Velleman says, "In harboring special dispositions toward himself, the immoral agent becomes resistant to a fully general and simple description, thus depriving himself of an intellectually satisfying self-conception" (p. 306). I do not deny that Velleman is drawing our attention to a real problem for immoral agents. Harboring special dispositions toward oneself is not the crux of the problem, though. One might consistently (and for good reasons) hold that everyone should hold special dispositions toward themselves. In particular, one might consistently hold that all persons should feel especially responsible for their own actions. Still, Velleman has a point. People typically do want to think of themselves as having done what was right, and doing what they would regard as obviously wrong if someone else had done it creates a tension. People sometimes resolve the tension through self-deception.

Other variations of the Kantian argument try to show that we should be moral not because immorality would have bad psychological consequences but rather because immorality involves a

kind of logical error. Regarding a rational egoist who acknowl-
edges that it is in his best interest for people like him to treat moral
reasons as overriding, Kurt Baier says, "If he thinks that moral
reasons ought to be recognized and treated as overriding, but then
fails to treat them thus, he acts contrary to what he himself rightly
believes reason requires, and so acts contrary to reason" (1978,
p. 249).

Baier anticipates the response that his argument "does not show
that being immoral is necessarily contrary to reason—for being
immoral, far from being irrational, is often perfectly rational"
(1978, p. 249). But, Baier claims, this objection makes the mistake
of rebutting a stronger claim than he is actually making. Of the
immoral person, Baier says, "I am not of course arguing that he is
acting irrationally. I am merely arguing that he is acting contrary to
reason though not in the particularly flagrant way involved in irrationality" (p. 250). So, as Baier (to his credit) admits, if the failure
he describes is "contrary to reason" at all, the sense in which it is
contrary to reason is so weak that it leaves open whether such
failures are irrational.

Other proponents of the argument have been less candid about
its weakness. According to Alan Gewirth, his *dialectically necessary method* begins with premises that "every person logically
must accept simply by virtue of being an actual or prospective
agent. The argument proceeds to show that, by accepting these
agency-necessitated statements, every actual or prospective agent is
logically committed to accept a certain supreme principle of morality" (1991, p. 74). The premise with which Gewirth begins, the
premise that is supposed to be logically inescapable, is:

1. I must have freedom and well-being.

Gewirth then offers the following formal argument (p. 76).

2. Suppose, for argument's sake, we deny that I have rights to
freedom and well-being.
3. In that case, it is permissible that others interfere with my freedom and well-being.
4. In other words, it is permissible that I not have freedom and
well-being.
5. Therefore, it is not true that I must have freedom and well-
being.

6. But since (5) contradicts (1), we must reject the supposition (2) that led to (5). Therefore,

7. I have rights to freedom and well-being.

Since I could not avoid asserting the necessity of my freedom and well-being, and since the grounds on which I could not avoid asserting it are equally available to all persons, I must acknowledge that each person has a right to freedom and well-being.

Many readers will have seen this sort of argument before, and we will not pause here to rehearse it in detail. We could question its validity, since it seems to leap from the premise that I must *have* freedom and well-being to the conclusion that I must *claim a right* to freedom and well-being.[1] Had we thought the argument form was valid, we could have questioned the argument's soundness, since the premise "I must have freedom and well-being" is hardly a truism.[2] But leave such questions aside. Suppose that, were we to look sympathetically at the details of the argument, we would be convinced that the argument is sound; we would concede that Gewirth has a notion of logic from which it follows that, to be logical in that sense, you have to be moral. Would the argument's soundness imply that we should be impressed by it? Not necessarily. The argument constitutes a reason for flesh-and-blood people to be moral only if they have reason to be what Gewirth calls logical. But no one has reason to be what Gewirth calls logical: not logicians, not egoists, not committed moral agents—no one. Of course, ignoring standard logic can be perilous. (This cup contains hemlock. Hemlock is poison. Therefore, if I drink from this cup . . .) But what Gewirth calls logic is not standard logic; it is hard to imagine a situation in which ignoring it would be perilous in the way that ignoring standard logic can be perilous.

To answer a person's "why be moral" question, we need to show that he or she has reason to be moral. If we try to answer by arguing that being moral is *rational*, we had better make sure he or she

[1] The argument has been so questioned by Rüdiger Bittner (1989, p. 28).

[2] If 'must' is interpreted normatively, then premise (1) becomes equivalent to a claim that I ought to have freedom and well-being, In that case, the argument assumes what it is supposed to prove. If 'must' is interpreted descriptively, then (1) means that I need freedom and well-being in order to prosper. So, interpreted, (1) is probably true. But Alan Gewirth's (1991) formal argument asserts that (5) contradicts (1), and if (1) is merely descriptive (albeit logically inescapable), then contrary to appearances, (5) does not contradict (1). (5), as derived from step (4) is a normative claim.

has reason to be what we are calling rational. We may connect morality to what we call rationality, but unless people have reason to be what we call rational, the connection will be inconsequential. We will have connected morality to something that there is no reason to be, and therefore the connection will give people no reason to be moral, either.

The following sections bring together the main conclusions of previous chapters, showing how they point to an answer to the "why be moral" question. In outline, the argument is simple. Instead of simply assuming we have reasons to be rational, I argue first that beings like us in situations like ours have reasons to be reflectively rational, and second that reflectively rational agents have reason to be moral. Therefore, to whatever extent the "reason to" relation is transitive, we have reason to be moral. That does not mean people always will be moral. The conclusion is less giddy than that, for it does not assume people always will be reflectively rational. But it leaves us with a suggestion that most immorality has its source in the fact that we are not always reflectively rational.

THE ARGUMENTS OF PART I

Grounding morality in a conception of rationality is impressive only if the conception of rationality is one that motivates us or that we have reason to try to live up to. Means-end reasoning is motivationally potent, but we get from means-end reasoning to morality only when means-end reasoning becomes reflective. When instrumental rationality evolves into reflective rationality, it becomes motivationally potent in a different way. In effect, reflective rationality appeals not only to ends we have but also to ends we have reason to develop, given ends we have. The trick, then, is to show that it serves our ends for our means-end reasoning processes to become reflective. That was the task of Part I.

Chapter 1 proposed that rational choice involves seeking effective means to one's ends. Rationality, even conceived in means-end terms, does not require us always to be seeking means to our ends, for the activity of seeking is sometimes counterproductive. Further, Chapter 2 argued, rationality does not commit agents to a maximization strategy. Maximization is a means to an end, and it is not always an effective means.

In a way, this should not be surprising. Natural selection does not build in a bias in favor of optimizers. On the contrary, species most highly adapted to their ecological niches are the first to go extinct when the environment changes. It is species with merely satisfactory levels of adaptation to particular ecological niches that survive environmental change. As with species, so with individual agents. Maximization is a strategy, and strategy is a means to an end. How well it serves its purpose is an empirical matter. Agents who satisfice rather than optimize with respect to prevailing conditions are less likely to waste precious resources optimizing with respect to conditions that are bound to change.

Also, Chapter 2 explained, it is rational to pursue local goals under self-imposed constraints. Such constraints need not be the same as moral constraints, of course. The point, though, is that we cannot say morality is irrational simply in virtue of requiring us to operate under self-imposed constraints. Nor can we say morality and rationality are inconsistent purely in virtue of rationality requiring us always to be seeking maximally effective means to our own ends, for rationality requires no such thing.

Chapter 3 argued that ends themselves can be assessed as rational or otherwise. More specifically, their adoption as ends can be evaluated as means to what I called maieutic ends. Reflective rationality involves criticizing ends as well as means, and one way to understand how even final ends could be subject to rational criticism is to suppose that maieutic ends could be achieved in the process of acquiring final ends. Chapter 4 considered how alternative means to our maieutic ends might be compared.

Those who are naturalistically inclined might wonder: If our biologically given goal is simply to replicate our genes, then why do we have any goals beyond the goal of replicating our genes? Presumably because some goals are best promoted by something other than their pursuit. Some goals are achieved by oblique means, by the development and exercise of capacities to pursue different goals. Organisms evolved a will to survive probably because it turned out that beings with a will to survive were better replicators than beings with no goals beyond a will to replicate.

Over generations, species adapt to changing environments through natural selection, but the development of cognitive capacities gave animals increasing behavioral flexibility. Changes in behavior were no longer a matter of selective pressures operating on a population's hard-wired behavioral mechanisms over generations;

instead, individual organisms themselves could adapt their behavior to changing circumstances. At some point, a capacity for reflection emerged as well, perhaps as a by-product of increasing cognitive capacities. With that capacity for reflection came increasingly complex sets of goals. A purely instrumental conception of rationality will be static, with no resources to explain how a child satisfies his or her self-regarding desires by gradually developing them into something more mature. But the models of reflective rationality developed in Chapter 3 explain how the child's maturing cognitive capacity could help drive the maturation of an initially childish set of goals.

Instrumental rationality says nothing for or against morality. This is crucial, because the instrumental conception makes it appear that we cannot get from rationality to reasons to be moral unless we beg the question; either we assume we just happen to have a preference for being moral or else we build morality into our conception of rationality. But no conception of (and no preference for) morality is built into the concept of reflective rationality. What is built in is a recognition of certain facts about human nature in a social context. Specifically, we begin with an end of survival, but in a social context, bare survival generally is too easy. Our commitment to survival will be undermined unless we replace it with something more complicated that engages the excess cognitive capacity that will otherwise dwell on bare survival's pointlessness. With the emergence of a more complicated corpus of ends, survival acquires its point. It becomes part of something bigger than bare survival. It becomes a means to further ends, thereby acquiring a rational justification.

Jean Hampton says, "The *only* way to establish that there is such a thing as a noninstrumental, evaluative side of human reason is to argue that the evaluation has been covertly present in the instrumental model all along" (1992, p. 219; emphasis added). This is a plausible position, on its face; however, the argument of Chapters 3, 4, and 5 shows that there is a least one other way. The emergence of the noninstrumental, evaluative side of human reason is, or or at least can be, normatively grounded in pure means-end reasoning, given my descriptive suppositions about human psychology. And, as a separate issue, the model does not simply assume we rationally ought to pursue the end of survival, or any other end. Rather, the model posits that the end of survival in fact

251

drives most of us (whether or not it ought to) to develop complicated chains of ends. If the end of survival acquires a rationale, it will be in virtue of becoming a means to further ends. And if the chain circles itself, as explained in Chapter 3, then every end in the chain will have acquired a rationale. There will be no end the normative force of which is simply taken as given.

Chapters 4 and 5 argued that our maturing corpus of self-regarding ends is served by supplementing it with goals that go beyond static self-interest to embrace reflective self-regard and concern for others. In addition, accepting principled commitments, particularly those involving respect for others, is part of belonging to a community and, thus, coming to be part of something bigger than oneself, thereby giving a new kind of value to our latent productivity. From Part I emerges the conclusion that rationality can make, and indeed tends to make, room for the kinds of substantive ends and self-imposed principled commitments that, for an individual agent, constitute being moral.

The argument may not show that other-regard is rationally necessary, but it does more than show merely that other-regard is consistent with being rational. The upshot, rather, is that beings like us have powerful reasons not to regret our tendency to be other-regarding. Thrasymachus (as I envision him) really is missing out on something precious, but it is precious to us, not to him. It gives us reason to be glad we are not like him, even though it may not give him reason to wish he were like us. In lacking the concerns that energize the rest of us, Thrasymachus does not feel he is missing out on something precious, for he has lost or has never developed his capacity to find it precious.

Thrasymachus's choices have shaped him in such a way that, given the current state of his goals and desires, and given an inability on his part to reflect on the poverty of his goals and desires, the things he does in pursuit of them may well be instrumentally rational. People who do not respect their own ends have a powerful incentive to be unreflective, and bad people typically are unreflective. That may explain how they can dismiss the moral life without a second thought. They *need* to dismiss it without much thought, because stopping to honestly think about it might be unbearable. But the fact that immorality can be instrumentally rational for an incorrigibly unreflective person need not prevent us from talking about reasons to be moral for people like us. It need not prevent us from talking about our reasons to be thankful that we are not like Thrasymachus.

THE ARGUMENTS OF PART II

Whereas Part I argued that rationality makes room for morality, Part II argued that morality in turn makes room for the kinds of ends and strategies that tend to go with being rational. Chapter 6 argued that it makes sense to ask "why be moral" and that morality, at the level of recognition rules, is teleological. The predicate 'good' normally is understood relationally, as when one says this hammer is good for pounding these nails, or that road is good for getting to that destination, and so on. The concept is essentially teleological. When speaking of ethics, of course, we also use normative predicates in a nonrelational way. As a result, ethical discourse often is not in any obvious way teleologically grounded.

Nonetheless, it can serve a deeper purpose to accord some things a nonrelational normative status. We care about others not because caring about others is reflectively or even collectively rational; rather, we care about others, period. Sometimes, we do things because they are right, period, but that kind of steadfastness, that kind of noninstrumental commitment, has instrumental value. Noninstrumental caring is what gives Kate more to live for. By hypothesis, the instrumental value is not what motivates truly moral people, but we see their noninstrumental motivation as moral precisely because we can see the underlying telos of that kind of commitment. We can see how that kind of commitment fits into the lives of human beings living together. The idea that there can be such a thing as a noninstrumental rightness, the sense of rightness that seems most fundamentally ethical, thus becomes explicable.

What is being questioned when we ask "why be moral"? Chapter 6 argued that the philosophical energy spent on the question over the millenia presupposes that the decision to be moral has consequences and that we care about those consequences from a first-person plural perspective. To ask "why be moral" is to ask for reasons to care, from a singular perspective, about things we already acknowledge having reason to endorse from a plural perspective.

What, then, are our grounds for endorsement from a plural perspective? That is where moral dualism comes in. Reflective rationality matters to us in a way that goes beyond how it bears on our self-regarding concerns. We endorse people being more reflective and we do so independently of how their becoming more reflective affects us. Being reflectively rational will make them, as well as the people around them, better off. Moral dualism's personal strand makes room for reflective rationality by building reflective rationality into its recognition rule, endorsing personal goals in terms of whether pursuing them shapes one's character in a reflectively rational way.

Reflective rationality, though, is not all there is to morality. Morality is a cluster concept ranging over social as well as psychological phenomena. And as a social phenomenon, there is more to morality than the personal conduct of human atoms in the void. There is also the social matrix in which moral agents are embedded. That matrix carries some of the burden of giving morality its content and of bringing morality to bear on the choices of moral agents. Some institutions constrain us in ways that make us generally better off, thereby giving us reasons to endorse those constraints from a first-person plural perspective. You may have deontological or utilitarian or egalitarian or elitist ideas about how institutions ought to function, but if functioning in those ways would make people generally worse off, then we have decisive reason to condemn them from a first person-plural perspective. For us to have a moral reason to implement any such ideas through social structure, such implementation will have to constitute a way of serving our common good.[3]

Chapter 7 concluded that if serving the common good is a recognition rule for the morality of institutions, then moral institutions are those that give human agents reasons to act in ways that serve

---

[3] Thomas Nagel seems to assume that if we all took an impersonal perspective, we would all see things the same way, namely, a radically egalitarian way (1991, p. 64). Nagel speaks as if our fundamental moral and political problem is to reconcile our separate personal perspectives with *Nagel's* impersonal perspective, as if there were no other. On the contrary, Nagel's view is not like mine, and his view does not become like mine even when we both abstract from our personal concerns. Different people not only have different ideals for themselves as individuals but they also have different ideals for themselves (and for others) as a group. Reconciling our impersonal perspectives is a huge problem. And the most excruciating aspect of this problem, perhaps, is that from some people's points of view, it evidently appears permissible to pursue their ideals by exploitative means.

the common good. Moral social structures serve the common good not by producing goods but rather by facilitating the production of goods by people, and one of the main ways in which institutions facilitate production is by removing impediments to peaceful individual productivity, impediments that people might otherwise create for each other. The point of social structures is to facilitate individual self-improvement—not to eliminate individual self-improvement and replace it with something else. Moral social structures facilitate individual self-improvement by minimizing the extent to which people interfere with each other in their efforts to improve themselves and by helping to create conditions under which those efforts are mutually supportive.

Part of the point of social structure is to create conditions under which regard for others can be self-affirming. Samuel Scheffler may have something similar in mind when he says, "If morality is fundamentally a humane phenomenon, then not the least of the ways in which this is so is that it encourages decent human beings to contribute to the development of societies in which it may be easier for rational agents to be decent human beings" (1992, p. 145). Moral social structure gives us incentives and opportunities to pursue our own flourishing in ways that make the people around us better off as well. They also give us incentives to avoid pursuing our own interests in ways that make others worse off. The resulting degree of coincidence between morality and self-interest is not a matter of necessity, neither is it merely a coincidence. On my theory, for a social structure to be moral is for it to have a built-in tendency to give us reasons to act in ways that serve the common good.

David Gauthier notes that if one is in a parametric environment (a game in which people play according to a fixed pattern, not adapting to how other people are playing) then rationality requires straightforward maximization (1986, p. 183).[4] Now, I deny that rationality requires straightforward maximization in parametric environments. We may have reason to satisfice or to maximize within self-imposed constraints, including constraints that express respect for others. Nevertheless, there is a major lesson here. Al-

---

[4] I will not try to add to the wealth of commentary now available on David Gauthier's (1986) book. For starters, though, one might want to consult Peter Vallentyne (1991).

though parametric environments do not rationally require straight-forward maximization, straightforward maximization is still what they tend to elicit. The lesson, therefore, is that collectively rational social structures tend not to put people in a parametric environment. Collectively rational social structures tend to put people in situations where they respond to each other's behavior and encourage each other to act in collectively rational ways.

One way to make a constraint collectively rational is to back it up with external sanctions that induce people to act in collectively rational ways. External sanctions help make it individually rational to comply with collectively rational constraints. There are limits to the motivational potency of practically feasible external constraints, though. This is true even for a social structure like criminal law, the whole point of which is to motivate people via the threat of extreme sanctions. Therefore, collectively rational social structures must have other ways of structuring incentives in such a way that people actually react to them in a manner that tends to serve the common good. And they do. Even the fabled Ring of Gyges, which makes its wearer immune to external sanctions, would not completely prevent social structure from being motivationally efficacious, because moral incentive structures are often positive reinforcers. They do not work solely, or even mainly, by threat.[5]

As the previous section pointed out, showing that amoralists like Thrasymachus are irrational is neither necessary nor sufficient to show that being moral is rational for people like us. Still, Thrasymachus is part of the social order, and moral social structures take his presence into account. The interpersonal strand of morality constrains rationality to some extent, yet it is in the nature of social structures to serve the common good by working with individual rationality rather than against it. This strand deems moral only those structurally embedded constraints that actually give individuals the incentive and the opportunity to pursue

[5] The Ring of Gyges, as discussed in Book II of Plato's *Republic*, was supposed to give its bearer the power to render himself invisible, which in turn was supposed to make the bearer all-powerful, which in turn was supposed to ultimately corrupt the bearer. (J.R.R. Tolkien's *Lord of the Rings* is, I presume, directly inspired by this myth.) In passing, it seems to me that, because power tends to corrupt, the great danger to a person of absolute power would be the risk of being corrupted by that power and thereby losing his or her basis for self-respect.

their own projects in peace. Social structures that serve the common good are essentially adapted to the real features of human agents, including their pronounced tendency to be self-regarding. Meanwhile, reflectively self-regarding agents often deliberately adapt themselves to moral social structures—they become parts of social structures that serve the common good—as they reflect on their reasons to be peaceful and productive members of the community, to affirm themselves through honest rapport with others, and to be persons of forthright principle, not just persons of prudence. While it may not exactly pay to be moral, it is not too far from the truth to say being moral is a prior condition for anything paying. Being moral is something we need to do in order to merit self-regard.

Chapter 5 suggested that being moral need not involve expressing concern for literally everyone, although it does involve having a universal respect for others. Chapter 7 went on to argue that, from a plural point of view, we have reason to endorse opportunities to pursue parochial concerns, the kind of concerns people are willing and able to pursue, and at the same time we have reason to endorse nonparochial respect. People are capable of the latter, and some people achieve it. We do not have to remake human nature to achieve universal respect in the way that we would have to remake human nature to achieve universal concern. As we are, parochial concern and universal respect serve our ends.

So, the morality of other-regarding concern is complicated, and limitless concern is not a prerequisite of being moral. Nonetheless, morality is still demanding in two ways. First, it demands that we be reflectively rational, which is not an easy demand to meet. Second, it demands that we conform to interpersonal constraints that serve the common good as they work through social structure. It is in the nature of moral social structures that they do not cut against individual rationality in gratuitous ways. But that does not mean they do not cut against individual rationality at all. They are such as to induce collectively rational behavior in the normal run of cases, and they do this by minimizing the gap between individually and collectively rational behavior in the normal run of cases. A gap may still exist even in normal cases, however, and the gap can widen in cases that are not normal. Thus, moral constraints may be demanding even in normal cases and more so in abnormal cases. Nevertheless, reflectively rational people have a kind of individual rationality that will tend to close such gaps. Faced with situations in which they could get away with murder, they will not want to, for they recognize that (among other things) they have an interest in being the kind of person who does not have dark secrets.

From a singular perspective, we have reason to embrace personal morality, to choose and pursue our goals in reflectively rational ways. And we have indirect, incomplete, and contingent reasons to embrace interpersonal morality, to pursue our goals within the constraints imposed on us by collectively rational social structures. The better the institutions, the more complete our answer to the "why be moral" question, generally speaking. Likewise, the more reflectively rational the person, the more complete the answer, again generally speaking.

As explained in Chapter 6, the fact that we care about the "why be moral" question presupposes the possibility of divergence between what we have reason to do from a first-person singular perspective and what we have reason to endorse from a first-person plural perspective. "Why should we be moral" and "why should I be moral" are different questions. It is because we always have an answer to "why should we be moral" that we find it so disturbing that we do not always have an answer to "why should I be moral." It is from our plural perspectives that the contingency of our first-person singular reasons to be moral strikes us as a threat. The history of attempts to answer the "why be moral" question is a history of attempts to explain why the apparent divergence between "we" and "I" perspectives is illusory—why, even from the first-person singular point of view, there are always compelling reasons to be moral.

But the apparent divergence is real. Some people in some situations have no compelling reasons to be moral. It is conventional to think of a successful answer to the "why be moral" question as one that convinces or ought to convince literally everyone to be moral. This convention is a mistake, because there are real reasons to be moral, and the real reasons are not reasons for everyone. To look for universal reasons is to look for something other than the real reasons. If we go looking for reasons for literally every human being to be moral, we go astray. The point should be to look for the real reasons to be moral, and not to presume of any particular reason that it will convince everyone, or even that everyone ought to be convinced. Let us look for the reasons people really have, and let us not mistakenly presume that genuine reasons must be reasons for everyone.

A Word about Eurocentrism

What does this imply about the project of showing that it is rational to be moral? Can a recognition rule, formulated in terms of what matters to us from a plural perspective, yield an action guide that not only has a moral claim on us but that also grips us from a first-person singular perspective? Answering the "why be moral" question involves drawing out such connections as exist or can be created between our separate grounds for endorsement from singular and plural perspectives. Unlike David Gauthier, I think the gulf between morality and rationality would be vast for a being like Homo economicus.[6] For beings with a psychology like ours, however, the gulf may be narrow enough to bridge.

When I speak of beings with a psychology like ours, one might wonder how widespread I take our psychology to be. The book speaks to people in a position to read works of twentieth-century Western philosophy. None of us is in any position to know whether my conclusions apply, or how they would sound, to people whose circumstances or interests or worldviews are utterly unlike ours, but my conclusions are meant to speak to beings like us. As an account of morality, rationality, and the connections between them, this work is meant to apply wherever there are human beings, and wherever there are beings with the kinds of potentials and limitations that human beings have. I said both rationality and morality involve being conscious of how one's choices affect one's character. Would such claims have struck Aristotle or Confucius as coming from an utterly alien culture? I think not.

If Aristotle or Confucius did regard my theories of moral dualism and reflectively rational choice as coming from an alien culture, I would trust them not to jump to the conclusion that it has

---

[6] I do not mean to suggest that Gauthier views the connection between morality and individual rationality as merely contingent. Gauthier sometimes talks as if he has an independently specified conception of morality that he wishes to reconcile with individual rationality. At other times, though, he speaks as if morality could not consist in anything other than the constraints to which we are committed in virtue of seeking our own advantage in a social context.

no bearing on their own culture, for the fact that a theory emerges from a particular culture does not begin to suggest that the theory's validity is specific to that culture. It would be absurd to dismiss Euclidean geometry on the grounds that it came from a different culture. Perhaps less obviously, the point applies to theories of rationality and morality as well. My *examples* are geared to a late-twentieth-century Western audience with a working-class background, but the kinds of choices depicted in the examples are the kinds of choices that must be made by people everywhere. Had I been writing in another time and place, the book might have spoken of deciding where to hunt for food rather than where to hunt for an apartment. Nevertheless, the issue would have been the same. The need to make choices is not a culturally specific phenomenon. Talking *about* fundamentally different agents might require fundamentally different arguments, whereas talking *to* different audiences might call only for different examples, tailored to the audience's culture.

Perhaps this leaves a deeper worry unaddressed. Even if my theories exhibit no particular bias, perhaps a cultural bias lurks in the very idea of theorizing. Perhaps the urge to grasp morality in theoretical terms is itself a mistake. For what it is worth, I see no reason even to suspect that this is true, except for the fact that moral theorizing seems always to end in frustration. After all these centuries of effort, a deep, comprehensive, and plausible theoretical grasp of morality still eludes us. Yet I am glad that, despite the elusiveness of deep and comprehensive theories, people keep looking. Over the centuries, such frustration no doubt led some people to stop looking for deep theoretical truths in medicine, meteorology, mathematics, and so forth, but I am glad it did not stop everyone. I am glad that people still search for a deeper understanding of morality. I am self-conscious about my attempt to construct a moral theory, partly because it might be seen as thoughtlessly following in the footsteps of other theorists. I have tried to avoid preconceptions about how deep or how comprehensive a moral theory must be in order to illuminate its subject matter. How much of my theory will I still believe ten years from now? I do not know, but the bare fact that my theory is a theory probably will never strike me as a point against it. Time will tell.

My answer to the "why be moral" question is addressed only to people who are reflective enough to earnestly ask the question. If there are whole cultures in which the question does not arise, then the question does not arise. But if and when people become reflective enough to ask the question, my answer will be relevant to them in virtue of that capacity for reflection.

Of course, it is not necessary for every issue raised to apply to everyone, or even to every culture. The agent dimension need not be universal. Some of the issues discussed here arise as issues only among people with time to think, for example. Not everyone does. Still, leisure time is hardly peculiar to late-twentieth-century Western culture. Further, even when the issue is universal, the examples used to illustrate it must still be tailored to the audience. For twentieth-century Western audiences, Kate's choice of careers nicely illustrates various arguments. Had I been addressing an audience for whom division of labor and the emancipation of women were alien and unnatural concepts, it would have been a bad example, although the arguments it illustrates would have been no less valid. The argument is addressed to philosophically inclined members of late-twentieth-century Western culture, but the argument is about beings with the capacity for reflection, wherever and whenever they may be found.

Concluding Remarks

The strategy of this book, Chapter 1 announced, was to explore the extent to which morality and prudential rationality make room for each other. The model of reflective rationality developed in Part I showed how integrity and regard for others fit into the lives of humanly rational agents. Moral dualism, as developed in Part II, depicts morality as making room for projects that develop one's character in a reflectively rational way, so long as those projects are pursued within constraints that work through social structures in collectively rational ways. Moreover, Chapter 7 argued, structurally embedded constraints are collectively rational only insofar as they induce individual agents to act in collectively rational ways, which is to say that they do what they can to make it individually rational to act in collectively rational ways. The implication is that morality and rationality make room for each other in a variety of ways.

In concluding that morality and rationality make room for each other, am I claiming merely that morality and rationality are consistent? Or, am I claiming that being moral is a way (perhaps in some circumstances the only way) of being rational? On a case-by-case basis, even the weaker claim sometimes fails to hold. On the other hand, this book has argued that the stronger claim (that being moral is a way of being rational) holds true as a general rule, both as applied to particular cases and also as a general rule for shaping one's life and character. Thus, it may not matter that there are cases where the weaker claim is false, for these may not be important enough from the global perspective to justify leaving one's plans and one's character—the core of one's identity—in suspense while waiting to see if such situations arise.

The upshot is that morality is fairly well reconciled with reflective rationality. And the concept of reflective rationality is by no means peculiar. Normal people are better off being reflectively rational, and normal people are capable of being reflectively rational much of the time. The idealization of self-interest represented by my model of reflective rationality is genuinely an ideal, for it is genuinely something to which we have reason to aspire, not only from our singular perspectives but from our plural perspectives as well. It would be prudent and moral to try to take the kind of self-interest we have and make it more reflective. We advise our friends to do the right thing. We raise our children to be moral. That we can do such things with a clear conscience presupposes that we do not believe we are advising people, or raising our children, to be irrational.[7]

Unfortunately, morality is by no means fully reconciled with human frailty. Even after we make moral commitments, we are constantly having to reaffirm them. Matters of character and virtue, commitments built up partly through habit, enter into particular choices, yet we find ourselves free in many cases involving our most important choices. Kate can tell herself she will lie only when it is important, and that one lie does not a liar make. The trouble is, she can remember also telling herself she would miss her morning jog only when it was important, and it has now been three years since her last morning jog. If Kate wants to be honest as a way of life, she will have to be honest as a way of life, which means

---

[7] The point is from Robert M. Adams (unpublished).

she will have to be ready to affirm her choice even in cases where it really matters.

We are not always up to the demands of morality partly because we are not always up to the demands of reflective rationality. Even if reflective rationality is normal, it is still an achievement. So, my account explains rather than ignores the fact that immorality is not rare. We have reasons to be reflectively rational. Reflectively rational people have reasons to be moral. The reasons are overwhelming at neither step, but they are there.

This is somewhat comforting, but not unrealistically so, for it leaves us to face the fact that we are by nature shortsighted. We are creatures of evolution, and it is more natural for us to worry about immediate physical threats than about the impacts of our actions on our characters. Sometimes we are caught off guard, revert to "fight or flight" mode, and do things we later regret. We have ample reason to strive to be bigger than that, but the fact that we have reason to strive is no guarantee of success. The connection between rational choice and moral agency is deep and pervasive, nonetheless, it is tenuous and easily lost from sight.

The conflict we have to live with—a conflict within ourselves and a conflict within our relationships—is a conflict not so much between morality and rationality per se as between morality and an instrumental rationality employed in service of shortsighted and superficial ends that we would be better off rejecting. Thus, when we are in statically rational mode, thinking of a situation in terms of how it threatens our careers rather than in terms of how it tests our characters, the ends we have in that mode may sometimes be best served by skirting collectively rational social structures when the opportunity arises, as it sometimes will.

We have a problem that Homo economicus does not, namely, that we sometimes lack the strength of will to do what is in our best interest. Sometimes we fail morally not so much because we lack sufficient reason to be moral as because we lack sufficient strength to be moral. Telling the truth sometimes takes more courage than we can muster, even when we foresee being intensely disappointed with ourselves if we lie. Consider how weak we can be in situations where we are afraid or embarrassed to tell the truth. We react to the possibility of making a bad impression as if the situation were a threat to our physical health. This is a mistake, for what is really at stake is usually too subtle to be properly addressed by such reactions. Covering up the truth in overreaction to perceived threats to our standing in other people's eyes is self-defeating; it walls off the possibility of our real selves being affirmed by those we are deceiving. Nevertheless, it takes a certain strength of character to act in our reflective self-interest. Similarly, developing one's talents is morally demanding; seeing where one's talents lie requires honest self-appraisal, and turning raw talent into practiced skill takes courage and perseverance. Being rational in a full-blooded sense—developing oneself in a way that is true to oneself—is a profoundly demanding activity.

* References *

Ackrill, J. L. 1980. "Aristotle on Eudaimonia." In *Essays on Aristotle's Ethics*, edited by Amelie O. Rorty. Berkeley: University of California Press.

Adams, Robert M. Unpublished. "Moral Faith."

Akerlof, George A., and Dickens, William T. 1982. "The Economic Consequences of Cognitive Dissonance." *American Economic Review* 72:307–19

Anscombe, G.E.M. 1958. "Modern Moral Philosophy." *Philosophy* 33:1–19.

Aristotle. 1985. *Nicomachean Ethics*. Translated by Terence Irwin. Indianapolis: Hackett. First published ca. 340 B.C.

Badhwar, Neera Kapur. 1993. "Altruism versus Self-Interest: Sometimes a False Dichotomy." *Social Philosophy and Policy* 10:90–117.

Baier, Kurt. 1958. *The Moral Point of View*. Ithaca: Cornell University Press.

———. 1970. "Why Should We Be Moral?" In *Readings in Contemporary Ethical Theory*, edited by K. Pahel and M. Schiller, pp. 427–41. Englewood Cliffs: Prentice Hall.

———. 1978. "Moral Reasons and Reasons to Be Moral." In *Values and Morals*, edited by A. I. Goldman and J. Kim, pp. 231–56. Dordrecht: D. Reidel.

Bittner, Rüdiger. 1989. *What Reason Demands*. New York: Cambridge University Press.

Bradley, F. H. 1927. *Ethical Studies*. Oxford: Oxford University Press. First published 1876.

Bratman, Michael E. 1990. "What Is Intention?" In *Intentions in Communication*, edited by P. Cohen, J. Morgan, and M. Pollack. Cambridge: MIT Press.

Bricker, Phillip. 1980. "Prudence." *Journal of Philosophy* 77:381–401.

Broadhead, Robert S., and Douglas D. Heckathorn. Unpublished. "Community Outreach to Combat AIDS among Drug Injectors."

Broadie, Sarah. 1991. *Ethics with Aristotle*. New York: Oxford University Press.

Brock, Dan W. 1977. "The Justification of Morality." *American Philosophical Quarterly* 14:71–78.

Buchanan, Allen. 1991. *Secession*. Boulder: Westview.

Butler, Joseph. 1874. *Fifteen Sermons*. Oxford: Clarendon. First published 1726.

Coleman, Jules L. 1988. *Markets, Morals, and the Law*. New York: Cambridge University Press.

———. 1991. "Rules and Social Facts." *Harvard Journal of Law and Public Policy* 14:703–25.

———. 1992. *Risks and Wrongs*. New York: Cambridge University Press.

Cooter, Robert D. 1991. "Inventing Market Property: The Land Courts of Papua New Guinea." *Law and Society Review* 25:759–801.

Danielson, Peter. 1992. *Artificial Morality*. New York: Routledge.

Elster, Jon. 1984. *Ulysses and the Sirens: Studies in Rationality and Irrationality*. Rev. ed. Cambridge: Cambridge University Press.

Falk, W. D. 1986. " 'Ought' and Motivation." In his *Ought, Reasons, and Morality*, pp. 21–41. Ithaca: Cornell University Press.

Feinberg, Joel. 1981. "Psychological Egoism." In *Reason and Responsibility*, edited by J. Feinberg, pp. 498–508. Belmont: Wadsworth

Foot, Philippa. 1978. *Virtues and Vices*. Berkeley: University of California Press

Frank, Robert. 1988. *Passions within Reason*. New York: Norton.

Frankfurt, Harry. 1992. "On the Usefulness of Final Ends." *Iyyun* 41: 3–19.

Freeman, Samuel. 1991. "Contractualism, Moral Motivation, and Practical Reason." *Journal of Philosophy*. 88:281–303.

Fumerton, Richard A. 1990. *Reason and Morality*. Ithaca: Cornell University Press.

Galston, William A. 1991. *Liberal Purposes*. New York: Cambridge University Press.

———. 1993. "Cosmopolitan Altruism." *Social Philosophy and Policy* 10:118–34.

Gauthier, David. 1986. *Morals by Agreement*. Oxford: Oxford University Press.

———. 1990. *Moral Dealing*. Ithaca: Cornell University Press.

Gewirth, Alan. 1991. "Can Any Final Ends Be Rational?" *Ethics* 102: 66–95.

Gibbard, Allan. 1990. *Wise Choices, Apt Feelings*. Cambridge: Harvard University Press.

Gintis, Herbert. 1974. "Welfare Criteria with Endogeneous Preference: The Economics of Education." *International Economic Review* 15: 415–30.

Goodin, Robert E. 1992. *Motivating Political Morality*. Cambridge: Blackwell.

Griswold, Charles L. Forthcoming. "Platonic Liberalism: Self-Perfection as a Foundation of Political Theory." In *Contré Platon*, edited by Monique Dixsaut. Paris: Vrin.

Hammond, Peter. 1976. "Changing Tastes and Coherent Dynamic Choice." *Review of Economic Studies* 43:159–73.

Hampton, Jean. 1992. "Rethinking Reason." *American Philosophical Quarterly* 29:219–36.

———. 1993. "Selflessness and the Loss of Self." *Social Philosophy and Policy* 10:135–65.

Hardie, W.F.R. 1967. "The Final Good in Aristotle's Ethics." In *Aristotle*, edited by J.M.E. Moravcsik, pp. 297–322. Garden City: Anchor.

Hardin, Russell. 1988. *Morality Within the Limits of Reason*. Chicago: University of Chicago Press.

———. 1994. "My University's Yacht." *Nomos* 36:205–27.

Harsanyi, John C. 1982. "Morality and the Theory of Rational Behavior." In *Utilitarianism and Beyond*, edited by A. Sen and B. Williams, pp. 39–62. New York: Cambridge University Press.

———. 1985. "Does Reason Tell Us What Moral Code to Follow and, Indeed, to Follow Any Moral Code at All?" *Ethics* 96:42–55.

Hart, H.L.A. 1961. *The Concept of Law*. Oxford: Clarendon.

Herman, Barbara. 1983. "Integrity and Impartiality." *Monist* 66:233–50.

———. 1985. "The Practice of Moral Judgment." *Journal of Philosophy* 82:414–36.

Hobbes, Thomas. 1962. *Leviathan*. New York: Macmillan. First published 1651.

Hoffman, Paul. 1987. "The Man Who Loves Only Numbers." *Atlantic Monthly*. (November): 60.

Hume, David. 1978. *A Treatise of Human Nature*. Oxford: Clarendon. First published 1739.

———. 1983. *An Enquiry Concerning the Principles of Morals*. Indianapolis: Hackett. First published 1751.

Irwin, T. H. 1993. Review of Broadie (1991). *Journal of Philosophy* 90:323–29.

Kagan, Shelly. 1989. *The Limits of Morality*. New York: Oxford University Press.

Kant, Immanuel. 1981. *Grounding for the Metaphysics of Morals*. Indianapolis: Hackett. First published 1785.

Kavka, Gregory S. 1985. "The Reconciliation Project." In *Morality, Reason, and Truth*, edited by D. Copp and D. Zimmerman, pp. 297–319. Totowa: Rowman and Allanheld.

Kukathas, Chandran. 1992. "Are There Any Cultural Rights?" *Political Theory* 20:105–39.

Kymlicka, Will. 1989. *Liberalism, Community, and Culture*. Oxford: Oxford University Press.

———. 1992. "The Rights of Minority Cultures." *Political Theory* 20:140–46.

Lear, Jonathan. 1992. "Inside and Outside the Republic." *Phronesis* 37: 184–215.

Levi, Isaac. 1986. *Hard Choices: Decision Making under Unresolved Conflict*. New York: Cambridge University Press.

Long, Roderick. 1992. "Mill's Higher Pleasures and the Choice of Character." *Utilitas* 4:279–97.

Louden, Robert. 1992. *Morality and Moral Theory*. New York: Oxford University Press.

Lyons, David. 1991. *In the Interest of the Governed: A Study of Bentham's Philosophy of Utility*. New York: Oxford University Press.

McClennen, Edward F. 1988. "Constrained Maximization and Resolute Choice." *Social Philosophy and Policy* 5:95–118.

McCord, Joan. 1982. "The Cambridge-Somerville Youth Study: A Sobering Lesson on Treatment, Prevention, and Evaluation." In *Practical Program Evaluation in Youth Treatment,* edited by A. J. McSweeny, W. J. Fremouw, and R. P. Hawkins, pp. 11–23. Springfield: Charles C. Thomas.

MacDonald, Scott. 1991. "Ultimate Ends in Practical Reasoning: Aquinas's Aristotelian Psychology and Anscombe's Fallacy." *Philosophical Review* 100:31–65.

McDowell, John. 1978. "Are Moral Requirements Hypothetical Imperatives?" *Proceedings of the Aristotelian Society* 52 supp:12–29.

MacIntyre, Alasdair. 1979. "Why Is the Search for the Foundations of Ethics So Frustrating?" *Hastings Center Report* 9:15–22.

March, James G. 1988. "Bounded Rationality, Ambiguity, and the Engineering of Choice." In *Decisions and Organizations*, edited by J. G. March, pp. 266–93. New York: Basil Blackwell.

Mill, John S. 1974. *On Liberty*. Harmondsworth: Penguin. First published 1859.

———. 1979. *Utilitarianism*. Indianapolis: Hackett. First published 1861.

Moore, G. E. 1903. *Principia Ethica*. Cambridge: Cambridge University Press.

Morris, Christopher W. 1988. "The Relation between Self-Interest and Justice in Contractarian Ethics." *Social Philosophy and Policy* 5:119–53.

———. Unpublished. "State, Sovereignty, and Nation."

Nagel, Thomas. 1970. *The Possibility of Altruism*. Oxford: Clarendon Press.

———. 1986. *The View from Nowhere*. New York: Oxford University Press.

———. 1991. *Equality and Partiality*. New York: Oxford University Press.

Nelson, Alan. 1986. "Explanation and Justification in Political Philosophy." *Ethics* 97:154–76.

Nelson, William N. 1990. *Morality: What's In It for Me?* Boulder: Westview.

Nielsen, Kai. 1989. *Why Be Moral?* Buffalo: Prometheus.

Nozick, Robert. 1993. *The Nature of Rationality*. Princeton: Princeton University Press.

Oakeshott, Michael. 1991. *Rationalism in Politics*. Indianapolis: Liberty Press.

Olen, Jeffrey. 1988. *Moral Freedom*. Philadelphia: Temple University Press.

Palmer, Tom G. 1989. "Intellectual Property: A Non-Posnerian Law and Economics Approach." *Hamline Law Review*, 12:261–304.

Parfit, Derek. 1984. *Reasons and Persons*. New York: Oxford University Press.

Pettit, Philip. 1984. "Satisficing Consequentialism." *Proceedings of the Aristotelian Society* 58 supp.:165–76.

———. 1991. "Decision Theory and Folk Psychology." In *Foundations of Decision Theory*, ed. Michael Bacharach and Susan Hurley, pp. 147–75. Cambridge: Basil Blackwell.

Plato. 1974. *Republic*. Translated by G.M.A. Grube. Indianapolis: Hackett. First published ca. 390 B.C..

Pollock, John L. 1984. "How Do You Maximize Expectation Value?" *Nous* 17:409–21.

Postema, Gerald. 1988. "Hume's Reply to the Sensible Knave." *History of Philosophy Quarterly* 5:23–40.

———. Unpublished. "Conflict, Conversation, and Convention: Reflections on Hume's Account of the Emergence of Norms of Justice."

Prichard, H. A. 1968a. "Does Moral Philosophy Rest on a Mistake?" In his *Moral Obligation*, pp. 1–17. London: Oxford University Press. First published 1912.

———. 1968b. "Moral Obligation." In his *Moral Obligation*, pp. 87–163. London: Oxford University Press.

Rawls, John. 1955. "Two Concepts of Rules." *Philosophical Review* 64:3–32.

———. 1971. *A Theory of Justice*. Cambridge: Belknap.

———. 1980. "Kantian Constructivism in Moral Theory." *Journal of Philosophy* 77:515–72.

Raz, Joseph. 1986. *The Morality of Freedom*. Oxford: Oxford University Press.

Resnik, Michael. 1987. *Choices*. Minneapolis: University of Minnesota Press.

Russell, Bertrand. 1954. *Human Society in Ethics and Politics*. London: George Allen and Unwin.

Sayre-McCord, Geoffrey. 1989. "Deception and Reasons to Be Moral." *American Philosophical Quarterly* 26:113–22.

———. 1994. "On Why Hume's 'General Point of View' Isn't Ideal—— and Shouldn't Be." *Social Philosophy and Policy* 11:202–28.

Scanlon, T. M. 1982. "Contractualism and Utilitarianism." In *Utilitarianism and Beyond*, edited by A. Sen and B. Williams, pp. 103–28. New York: Cambridge University Press.

Scheffler, Samuel. 1982. *The Rejection of Consequentialism*. New York: Oxford University Press.

———. 1992. *Human Morality*. New York: Oxford University Press.

Schmidtz, David. 1990a. "Justifying the State." *Ethics* 101:89–102.

———. 1990b. "Scheffler's Hybrid Theory of the Right." *Nous* 24:622–27.

———. 1991. *The Limits of Government: An Essay on the Public Goods Argument*. Boulder: Westview.

———. 1992. "Rationality within Reason," *Journal of Philosophy* 89:445–66.

———. 1993. "Reasons for Altruism." *Social Philosophy and Policy* 10:52–68.

———. 1994. "Choosing Ends." *Ethics* 104:226–51.

Sen, Amartya. 1990. "Rational Fools: A Critique of the Behavioral Foundations of Economic Theory." In *Beyond Self-Interest*, edited by Jane Mansbridge, pp. 25–43. Chicago: University of Chicago Press.

Seung, T. K. 1993. *Intuition and Construction*. New Haven: Yale University Press.

Seung, T. K. and Daniel Bonevac. 1992. "Plural Values and Indeterminate Rankings." *Ethics* 102:799–813.

Sidgwick, Henry. 1962. *The Methods of Ethics*. 7th ed. Chicago: University of Chicago Press. First published in 1907.

Simon, Herbert A. 1955. "A Behavioral Model of Rational Choice." *Quarterly Journal of Economics* 69:99–118.

———. 1979. *Models of Thought*. New Haven: Yale University Press.

Singer, Peter. 1978. "Rights and the Market." In *Justice and Economic Distribution*, edited by J. Arthur and W. Shaw, pp. 207–21. Englewood Cliffs: Prentice Hall.

Slote, Michael. 1989. *Beyond Optimizing: A Study of Rational Choice*. Cambridge: Harvard University Press.

Smart, J. J. C., and Bernard Williams. 1973. *Utilitarianism: For and Against*. Cambridge: Cambridge University Press.

Smith, Holly. 1991. "Deciding How to Decide: Is There a Regress Problem?" In *Foundations of Decision Theory*, edited by M. Bacharach and S. Hurley, pp. 194–219. Cambridge: Basil Blackwell.

Spencer, Herbert. 1969. *Social Statics*. New York: Augustus M. Kelley. First published 1850.

Stocker, Michael. 1990. *Plural and Conflicting Values*. New York: Oxford University Press.

Thornton, J. C. 1970. "Can the Moral Point of View Be Justified?" In *Readings in Contemporary Ethical Theory*, edited by K. Pahel and M. Schiller, pp. 443–53. Englewood Cliffs: Prentice Hall.

Titmuss, Richard M. 1971. *The Gift Relationship*. New York: Vintage.

Toulmin, Stephen. 1970. "The Logic of Moral Reasoning, and Reason and Faith." In *Readings in Contemporary Ethical Theory*, edited by K. Pahel and M. Schiller, pp. 416–27. Englewood Cliffs: Prentice Hall.

Ullmann-Margalit, Edna, and Sidney Morgenbesser. 1977. "Picking and Choosing." *Social Research* 44:757–85.

Vallentyne, Peter, ed. 1991. *Contractarianism and Rational Choice*. New York: Cambridge University Press.

Velleman, J. David. 1989. *Practical Reflection*. Princeton: Princeton University Press.

Wahl, Richard W. 1989. *Markets for Federal Water: Subsidies, Property Rights, and the Bureau of Reclamation*. Washington, D.C.: Resources for the Future.

White, Robert. 1971. "The Urge towards Competence." *American Journal of Occupational Therapy* 25:271–74.

Williams, Bernard. 1985. *Ethics and the Limits of Philosophy*. Cambridge: Harvard University Press.

Wiltshire, Roderick. Unpublished. "The Wrong and the Good."

Wittgenstein, Ludwig. 1958. *Philosophical Investigations*. New York: Macmillan.

271

* Index *

273